THE CRUISING WOMAN'S ADVISOR

How to prepare for the voyaging life

DIANA JESSIE

forewords by TANIA AEBI *and* LIN PARDEY

SECOND EDITION

 Mc Graw Hill

INTERNATIONAL MARINE / MCGRAW-HILL
CAMDEN, MAINE ■ NEW YORK ■ CHICAGO ■ SAN FRANCISCO
LISBON ■ LONDON ■ MADRID ■ MEXICO CITY ■ MILAN ■ NEW DELHI
SAN JUAN ■ SEOUL ■ SINGAPORE ■ SYDNEY ■ TORONTO

The McGraw·Hill Companies

1 2 3 4 5 6 7 8 9   DOC DOC   9 8 7

© 1997, 2007 by Diana B. Jessie

Library of Congress Cataloging-in-Publication Data
Jessie, Diana.
The cruising woman's advisor : how to prepare for the voyaging life / Diana
Jessie ; forewords by Tania Aebi and Lin Pardey. —2nd ed.
p.   cm.
Includes bibliographical references and index.
ISBN-13: 978-0-07-148558-6 (pbk. : alk. paper)
ISBN-10: 0-07-148558-9 (pbk. : alk. paper)
1. Boating for women. 2. Boat living. I. Title.
GV777.57.J47 2007
797.1082—dc22   2007013440

ISBN-13: 978-0-07-148558-6
ISBN-10: 0-07-148558-9

Questions regarding the content of this book should be addressed to
International Marine
P.O. Box 220
Camden, ME 04843
www.internationalmarine.com

Questions regarding the ordering of this book should be addressed to
The McGraw-Hill Companies
Customer Service Department
P.O. Box 547
Blacklick, OH 43004
Retail customers: 1-800-262-4729
Bookstores: 1-800-722-4726

Title page photo courtesy Billy Black. All other photographs courtesy the author
unless otherwise indicated.

DEDICATION

For the women who want to control

their destinies, and for the partners with

whom they share their lives

CONTENTS

CONTENTS

CONTENTS

CONTENTS

FOREWORD TO THE SECOND EDITION

BY TANIA AEBI

TWENTY-ONE YEARS AGO, I had one year's worth of memory and knowledge of actual sailing on the oceans to draw from while preparing for my circumnavigation. What was lacking in personal experience I tried to get through books. As far as reading material went, the words of David Lewis, Robin Lee Graham, the Hiscocks, Tristan Jones, Robert Manry, Ann Davis, and Naomi James fed my hunger to absorb as much as possible about sailing. These people were adventurers who wrote about bravely suffering the elements, surviving hairy situations, and being endlessly resourceful. I read with dismay as they dealt with extraordinary difficulties like broken rudders, dismastings, tremendous storms, unfriendly natives and officials, then carried blithely on to round another one of the Capes. It took every optimistic fiber I had to keep believing the stories were about extremes, not the norms that average cruisers sailing the average trade wind passages would encounter.

I tried reading between the lines to glean information from their exploits in terms of what tools to bring, how to provision, and what to expect from the big wide world, but aside from teaching to expect the worst, what these books offered the layperson was pretty limited. These were *stories*, not *manuals* on how to live the stories. They were for inspiration and entertainment, not instruction and troubleshooting. Unless a problem like a clogged head or a busted seacock added to the dramatic narrative tension, there was very little elaboration on the mundane yet infinitely more important details of practical daily matters in the average liveaboard life—where to learn about basic points of sail, electricity, plumbing, and maintenance, how to deal with seasickness, how to make friends, how to maximize comfort with limited space, how to keep in touch with people back home.

Aside from Tristan Jones's Tupperware endorsement, I really can't remember anything in the books from back then that suggested ways to make a boat into a safe and comfortable home instead of a ruggedly strong ride to get through one trial after another. Even though boats are always referred to in the feminine, the literature and reference books were almost entirely about the men who thrived on challenges, facing down death, surfing on the edge of reason, and surviving to tell the tales. In those days, even for women sailing with partners and spouses, the topic of more domestic female concerns wasn't recognized as a subject unto itself, separate from the inherently rough-and-ready masculine nature of the sailor and boats. Also, my situation was unusual; women and girls didn't just take off on their own, so fat chance that I was going to find a how-to manual for the nurturing girlie guidance I needed.

But that was then. Nowadays, things are different. More and more people, of all types and appetites for adventure, have gotten up from the armchair and are out there cruising, especially couples, and the market has exploded with ways to satisfy hunger for female-centered knowledge. Enter *The Cruising Woman's Advisor*, so usefully filling a void that this second updated edition needed to be assembled. In this book, Diana Jessie offers oodles of motherly wisdom and sisterly advice gained by years of her own experience, supplemented and broadened by testimonials and insights from other notable women cruisers of all ages. She dispenses information and brings clarity to the unknown in ways that make the female initiate to the world afloat feel safer and less fearful, feelings that are direct results of the calming balm of knowledge.

When you read how some couples have cruised for many years without ever being in a frightful storm (because passages can be seasonally timed for good weather), when you read about strategies couples use to stay happily together (because nothing tests a relationship more than mandatory teamwork in radically close quarters), when you read about ways to deal with seasickness (because treatments do exist), when you read about other people's fears (because, honestly, we all have them), when you are given plenty of practical information about medical issues, communications, taking care of children, provisioning, and stowing (because these are the concerns we face on boats way more often than pirates and storms), then cruising becomes normalized and more accessible to everyone. And since not even the most seasoned sailor can recall or know everything, a book like Diana Jessie's offers guidance as good as the best self-steering system.

As I read *The Cruising Woman's Advisor*, I kept thinking that, in spite of all the miles under my keels, this book would be a resource I'd turn to before planning any major voyage. For instance, I'm currently hatching a plan to take my two boys out to sea for a year before they leave the nest. Out there with them, circumstances would be way different from what past cruising lessons have taught me, with new things to learn. Now I'd be a mother thinking about education, entertainment, health, comfort, and safety issues regarding their welfare.

So I found myself taking notes, grateful for the hint to take extra pairs of prescription glasses for my son who wears them, and for the list of homeschooling options. Reminders to make sure during the outfitting phase that all the appropriate guidebooks are shelved, that the galley components are in order, and that the head is working properly are equally as important as recommendations to invest time in ensuring a reliable engine, good rigging, and figuring out how to manage relationships aboard.

Turning from one page to the next of thoroughly thoughtful and impressively laid out advice, I kept thinking, "Diana has covered everything! This book is the definition of comprehensive." For the average woman who is just starting out, a little nervous and intimidated, even the most seemingly obvious piece of information could be completely pivotal for her. Perhaps learning that it is possible to bring along a hand-crank clothes wringer might be just the ticket she needs to smooth the waters into a way of life that knows no rival or better teacher.

In the end, one thing is certain. Whether this new cruiser relates to Dawn Riley—or Ginger, Mary Ann, or Mrs. Howell—reading is the first step for her fear or doubt to get replaced by curiosity, then curiosity by the experience that is beyond all books and advice. After she finishes *The Cruising Woman's Advisor*, has absorbed the theory, taken all the notes and strength she can extract from it, then it will be time to turn off the light, get up from the armchair, and go out and live the above-average life about which Diana Jessie writes.

CORINTH, VERMONT, NOVEMBER 2006

FOREWORD TO THE FIRST EDITION

BY LIN PARDEY

IT IS 1987. We are at our home base in New Zealand, *Taleisin* swinging to her mooring just beyond the windows. Three women, with seven circumnavigations and who knows how many thousands of miles under their belts, sit cross-legged on a bunk, talking of lives dominated by voyaging. Susan Hiscock recalls her most worrisome moments, aground in the Torres Straits, dozens of miles from the nearest settlement—the story turns hilarious as she tells of a boatload of missionaries happening by. Their assistance turned a possible disaster into a great story. "Eric always told people he'd *truly been saved*," she quips. Patience Wales, on her second circumnavigation, tells of the drama created by trying to be both a roving magazine editor and a voyager as she explored the communicationless, exotic outer Solomon Islands. Then I can't help but add my most worrisome moments—when amazing 100-mile-per-day currents swept us past Japan.

As I listened to our concerns back in 1987 I remember thinking how different they were from those of people (women, especially) who are first contemplating a cruising life. Like Diana Jessie, I have been in front of groups of women who asked each and every one of the questions covered in this book.

Although my answers to some questions may have been different in detail to those you read here, this reflects only differences in lifestyle or cruising style. For example, because we rarely cruise with crew, we carry sufficient water and have special facilities for luxurious (by cruising standards) showers on a daily basis at sea; because Larry and I dislike telephones and went cruising to avoid them, naturally we also avoid transmitting radios.

But the information Diana offers is not only useful and accurate; it also stresses an often ignored fact that the 1987 intimate meeting of three long-term cruising women illustrated for me—cruising is a participation sport. The more both partners get involved, the larger the rewards. Furthermore, sailing and the amazingly simple but efficient floating machine you will live on provide the key to exploring the world on an enjoyable, affordable long-term basis.

Diana will, as you read her well-organized ideas, encourage you and your mate to become more knowledgeable about your sailing home and conveyance; more aware of its inherent sail-powered reliability and its hidden pleasures.

No book, no seminar, can answer every question you may have—and when you finish this book you'll probably still wonder, "Should I go cruising, will I find it fulfilling, fun, exciting? Is it worth the risk?"

Diana Jessie definitely feels it is. I'm still looking forward to the next sailing adventure, the next landfall after thirty years of voyaging. Each long-term voyager we meet seems completely comfortable with the only possible answer to those really big questions. By choosing to avoid risk, you may be taking the biggest risk of all.

HONG KONG, 1997

PREFACE

WHEN YOU'RE YOUNG, a decade is a long time. However, as we age those decades go to "fast forward." We change without noticing it. Suddenly, one day, there is a wrinkly old face staring back from the mirror. How did that happen? When friends say, "Don't you think you're getting too old for this lifestyle?" it shakes us, and then we answer, "No." Our constant is still living aboard and cruising. There is nothing else we would rather do. A decade has passed since I wrote *The Cruising Woman's Advisor: How to Prepare for the Voyaging Life*, and times have changed.

We know that cruising has changed. Many more people are going cruising, both coastal and bluewater. We have more discretionary income and live a lifestyle that offers the chance to select from the buffet of adventure. Hooked by "reality" television, we go through life with a list of options for adventure about which we used to just dream. Electronic advances, bigger boats, and an unquenchable thirst for something new have created a different kind of cruiser. Many new owners have never been on a boat, and they begin with 50-footers. Armed with money and a desire for excitement, novices set off cruising with minimal skills and experience. Unfortunately, when many of these cruisers find disaster, not adventure, the challenges fade.

This second edition grew out of the need for newbies to get beyond the novice stage. Many more women are sharing and participating in the cruising experience instead of staying home or just sitting in the cockpit. Indeed, many women have become the architects of the venture rather than "the mate." Another phenomenon is finding that the man, who originally wanted to cruise, has changed his mind. He wants to go back to his milieu while she has fully adjusted to the cruising life and wants to continue.

Cruising is not limited to sailing anymore. Many baby boomers have discovered they want to continue to enjoy cruising, but they also want more physical comfort than their sailboat can offer. Larger powerboats, trawlers, and converted fishing vessels are capable of extensive coastal cruising, and some have the fuel capacity for ocean voyaging. E-mail systems allow almost uninterrupted connection with those at home. Cruisers raise and educate children aboard, the same way many families do with land-based homeschooling. Pets are common aboard cruising vessels; they are family, too.

In this second edition, I have added more participants and updated my conversations with those women who were so helpful ten years ago. The cruising children who were babies and toddlers in the first edition are now college students, professionals, and parents. Many of the participants are grandmothers.

The original participants and the new interviewees were endlessly gracious and willing to answer my calls and make suggestions. The women who have conquered powerboats give me hope.

I want to thank Jonathan Eaton once again for his support; Bob Holtzman for being my editor, clearing the path, and answering endless questions; Margaret Cook, editing manager, and Jane Curran, copyeditor, for their patience and useful suggestions; and International Marine for believing in books. Marilee Shaffer, owner of Waypoint, and Don Melcher, owner of H.F. Radio On Board, the partners of Complete Cruising Solutions, had all the answers on things electronic and the patience to help me. Terri Parrow, vice president of BoatU.S. Internet Operations, found resources galore through her many contacts that she generously shared. Grateful hugs for my ever-present sounding board, Donna Green-Tye, sailor, editor, and daughter extraordinaire, who was on call from beginning to end, fielding question after question.

Finally, all those things I said about my husband a decade ago are still true. His strength, skill, and humor make him a great partner—wherever we may be. He persevered and continued without being privy to this second edition. While I wrote, he labored restoring our new home, a 1974 wooden Grand Banks Alaskan 53, so we can return to the cruising fleet. Jim, you are the best of the best.

INTRODUCTION

CRUISING IS EXOTIC in the eyes of many and a complete mystery to others. Women who go cruising know that this adventure is unique. How we travel, the people we meet, and the risks we take are anything but ordinary. The sheer number of cruisers offers us the opportunity to see the different styles and attitudes of cruisers.

This book was written to encourage and support women at all stages of their cruising lives: from those who are dreaming about cruising to those who have already left. It was also written for the man who wants a woman to go cruising with him and wants to understand her concerns.

In the first chapter I try to describe the difference between cruising as an event and as a lifestyle. The event approach is not new, but it hasn't received the attention that the assumed permanent lifestyle cruising has. In the second chapter, I delve into the dream and look at what happens when dreams don't come true.

The next few chapters define the basics of what you need to know before you settle into long-term or long-range cruising under power or sail: what skills you need, what type of boat to get, and how to handle issues including bad weather, security, and health.

When you go cruising there are additional considerations that vary with your personal lifestyle. There are a number of chapters you can read or skip depending upon your individual plan. If you take children and pets along, how are their needs integrated into cruising? Are your parents approaching an age at which they will require assistance from you? Will you need to be in communication with family, friends, and colleagues? Will you be earning a living as you cruise?

Finally, I address those things that make your experience very personal: turning your boat into your home, keeping your heirlooms and treasures safe, personal hygiene aboard, expanding your experience, and your obligations and responsibilities.

When it comes to learning, men seem inclined to find a guru or hero and stick with that one set of ideas. Women prefer to collect information as part of the education and decision-making process. With that in mind, some of the women who offered experiences and ideas in the first edition are still included. It was fun and enlightening to find new participants who have experience with electronics, own and operate powerboats, and have cruised to new venues. Some participants have served in the military, some made the transitions from sail to power, some have full-time careers, and some teach and write. All of them contributed to this effort. I hope you will take a moment to look through the Participants section and get acquainted with each of them.

PARTICIPANTS

GAIL AMESBURY and her husband, Don, cruised Europe, Africa, and the Caribbean. Their three children were educated in boarding schools in England and spent holidays cruising with their parents. After Gail and Don sold their boat, they settled down in Florida to see the last of their children established and independent. They currently live in the British Virgin Islands.

NANCY BISCHOFF cruised in the Pacific with her husband, Kurt, and their two sons on board a Tayana 37. The boys grew up on the boat and experienced life as cruisers. Teenagers are frequently alienated from their families, but the Bischoffs are proof that parents and children can remain close as children grow older. Nancy and Kurt, now grandparents, just returned from a second voyage without their now-grown sons.

GAIL BOWDISH, M.D., an emergency medical specialist based in a city hospital in Minnesota, raced her Islander 36 on the Great Lakes. Now the owner of a C&C 33, she continues to race, began teaching sailing in 2005, and eventually hopes to become a full-time liveaboard. As a doctor and sailor, she is knowledgeable about the health concerns that women have while cruising in areas far away from immediate help. She provides helpful advice and insight on several important health issues.

SALLY BEE BROWN is a contributing editor to *PassageMaker* magazine and writes for other magazines based in the Pacific Northwest. Her boat career started as a "go-along," but that changed.

When she and her husband purchased an Ocean Alexander 43, she decided to learn all she could about operating a powerboat. She is in a constant learning mode and performs the docking maneuvers more than 90% of the time. As they look for their next boat, she favors a 42-foot Nordic Tug. She is a strong advocate for partnership cruising. Her thoughts on being fearful are most insightful.

LOUISE BURKE started sailing with her husband in 1968 and worked with him taking guests on charter boats and delivering boats from port to port. After her husband's death, she acquired her captain's license in 1973 and continued to skipper charter boats and go racing. In 1976 she became the sailing master of *Mistral*, an 82-foot Herreshoff schooner sailing out of the United States Naval Academy, and the first woman to teach sailing at the school. After leaving the academy, she continued sailing and training other women as instructors.

BARBARA COLBORN started sailing in her thirties with her husband, David, on a MacGregor 26. They put their boat on a trailer and hauled it to different parts of the country. Chartering in the Caribbean got them interested in going cruising. In 1994 they began their first long cruise. They cruised for fourteen months, traveling to Mexico, the Hawaiian Islands, and back to California. Barbara offers a fresh and positive perspective. She self-published two books about her experience, *A Sailor's Devotional* and *Crossing the Horizon: One Couple's Mid-Life Adventure*. Her cruising experiences inspired her to devote herself to more evangelical work.

CAROL CUDDYER cofounded Sea Sense in 1989 with Patti Moore (see below) in response to the increasing demand for women teaching women how to sail. They have expanded into powerboat instruction, and both of them have 100-ton licenses. Carol teaches sailing and powerboating in a variety of locations in the United States and Europe. With powerboats, she

and Patti prefer to teach on the student's boat because of the r
ber of systems and variations among powerboats. Whether the boat
is power or sail, when it comes to operating a boat Carol's philoso-
phy is "The Woman's Place Is at the Helm."

 PAULA DINIUS is a survivor of the infamous
Queen's Birthday Storm, which struck a group of
boats sailing from New Zealand for Tonga in June
of 1994. *Rescue in the Pacific* by Tony Farrington tells
the story of the storm and its survivors, and is must-reading for all
cruisers. Her husband, Dana, was severely injured in the storm, and
they finally abandoned their boat when a container ship was able
to rescue them. Later the boat was salvaged but subsequently was
lost in a fire. She and Dana are now divorced, and Paula lives and
works in a rural setting in Oregon close to her family. Although she
no longer sails, she still loves the ocean.

 ALISON FISHEL started sailing at age 7, racing with
her dad and brother. In high school, she built an El
Toro of wood that "always leaked." In 1991 she married Bill, who was retired and had no hobbies. Alison
told him, "You need to find something you like." His response was, "Do
you like boats?" After a series of boats, they wanted to go cruising and
decided they needed a trawler. They saw an advertisement in June 2000
for Ocean Ventures and ordered a boat, but the company went belly-up
before completing the boat. In September 2003 Alison and Bill moved
the unfinished boat to YachtSmiths International in Dartmouth, Nova
Scotia, and in August 2004 they launched it. After waiting more than
four years, it took four months to bring her home to San Francisco Bay.
They are happy cruising and living aboard this handsome steel trawler.

 **LURA FRANCIS** and her husband, Jack, circum-
navigated in a 32-foot boat that they finished them-
selves. Lura was plagued with major health problems
for nearly ten years before cruising, but that did not
deter her from realizing the cruising dream she and
her husband had planned. Shortly after returning

from their voyage and retiring to their home in the California Sierras, Jack died of a heart attack. Lura's joy and pride in the voyage she and Jack took together still brings a sparkle to her eyes.

 LINDA FRASER made the transition from sailing to power cruising in her thirties, an earlier age than most. She and her husband, Andrew, bought their dream boat, a Hans Christian 38, and cruised from San Franciso to Acapulco and back. She said they spent too much time trying to maintain all of the wood, which took away from the fun. They decided that they wanted more space and began looking at pilothouse sailboats. They also wanted to have some protection from the elements and finally decided that a powerboat made sense because it had more living space and good protection. They now cruise a 46-foot Nordhavn with their dogs, Quincy and Bob, and have no brightwork to varnish.

 **KATIE HAMILTON** has been boating since 1969 when she and her husband, Gene, bought their first boat, a 28-foot sailboat. Since then they have had a 32-foot sailboat (Vanguard), a 41-foot sailboat (Rhodes 41), a 42-foot trawler (Grand Banks), a J/24, and a 35-foot sailboat (C&C), and they currently own a 36-foot trawler (Grand Banks). Over the years, she says she has learned by cruising many miles, making many mistakes, and continually learning as they cruise the Great Loop Cruise, which includes the Intracoastal Waterway and the inland river system and the Great Lakes. She and her husband have recently published *Coastal Cruising Under Power*, an excellent book for the beginning or transitional cruiser.

 IRENE HAMPSHIRE raised her two sons on a small boat in Southern California. She spends most of her cruising time helping her mate, Jon Shampain, deliver boats to different ports. Her oldest son, Erik, now 28, followed his father's example as a professional sailor. Her younger son, Shawn, has started a career combining ceramics and glassblowing. She makes her home on a Grand Banks 36.

RÉANNE HEMINGWAY-DOUGLASS wrote the amazing book *Cape Horn: One Man's Dream, One Woman's Nightmare* more than twenty years after making that passage. Her candor about the experience and about her family relationships is bold and informative. Still married and still adventurous, she and her husband, Don, have sold Fine Edge, a small publishing company, to spend more time cruising. Réanne and Don are the authors of the *Exploring* series, cruising guidebooks for the entire North American Pacific coast. They live on Fidalgo Island in Washington State and spend summers on their research vessel, *Baidarka*.

NANCY JEWHURST cruised full-time on board a Traveler 32 with her husband, Victor, and her son, Kyle. When Kyle reached age 12, the family moved ashore to provide him social and school opportunities Nancy felt he needed. She exudes joy and enthusiasm about cruising because she believes the lifestyle gives her a closeness with her family that might not be possible in any other kind of life. Kyle now attends UCLA. Nancy and Vic still spend time on *Charisma* each year.

GAYLE JONES is certified by the American Council on Exercise (ACE) as a personal trainer. She has had a private studio for the past eight years. She makes her home in Gig Harbor, Washington. She is a great example of how exercise keeps you fit and happy. She enjoys powerboating with her husband, Tom.

JANE KENNY has to be classified as a racing sailor *and* a cruising powerboater. She and her husband, Geves, have a home base in San Diego where they race Sabots, regularly beating all comers. They became powerboaters when a friend asked them to write an operations manual for a 52-foot DeFever. They didn't know anything about powerboating but learned rapidly. They went on to own an Ocean Alexander 43 for twelve years and kept it in Mexico for cruising. A Tollycraft 34 currently used in Green Bay and soon to be moved to the West Coast has replaced it.

 BARBARA MARRETT is a contributing editor to *Cruising World* magazine. She and John Neal sailed the South Pacific extensively in his Hallberg-Rassy 31. They published an account of their experiences in *Mahina Tiare*. Barbara has her USCG license and actively participates in many women's sailing events. She lives in the San Juan Islands.

 PATTI McKENNA has spent all of her life on or near the water. Her father was in the U.S. Coast Guard, and she and her sister, Terri Parrow (see below) grew up powerboating. When the family moved to New Jersey, Patti was introduced to boating on the ocean. As an adult, she joined the U.S. Coast Guard. After a five-year stint teaching others about safety and handling powerboats, she returned to civilian life. She still lives and works around boats and currently enjoys her vintage 26-foot Pacemaker on the East Coast.

 PATRICIA MILLER RAINS is a licensed skipper who delivers yachts between the East Coast and West Coast of the United States via the Panama Canal. Her first cruises included some bad times, but she has since become more skilled and independent as a sailor. She is an editor and journalist and co-authored *The Boating Guide to Mexico* with her husband, John; the book, now in a third edition, is the definitive boating guidebook for Mexico.

 **PATTI MOORE** co-founded Sea Sense with Carol Cuddyer (see above). She came from a family of nonboaters and had her first taste of boating when she started sailing in her late twenties. She and her husband lived aboard and cruised up and down the East Coast. She and Carol discovered they had the same approach to boating and instruction. They started teaching

sailing, but the demand for power instruction increased in the mid-1990s. They teach wherever there is student demand. They operate from St. Petersburg, Florida.

 LAEL MORGAN is an accomplished photographer, author, and scholar. Her cruise from Boston through the Panama Canal up to Alaska in the early 1960s was the basis for her first book, *Woman's Guide to Boating and Cooking.* She and her then-husband, Dodge, made this long trip without the sophisticated electronics and onboard comforts available to cruisers today, but she still recalls her early experiences with great enthusiasm. A visiting professor in the Department of Communication, University of Texas at Arlington, since 2003, Lael worked as a journalist and has taught journalism for many years. She has written more than a dozen books, including *Good Time Girls of the Alaska Yukon Gold Rush,* which won her the title of Historian of the Year in 1988 from the Alaska Historical Society. She is currently researching a book with the working title of *Sex in Texas History.*

 PAT NOLAN operates Sistership, a sailing school in the Virgin Islands. She began her sailing career in Seattle, where she was active in the Seattle Women's Sailing Association and served as the organization's president in 1987. She is a strong advocate of women's sailing and is eager to help women find a place in the sport, as racers or as cruisers. Her theory on how women differ from men in their approach to sailing is an important contribution to the chapter on sailing skills. Pat was named an American Sailing Association Instructor of the Year in 2003 and 2004. In 2005, she was on the all-women's team (average age 50), that won the Bareboat V division at Antigua Race Week and was first overall out of 73 bareboats. No women's team has ever come close to that.

 LIN PARDEY and her husband, Larry, have sailed together for more than forty years, including both an eastabout circumnavigation via the great canals and a westabout circumnavigation via all the great southern capes. They still enjoy cruising on

Taleisin but now have a second love: *Thelma*, a 34-foot, 111-year-old, Bailey-designed gaff cutter that Larry bought Lin for her 60th birthday. They use *Thelma* during the Southern Hemisphere summer sailing season. Lin has been cruising most of her adult life and is practical and forthright in her comments. She has written and co-written with Larry several definitive books on cruising (see the bibliography). She also contributed the foreword for the first edition of *Cruising Woman's Advisor*. (Photograph by M. Marris)

TERRI PARROW and her sister, Patti McKenna (see above) grew up powerboating. She lives in Maryland and is vice president of BoatU.S. Internet Operations. She works with a huge variety of boating interests as well as being an avid recreational powerboater. Her job gives her a unique perspective on boating—political, manufacturing, safety, etc.—and access to many sources of information. She is responsible for the BoatU.S. "Ask the Expert" program on the Internet, which is open to all BoatU.S. members.

NANCY PAYSON fell in love with a man who promised to show her the world. She married Herb, and he kept his promise. Starting with little experience and learning as she sailed, Nancy has become an accomplished sailor. She is the epitome of what cruisers hope to be when they cruise: happy, warm, vital, and strong. Nancy and Herb now live in the San Juan Islands and still sail an Island Packet.

SUZANNE POGELL founded Womanship, the first sailing school for women and by women, in 1984 in Annapolis. The school is designed to give adult women hands-on opportunities to discover the joys of sailing and to gain and improve real skills; the ultimate goal is the confidence to take charge. The Womanship program was hailed by *Practical Sailor* as one of the two best sailing schools in the country. The school offers opportunities in twelve locations around the world. Although no longer actively involved in teaching sailing, Suzanne writes and lectures extensively on marketing to women.

DAWN RILEY is the most notable woman sailor in America, now taking part in her fourth America's Cup campaign as general manager for the French team. She has completed two Whitbread Round the World Races. She comments on sailing as she knows it and about starting at an early age to gain the independence she needed to take her to the top. Her book *Taking the Helm* is a great story of her experience skippering 60-foot *Heineken* with an all-female crew in the 1993–94 Whitbread Race.

KAREN RILEY met her future husband, Mike, while he was solo cruising on his 24-foot, motorless sailboat. They were married in Sri Lanka, and Karen gave birth to Falcon, their son, in Malta. They moved to a 39-foot boat while Falcon was a toddler. Falcon is now in college in California, and Karen and Mike are still cruising.

MIGAEL SCHERER is a writer and teacher. She has written several books, including *A Cruising Guide to Puget Sound and the San Juan Islands* (now in a second edition), *Back Under Sail*, and *Sailing to Simplicity*. For over thirty years, her cruising ground has stretched from Seattle to southeastern Alaska. Her special contribution to this book is describing how you can cruise, live, and work as a liveaboard. The 50-foot ketch she and her husband built is a satisfying place to live and work.

MICHELLE SIMON, M.D., is a pediatrician in Maryland and an enthusiastic sailor. She is a strong advocate for women in sailing and for women's health. She offers advice about caring for children while cruising to assist those who are considering entering the cruising life with the whole family. Divorced and still sailing, she looks forward to working with cruisers and helping them plan their health care.

MARJA VANCE along with her husband, Stephen, circumnavigated in the late 1970s aboard their Cal 2-27, *Twiga*, which they have since sold. Since then, they have worked aboard a variety of large boats as crew, including a 92-foot Nelson Merrick, a 100-foot canal barge, and a 96-foot McQueen. They are currently aboard the McQueen on the East Coast. They have managed to continue cruising by virtue of working as they go. Marja has some interesting comments on the changes she has made.

ELLEN VOYLES is a powerboater who has mastered the intricacies of a big boat. She started with skiboats with her two kids and husband, Glen. In 1992 Ellen and Glen helped as crew to deliver a Grand Banks 42. One thing led to another, and they now cruise aboard their own Grand Banks 46. Ellen learns by doing and continues to be the XO on their boat, overseeing haulouts, painting, and engine work. The recent elevation of Glen from captain to grandpa has cut into their cruising time.

PATIENCE WALES, editor emeritus of *SAIL* magazine, has circumnavigated twice. Now retired from the magazine, and living in Ipswich, Massachusetts, her view of cruising has not changed over the years, although her taste in boats has. She offers encouragement and direction on learning to sail, coping with fear, and gaining independence as a cruiser.

THE
CRUISING
LIFE

WHEN THE YOUNG WOMAN sitting next to me on the plane discovered that I lived on a boat and had spent my life cruising, she asked me how I slept, cooked, bathed, shopped, and worked—as if I had just arrived from Mars. When we parted, she told me that she could not imagine what my life was like, but that it sounded perfect.

Most people do not understand what it's like to live and cruise on a sailboat or powerboat, and their curiosity and amazement are always entertaining. They first try to understand the cruising life in the same day-to-day terms that define their lives. What is it like to live without a car, without a telephone, without daily contact with the rest of the world? But what is important to know goes beyond those day-to-day details. Cruisers' lives may seem as alien as life in outer space. But there is great joy in cruising. It is a life of adventure, challenge, and independence.

If you are considering becoming a cruiser, I am sure your questions are endless: What is cruising really like? Can I do it? Will I like it? Will it be horrible or wonderful? Women who have cruised along coastlines and across oceans, on big boats and small, for long periods of time and for short spans, all asked those same questions before they left.

Event or Lifestyle?

Until recently, it never occurred to me that some people set off on a voyage without the least bit of interest in being *cruisers*. These people go cruising because it is on a list of things they want to accomplish in their lifetime. They are prepared to take a given period of time, invest in a boat, sail from A to B, and then move on to the next event.

There is no rule that prohibits doing just that if you want. The problem is that because these people perceive their trip as a one-time thing, they look for the easiest way to accomplish something that is not easy. Generally, expense is not an issue in these situations because they are short term. Buying a big boat that will accommodate the creature comforts, the electronic gear, and the auxiliary engine, and fuel is easy. All they have to do is pay for it. Then they put fuel in the tank, food in the fridge and freezer, and leave.

This approach does not infringe on or change their lifestyle. It is similar to buying an RV and leaving home for a vacation. The difference is there are no white lines on the water, there is no AAA, and there is no 911. Even gunkholing along coastal waters can go from benign to treacherous in a matter of minutes, exposing you to danger.

These event cruisers see no need to learn about weather, battery maintenance, anchoring, or rescue procedures, among other things. As a result, those who travel with this perspective endanger other boaters out on the water. They expect others to take care of them when trouble occurs.

Lifestyle cruisers, however, are those who consciously choose to change their lives by moving aboard a boat and traveling. They probably consider the cruising life as some combination of a vocation and an education—but it is their life, not a brief interruption in their life, as event cruising is. They take responsibility for themselves and those around them. They recognize the risks of their life choice and prepare to handle them. They understand the need to be self-sufficient.

Most women are well suited to be lifestyle cruisers, since they generally understand that some situations are inherently dangerous. And they are hesitant about taking such risks without adequate preparation. When you take the time to learn what the risks are, you can prepare yourself. You will be living a different kind of life when you live on the water, so it's best to learn as much as you can before you go.

What Is the Cruising Lifestyle?

There is no single definition of the cruising lifestyle. The answer depends on whom you ask, for one of the best things about cruising is that it is a way of life that can be approached and managed in many different ways.

For me, cruising is the simple life. I live on a boat instead of living in a house or in an apartment. My possessions are few, and my living space is smaller than what you'd find in a typical mobile home. I do not spend hours cleaning, talking on the phone, or watching television. I share every day—in fact, nearly every minute—with my husband in this same space. We live day to day, planning what we want to do and where we want to go each day. It is rare that we use the phrase "I have to . . ." unless I am writing or the weather is bad.

We do not own suitcases because we take our home with us wherever we go, and we never have jet lag. Our dinghy is our "car" when we want to go ashore. We have no faxes or beepers on the boat, and our cell phone doesn't work offshore or in remote ports, so people either communicate with us face to face, send us an e-mail (see Chapter 10), or wait for us to turn on our radio.

Our boat is the focus of our lives. It is our home and our mode of transportation, and it holds everything we own. Whenever I have to be away from the boat, I am always anxious to return.

Cruising means moving from place to place. Some cruisers move from port to port, some cross oceans, and some travel around the world. The neighborhood changes constantly, and there is always a new place to visit, something new to learn, and new people to meet.

You may think cruising is a lonely life because you are always leaving people. But you always meet new people living the same life as you. You meet on docks and in anchorages, and you become friends because you share this unique lifestyle. As bluewater cruiser Nancy Payson says, "Your entertainment comes from friends and books, sharing with friends the adventures that you have."

Change is part of a cruising life. If you look forward to change, you will see cruising as an adventure. Lin Pardey says, "If you want adventure and freedom, I think you have to give up the perception of comfort and safety. There is no such thing as security in life. The only thing in life that's positive is change, so why not get out there and enjoy it? Accept change, and you can enjoy cruising."

Not everyone who cruises crosses an ocean or becomes a circumnavigator. Many cruisers live on board full-time and cruise coastal areas. Migael Scherer has lived on her boat in Puget Sound and cruised the Pacific Northwest and southeast Alaska for over thirty years. For her, cruising is not unlike being a career tourist. It is "spending time on the hook somewhere and then moving on to another place. You send yourself on a prolonged vacation. I like to be a long-term tourist. I want to be part of communities. Knowing people is important to me. A year is too short a time. It satisfies me to stay several years, then move."

Cruising does not have to be a permanent lifestyle. Combining a land life with cruising is the only way some couples and families can cruise. Cruising for a year may be their limit because they want to keep their children in school. They may have only a short sabbatical from work. They may have a limited budget and cannot stay away from land life and careers for too long. Some cruisers do not plan long trips because they are not sure the life is right for them. But whatever the length of your cruise will be, you should approach cruising as a lifestyle, not an event: learn as much as you can before you go, prepare as much as you can, be responsible, be open to new experiences, and—above all—enjoy!

Not all cruisers plan exactly what their cruising life will be until it actually happens. When she started cruising twenty years ago, Barbara Marrett, a contributing editor to *Cruising World*, viewed cruising as a way to adventure off to exotic places. "I didn't expect it to be a lifestyle, but I really enjoyed it much more than I could have imagined. It's not having a set schedule; it's being very open, embracing the unknown, and letting your life flow instead of directing it."

How we cruise, where we go, and the distance we travel vary, but the common threads between all cruising lives are adventure, freedom, challenge, and change. Whether you do it for the rest of your life or for one year at a time, you will grow and learn more about yourself and the world if you give cruising a chance.

Why We Go

When I asked women cruisers why they went cruising, I heard a variety of reasons for starting the adventure. When we begin, we all have our own individual reasons for cruising. After time, however, the women I spoke with seemed to share a similar commitment to cruising because of the opportunities it creates for travel, adventure, and independence.

"We went because of the adventure," said Lura Francis, an artist who shared the cruising dream with her husband, Jack. "Our whole married life had been going to concerts, going to the city, civic light opera, galleries, taking a picnic lunch and watching the boats on the bay. We used to say that someday maybe we would get a boat and go."

Many people dream about cruising; only some are fortunate enough to have their dream become a reality. Lura and Jack waited for the opportunity to fulfill their dream, sharing a cruising life after they had raised their family and retired.

Other women have cruised most of their adult lives. For them, cruising was not a future dream; it simply was life as they lived it. Lin Pardey was 20 years old when she started cruising. "I saw freedom in the life, unrestricted travel, and being free of material things," she says.

Now, more than forty years later, Lin talks about having a home base. (Long-term cruisers have a hard time using the word "house" when they talk about living on land.) "We will probably spend more time in our home base when we get older, but I can't picture putting away the boat and not going again. Maybe we'd build a little boat again, so we could manage. . . . We know people still cruising in their eighties."

A slide show led to Patience Wales's desire to cruise. "We wanted to get out of our lives and into different lives. So we saved all our money for six years, made our own beer, sold our houses, bought our boat, which was really too big for us because we didn't know what we were doing, and took off. I think I went, more than any other thing, for the adventure. It is like no other kind of traveling. That was in 1964. I was young and foolish. Now I'm old and foolish."

In the process of building their fourth boat in 1995, some of her feelings changed. Patience said, "I'm more blasé. I think I'm pickier. I know I'm less willing to be uncomfortable. But [cruising] really doesn't mean anything different from what it did the first time around."

I know many women who go along as a cruising mate. Paula Dinius said of her husband, "Dana was the real ramrod behind the whole thing. Because he was in a stressful position, for him it was a major escape. He dragged me through in the beginning, because I didn't have the passion he did. When we left, I was excited. I was excited about the adventure, but I was afraid of being on a boat at sea."

A first-time experience at anything can be daunting. Barbara Colborn, who was new to bluewater cruising ten years ago, talked to me immediately after returning from her first ocean voyage. "I wasn't sure that I wanted to cruise for the rest of my life, and we agreed on trying it for a year. Reading books is one thing, but actually being out there and experiencing it is another."

The beginnings of any experience are key to its outcome. But few of us can predict in the beginning what shape our cruising lives will take. I did not grow up sailing and did not see cruising as a lifetime dream—or even a short-term goal. Jim and I bought our boat as partners, figuring the financial obligation we shared was sufficient commitment to each other. We had lived on board for less than a year when I discovered, after reading a news article, that our boat was scheduled for the Transpacific Yacht Race to Hawaii. I exploded at Jim for not consulting me, but then we made a pact.

If the passage to Hawaii was not a good experience for me, Jim would buy out my half of the boat when we arrived in Honolulu. When we reached the Ala Wai dock in Honolulu, I announced, "I'm keeping my half."

That same summer the Australians won the America's Cup. We thought it would be a lark to sail to Australia to see the next competition, and so we went.

The two years we allotted for the voyage grew into a seven-year circumnavigation. Before we left we were married at the urging of family and friends, who worried about me traveling in countries where my rights as an unmarried woman might be in jeopardy. Twenty-seven years later, there is no doubt in my mind that cruising all over the world is—still—the most exciting thing I can do with the rest of my life.

Demands and Rewards

"The best times I've ever had in my life have been cruising; also, the most uncomfortable times I've ever had have been cruising," says Barbara Marrett. She tells potential cruisers that cruising can be both the best of times and the worst of times; she was warned before her first passage "not to expect a picnic. Experiencing ocean swells in a small boat can be very uncomfortable and frightening at times. So when I was miserable the first three days out, I was somewhat mentally prepared. . . . But the difficulty of sailing to the Galápagos and then Easter Island, our first landfalls, was repaid by the reward of exploring these incredible islands. I don't regret any part of the adventure, including the edge of the hurricane we passed through."

An early cruising lesson for me was learning to live with things that I cannot change. When Mother Nature has a bad day, I have to share it. Choppy seas, too much wind, not enough wind, heat, cold, heavy fog, broiling sunshine, and salty spray all have to be reckoned with at some point. Not only was it essential for me to learn to adapt to the conditions; I also had to acquire the grace to accept them.

A young man crewed with us for several thousand miles. One day we were becalmed within sight of our port, and our engine was not working. In frustration, he shook his fists and hollered like a child having a temper tantrum. When I questioned his behavior he said, "I have never felt so helpless."

I was unsympathetic at the moment, but I also have days when things do not work out the way I want. But the bonus, most cruisers discover, is that Mother Nature has many more good days than bad days. Those good days are our reward for enduring the bad ones.

Adjusting to cruising can take time. Barbara Colborn reminded me of some advice commonly given to new cruisers. She said, "People who have gone cruising said to give it at least a year, and I found that it was true. Five months into it, I was still uncomfortable about some things and wishing to be home now and then."

Several experienced cruisers have offered wise words about aspirations. The desire to take on a big trip easily fuels your enthusiasm and imagination, but sometimes it is not very realistic. Some people start out on a circumnavigation or a major passage and then discover it is not what they expected.

Migael Scherer offers advice to such cruisers. "Move slowly," she advises, "bite your trip into small chunks and do everything you can to build your confidence in yourself and your boat. Don't be afraid to turn back. There is no shame in turning back, and you should never regret it. Take those small steps first."

I believe if you feel insecure or unprepared for something, there is nothing wrong with rethinking your plans. Bad weather, inadequate navigation information, or boat-system failures can cause problems; those are the times to turn back to a safe harbor. Pride pushes people to do stupid things. Remember that there are no records at stake when you go cruising. The goal is your own enjoyment and satisfaction.

Cruising has its demands, but the rewards are many: exotic locations, adventure, excitement. For me, other rewards are the friends I have made along the way and the opportunities I've had to see history firsthand. Being a part of the natural world has also strengthened my belief in myself.

For Barbara Colborn, it took only a short time for her to see the rewards. When she was concluding her first cruising experience, she told me, "We've been out fourteen months and two passages, to Hawaii and back. I love it and I wish I didn't have to go back onto land and earn money. But I think it was important to say, 'Okay, we're going to try this for a certain period of time and see.' "

For Nancy Payson, one reward is spending time in new places. "[My husband] gets me to sail because I like to get to places and be there for a while. The sailing isn't the reason most women go. Certainly not initially. If they're lucky, they learn to love cruising."

For Lura Francis, cruising was a way to grow and learn. It was "a life where you have time to think, experience solitude, know yourself and your partner, grow together. It was being resourceful, finding out how to do everything from changing oil to making yogurt."

For me there is another reward that I did not anticipate. One day my husband said, "Cruising wouldn't be any fun if I didn't have you to share it with." Then he told me that the worst thing he could imagine—worse than sickness or losing the boat—would be not being able to remember all that we had experienced together.

I realized our partnership is very special. Maybe I could have had that relationship without cruising, but it is unlikely anyone will ever convince me of that. The roles cruising partners share may always be changing, but the commitment to the relationship is never in doubt.

2

HIS DREAM, HER DREAM, TOO

A LARGE MAJORITY OF WOMEN cruise with men. Whether they are married or not, the onboard relationship is critical to the success of the cruising experience. After interviewing cruising women about their relationships with the men they are with, it was clear that there is no single formula for success. There are certain elements, however, that are common to good onboard relationships.

The Raison d'Être

Most people dream about cruising before they turn the fantasy into a reality. When a couple shares the cruising dream, it is important that each has his or her own reasons for taking on the adventure. As Nancy Payson wisely advises, "Be sure you're doing it for yourself and not your husband, because you can get a lot out of [cruising] if you look at it this way. If you're going to be a martyr—and do it even though you want to keep the house or you don't think you'll like it—don't go."

We all have found ourselves the victims of self-fulfilling prophecies. We don't think we will like something, and sure enough, we don't. Nancy Payson cautions against prejudging: "I think women don't understand that you can enjoy yourself. You can get a big thrill out of all these things. You can learn and not be scared."

Migael Scherer understands that your motivation for cruising may not be exactly the same as your partner's, but she says, "Your reasons need to intersect to have a successful relationship and a successful cruise." In her experience, building their 50-foot ketch together from the keel up was a binding force in their relationship. "We learned to work together from the beginning. We had the same goal: getting the boat built. We still have some disagreement, but it's part of the teamwork."

Although Lael Morgan and her partner divorced after their cruise, she has a positive attitude about their experience. "Cruising was a dream for both of us right off the bat. Our chemistry worked. I loved the dream, the idea of doing it. That kept us together. It was far better than anything I could have imagined."

Cruising Roles and Relationships

Jim and I purchased our boat before we got married. I paid half and shared the upkeep. I came into the relationship having skippered my own boat for several years as well as racing with my first husband. There were many things I did not know about boats and sailing, but one thing I did know was that I did not enter into our boatownership as a first mate: We were partners.

I know from experience, however, that there can only be one captain at a time on any boat. Whether you are cruising or racing, one person has to be ultimately responsible. Especially in emergency situations, there is no time for a consensus.

Since my husband has more boating experience and skill than I do, he is the captain of our boat. We change our "titles" to suit certain situations. In foreign countries, we are listed as co-captains (or captain and pilot) to ensure equal status. I am the watch captain when we have a crew, and I am captain in my husband's absence. I refuse to be called the first mate. This has nothing to do with the tasks I perform—it has to do with my own perception of my role. I view myself as a partner and always have seen our relationship that way. In some ways that has made my transition to cruiser easier than it might be for some women.

As captain, my husband is in charge of the boat, but I question his decisions or plans if I believe there is good reason. If I think we need to reef because the boat is heeling too much, we usually reef. If conditions are poor for a designated departure date, my husband typically defers to my preference for delaying a start. He is not being macho and I am not being a wimp: My husband's tolerance for heavy weather, or his desire to move to a new port, causes him to look at the weather and other factors from a different point of view than mine.

Occasionally when I suggest a change, my husband points out a good reason why things should remain as they are. If, for example, I want to reef the mainsail, he may point out to me that the boat will be underpowered, and sailing will be more uncomfortable with reduced power in our sails. In those situations, we jointly assess the situation and determine the best course of action.

An emergency is never the time to challenge the captain or question his or her decisions. If I want an explanation, there is always time later to review our actions. If I see or hear something during an emergency that my husband misses, however, I offer the information, and he uses it in assessing the situation.

Despite the fact that no one calls me "first mate" more than once, I have taken on many of the traditional female tasks on the boat: cooking, provisioning, and bookkeeping. As my husband enjoys pointing out, I also am the manager, administrator, and chief executive officer. We could not go cruising if I did not handle those jobs.

My husband and I defined roles that work for us, and we function well with this relationship because we both can be what we want to be.

It is important to understand the roles you and your cruising partner will play. Many times those roles will follow the pattern you have already set on land. Women who have maintained a traditional role over a long period of time may find it difficult to change that pattern once they go cruising. If your husband or partner has been the leader in determining your course for the future, you may not want that to change.

Migael Scherer explains that while she takes on responsibility for the domestic chores, such as cooking and laundry, she has expectations about that role. "You need to make demands to meet your responsibilities. Food is the most important thing." If you do domestic duties on a boat, you are no less important than the person who handles the mechanical or deckhand duties.

Traditional roles work well for some cruising couples; others look beyond the traditional norms to learn what will work best in their cruising life. Lin Pardey, an experienced and competent sailor, understands how traditional roles develop. "We all fall into some traditional roles. The biggest fear is he may not know seamanship so you must back him up or take charge as needed."

As a novice cruiser ten years ago, Barbara Colborn expected that her husband, not she, would be captain. But, as she says, "As I learned more about weather and gained the confidence that comes with experience, we came to more equal footing."

Professional skipper Patricia Miller Rains knows that in order to ensure the safety of a vessel a woman needs to know how to be in charge. Patricia's first cruising relationship was not a happy one. Her partner "did not know much more about [cruising] than I did, but he had to be the captain. . . . He became a yeller. He'd never let me learn. He'd just scream and yell." Now, cruising with her husband, she has a happier relationship that suits her and ensures better safety for their vessel. "Most women grow up being conditioned to function as part of a team, and that's perfect. But for safety's sake, a husband/wife cruising team needs to rotate captain duties regularly, at least on a practice basis."

Patience Wales believes that taking on responsibility is the only way to really enjoy cruising. "Women are too dependent on the men they are cruising with. I feel very strongly about that. I've seen it over and over. Invariably [what] it comes down to [is that] she feels she is only an adjunct. She's an arm or a leg. She's not in any sense the main body or even a body that can support his."

For cruising men, the ability to trust a female cruising partner is crucial. Without trust, there is a weak link in the relationship. British cruiser Gail Amesbury makes the point very clear.

"The male attitude to the female on the boat is one of the biggest problems. If it's not right, that's when [the relationship] won't work. A man should lie down in the bunk and ask himself, 'Can I lie here for 48 hours and trust her?' If the answer is no, then he should wait until the answer is yes."

Taking on responsibilities can translate into pride and joy. "It's no fun to go along for the ride," Patience Wales says. "You should somehow be an important part of the crew. And if women would just understand that being in charge of something is fun, choose what they are going to do, and learn to do it well, that's the kick of it."

Communication Required

Many books and articles have focused on the different communication styles of men and women. Recognizing that there are differences can be a key factor in making the cruising partnership work.

Pat Nolan has taught men and women to sail, and she has watched how communication styles affect the way men and women function on a boat.

"Men communicate differently," she says. "They catch onto things in a different way. Men do things spur of the moment and don't do up-front talking about it. It causes problems because if no one knows what the job is, it ends with screaming and yelling." Couples sailing for a mooring buoy, for example, need to know who is doing what. They need to talk ahead of time, Pat advises. "That is the major difference: Let's talk about it. Women love to do it and men don't. [Men] assume you will know what they are thinking without telling you."

You may not agree with Pat's view of male and female communication differences and how they manifest themselves on a boat. But it is important to accept that there can be differences in communication styles. Be prepared to deal with them.

In her book *Cape Horn: One Man's Dream, One Woman's Nightmare*, Réanne Hemingway-Douglass describes how she struggled to keep communication open to maintain her family relationships—especially difficult with a combined family. Looking back on the voyage, she says, "With additional hindsight, I think counseling at that stage of our relationship (in the 1970s) would have proved unsuccessful. Don was too obsessed by *his* dream to practice adolescent psychology. His one thought was to form a strong crew—*not* to be a father. The boys wanted a *father*, not a captain; they also wanted adventure, not hard work.

"To this day, my younger son has never been able to read my book. 'It was too painful a period of my life,' he has told me. 'I don't want to reopen that chapter, Mom.' (His problems with Don, who is his stepdad, were also exacerbated by his seasickness.)

"Don has mellowed greatly in the intervening years, and although once in a while he has a bout of impatience, he can keep it in check a lot better now. I, on the other hand, have learned to communicate my limits: what responsibilities I *will* assume; what I will *not* (the latter when I feel I have never mastered a certain task). We both feel we're equal partners now—it's no longer his dream against my desires, and we enjoy cruising together immensely. Once in awhile I *do* have to remind him that I'm 50% owner of *Baidarka.*"

Misunderstood communication is common for cruising couples. You may find a given statement demeaning, or you may make a statement that is perceived as silly or unfair. Holding a grudge and allowing communication to become difficult puts your relationship in jeopardy.

Paula Dinius described how she and her husband handled communication on board when feelings were on edge and sensibilities were raw. "We had a pact when we were underway that things said on the boat don't count. If something is said that one of us can't forget, you have to take a shower, eat a meal, and take a nap before you can bring up what the other person said."

Seasoned cruisers recognize that being offshore creates certain stresses. Being clean, rested, and fed soothes your nerve endings and may change your perspective on a given situation.

Living the Dream

Good cruising relationships evolve over time.

Many cruising women have a situation similar to Nancy Payson's. "I deferred to him when we first started because he knew a lot more about it than I did," she says. "Now we are more [like] partners. He still has more strength than I do. He navigates because I don't like to. Our roles have evolved and we stick to them; they're comfortable."

Retired cruiser Lura Francis remembers how she and her husband, Jack, always functioned as a team. "We respected and trusted each other. He never put me down and I likewise for him. We [once] saw a couple anchoring and could hear the man screaming at the poor wife. Jack said, 'We aren't going to do that.' We developed hand signals. It takes lots of preparation and lots of work to be a team."

Because you depend on each other and are always together, cruising can cause a certain intensity for couples. In one way, cruising is an opportunity for couples—it is a way of life where you need to become a team and build trust and respect. Cruising can also be the test of a relationship. Many cruising women agree that a strong relationship on shore will remain strong at sea. A frail relationship is likely to fail.

For Nancy Jewhurst, who cruised with her husband, Victor, and their son, Kyle, cruising allows couples to spend a lot of time together when most couples on land seem to go separate ways. "He's out there with Little League. He has his hobbies, and the woman has hers. . . . In a cruising world, you have far fewer distractions, and it's a fairly intense life, which can be tough. But who knows how long we're here on this earth? I want to make the moments count. I think cruising moments count more than other moments."

Personal disputes that develop during cruising are often cited as reasons for divorce. Lael Morgan, who divorced from her husband after their cruise, believes cruising actually added to the longevity of her marriage. "I sailed with him later, and we are still good friends," she says. "We are both loners, and we lived separate lives."

For me, the trust and respect I enjoy in my relationship are earned commodities. My time, effort, and perseverance have paid off many times over.

Him

At some point, most of the women I have interviewed over the years tell me that cruising was his idea. That doesn't mean she disliked the idea, it is just a statement of chronology. A new twist in recent years caught me off guard. These are men who were the eager prime movers toward cruising, who decided in a year or two that they weren't happy. In contrast to my earlier findings, one of them wanted to go home—not her but *him.*

Here are three different scenarios we encountered within a few months. The first example is a couple we met who had spent about six months cruising and avoiding big towns. The wife was initially hesitant but had fallen in love with the boat, the routine, and the lifestyle. They decided to stop in Mazatlán, an old, established city on the Pacific coast of mainland Mexico. In a matter of days, the husband left the boat. He had decided that he wanted to live ashore and go back to being a contractor. His wife couldn't believe the change. She was determined to stay on the boat and continue cruising. They split up; she on the boat and he on land. She quickly found crew and continued cruising. He stayed in Mexico; he needed interaction that was more social and productive. He couldn't deal with the confinement and his perceived lack of accomplishment.

We became acquainted with the second cruising couple while we were staying in port in a slip while Jim recovered from shoulder surgery. She seemed happy and content with their lives. Almost daily, he came to the boat with some problem needing Jim's advice. With each visit, he was more upset. Finally, he came aboard one morning and announced, "The boat's for sale." He had put all new gear on the boat, from standing rigging to through-hull fittings, and had never realized that maintenance is a constant part of cruising—it never ends. His frustration with constant repairs caused him to give up. He decided they weren't going anywhere ever again on the boat. They packed up their personal belongings, left the boat with a broker, and bought tickets on the next plane home. She never commented on his decision. "Cruising is routine boat maintenance in exotic locations" is an oft-repeated saying, and if you cannot accept that truism, you are likely be very unhappy.

The third couple we encountered had planned to retire to cruising. She didn't learn anything about the boat or cruising and was not a boat partner. He had to chauffeur her to shore because she couldn't operate the dinghy. They had to stay in marinas so she had some freedom to come and go. But once ashore, she found her niche. She utilized her Spanish language skills and became the organizer and liaison between local communities and cruisers. She organized events, parties, flea markets, and was constantly busy. He was bored because he had anticipated sailing instead of staying for long periods near various villages. He finally announced that they were going back home because he couldn't find anything that he wanted to do. He wanted to return to what he knew because cruising wasn't the adventure he had sought. His wife was devastated. They returned home and sold the boat, leaving his wife only with memories.

These scenarios are sad. I don't know if they could have been avoided. The women had been the reluctant partner initially, but with time each woman had found a place and joy in the cruising life. Men who don't examine the whole picture may be sadly disappointed. It is essential that both partners share the responsibility and share the joy. If either partner is excluded from the dream, a cruising lifestyle may not be the right dream.

3

GETTING
STARTED

WHEN WE TAKE ON A NEW ACTIVITY, we formulate a list of questions in an attempt to visualize what will happen. This chapter answers frequently asked questions about cruising and being on the water. You may already have your own list of questions, and not all of them may be answered here. The answers to the questions in this chapter may increase your comfort level and resolve your doubts. Some of these topics will resurface in more detail in later chapters. Sailboats and powerboats have a lot in common. However, we'll discuss them in separate sections so you can read just what you need. We'll start with sailing.

Sailing

If you are not a sailor, it is likely that the first question on your list is, "How do I learn to sail?"

When I started cruising, I was surprised that some women were accompanying their husbands or boyfriends on cruises without knowing how to sail. As one woman cruiser told me, "I went along; I'm not a sailor. I went along all those years with the kids. I don't think I'm capable of taking charge of the boat." There always were others on board during passages, so she never felt in jeopardy. When there are more than two people on the boat, responsibilities tend to be shared. But I believe having several people share the responsibilities on a boat can contribute to a false sense of security.

As Barbara Marrett says of her first cruise, "I trusted John and his skill. I remember on our way out of the Strait of Juan de Fuca thinking, What would I do if there was a fire? What about a dismasting? I hadn't thought about certain emergencies until we were on the way out. I was involved with selling my business, saying goodbye to my friends. They had occupied my mind more than sailing had. I wished I had taken more sailing lessons and had spent some time singlehanding the boat." Barbara found a way to put her mind at ease: "I listed the emergencies I was concerned about and wrote down how we would handle them. I posted these instructions on a bulkhead near the radio so that in an emergency I could glance at the list as a reminder. Although we never had to use it, it gave me peace of mind."

With growing sailing experience and confidence in yourself, you lay the groundwork for successful cruising. Dawn Riley put it very simply: "I don't think anyone should be expected to feel comfortable and enjoy cruising if they don't know how to sail."

Where Do I Learn?

I am a believer in encouraging women to sail together, particularly to race together. I learned to sail without the benefit of a formal school. My first sailing experiences with my first husband were terrifying, and I grew to hate our 22-foot boat. I didn't learn well from him because I had no idea what the end result was supposed to be. In my first lesson, he told me, "Sail the boat around that buoy!" but I didn't know how.

After finally gaining some understanding of how to sail our boat, I was able to follow my first husband's instructions. But I was always intimidated by him and the boat, and I had no desire to take the helm or to be skipper.

Over a year later, we bought a 26-foot boat. At that time, my husband decided to spend time racing offshore on another boat. Our boat sat unused until a friend asked me if I would participate in a women's race. I pointed out that I didn't even know how to get the boat out of the berth, let alone sail it. She said, "We'll learn."

We got a crew together, pieced together what little we knew, and sailed in the race. We didn't hit anything or anyone. We were so exhilarated that we talked about racing the boat against men. Interestingly, we were encouraged by everyone we talked to.

There were six women on the boat, all of whom were married to or dating sailors. We decided not to ask boyfriends or husbands to teach us to sail, since other women had had bad experiences sailing with their partners. So we looked for instructors. The only men allowed on board were several instructors, who taught us specific skills.

Our instructors quickly discovered that we were serious students not afraid to ask questions. The interaction among the women on board made it easy to handle mistakes and keep our enthusiasm high. We did not become the season champions, but we had a good time.

As the skipper, I had to learn everything. Besides being on the helm during the races, I had to take care of the boat, lift and operate the outboard engine, and make lunch. It was great experience.

Think about the best way for you to learn, for you have several choices. Sail with your mate as your instructor; attend a sailing school, or find someone else to teach you, and then go back and sail with your partner. You also can learn on your own.

Your Mate as Your Instructor

If your husband or boyfriend teaches you how to sail, I believe you should be responsible for the program. Specify what you want to learn and in what areas you need to build your confidence.

Start by drawing up a list of things you want to know (see my list of basic skills later in this chapter). Your list may be very general in the beginning, but you can make it more specific as you learn. The important thing is to ask questions until you hear the answer you are looking for.

Sometimes a question is answered correctly, but the answer may not give you the information you really want. In one of our seminars, a woman asked, "What do I do when it is windy and the boat is heeling over too much?" She was told to let off the mainsheet, which is a way to reduce your heel. But from her facial expression, I could tell this answer did not tell her what she wanted to know. She wanted to know about more than the simple mechanics of heeling: She wanted to know what you do when there is too much wind and too much heel, and you feel insecure about not knowing what will happen next.

Asking questions of a spouse or a male friend teaching you to sail may intensify inherent communication problems in your relationship. If the question is about a specific procedure, the answer is specific. When you are looking for a whole body of knowledge, you need to ask a lot of questions.

Pat Nolan has witnessed the different ways men and women learn on a boat. "Women want to know what the procedures are going to be," she explains. "They want to know what is expected so they can process [the information] and be ready." Pat believes more people today are aware that men and women communicate differently, and women are becoming more assertive. "Instead of saying 'Okay, honey, whatever you say,' " Pat explains, "it's 'Hang on, let's talk about this.' "

Sailing in certain directions feels more comfortable than others. Being comfortable means feeling secure. This is the time to ask, "What makes sailing in some directions more comfortable than others?" If you're told, "Reaching and running are always more comfortable than beating," ask for an explanation. When are you reaching, running, and beating? Why does the wind seem different on these different points of sail? You'll have to understand these kinds of distinctions in order to control your environment better and make sailing a comfortable experience.

Each time you encounter something you don't understand, ask very specific questions. Your mate will quickly see that knowing how to control your environment is vital to your sense of security and comfort.

Not all of us are willing to learn from our mates in this way. If you try learning from your mate and the only result is frustration on both your parts, don't give up. Look for other ways to learn.

Sailing Schools

Sailing schools with professional instructors are a great way to learn, either by yourself or with your partner.

Taking lessons with your spouse may eliminate many potential problems. As Gail Amesbury says, "We learned side by side, starting at night school doing basic courses. It was a huge advantage. Neither one of us knew more than the other, and we relied on each other."

Lael Morgan, forty years after cruising from New England to Alaska, agrees. "Take courses together so you know what is involved. Most women don't have a clue about the danger, the difficulty, and the work [sailing] is." To add to her point, if you learn together, you are not in the situation of wondering how much the other person knows.

If you are a beginner sailing with an experienced partner, it's likely your partner will not want to take lessons. Be prepared to go out on your own and find a sailing school where you can learn the basics. Most prospective cruising women have jobs, families, and responsibilities. Finding the time and energy to learn how to sail will take a conscious effort, but rest assured that your effort will help you get more joy out of cruising.

You can start educating yourself while looking for the right school. One of the most important steps is to learn the correct names for boat parts and maneuvers. Begin that process on your own. If you have trouble remembering different parts of the boat, put labels on them. Learning the language of sailing is the first step to equalizing your relationship.

The Womanship sailing school developed the holistic concept of learning comprehensive cruising skills on board, rather than isolating specific skills to be taught one by one. Founder Suzanne Pogell describes this as "an accessible learning framework for women, who like the big picture of what they are aiming for." Suzanne's approach, format, and curriculum have been adopted by several schools that now specialize in teaching women. Among them are Sea Sense and Sistership (see the Resources appendix). These companies have received good press in a variety of publications.

Pat Nolan decided to start her own school, Sistership, in the Virgin Islands. An excellent sailor, she recognized that women learning together with women instructors had a different impact on the students. "When women sail with all women, they are more likely to express their concerns, their fears, and their lack of experience. Women are very open with each other about their needs but tend to be less so when there are men in the group. They don't want to appear inexperienced or fearful in front of the guys. Women are more likely to jump in and try something new in an all-women atmosphere."

Women-only schools offer basic instruction in sailing, docking, anchoring, checking engines, and navigation. In most courses, the school's emphasis is not to turn you into a member of an America's Cup crew. Instructors begin with basic skills and move to more advanced skills as the students are ready. A student's level of confidence at the end of the course often is the program's measure of success.

"I took a basic sailing course and then a liveaboard cruising class from Womanship," attests Gail Bowdish. "It was one of the most significant things in my life. I came home with a lot of confidence in handling the boat, and it worked for my self-esteem. I could take control over my life." Gail's reaction to a women's school is fairly typical.

There are alternatives to learning in a women-only school. US Sailing, the national governing body for the sport of sailing, put together a Keelboat Sailing Education program in concert with commercial sailing schools. The program is appropriate for adults who want to learn to sail keelboats at all levels, whether you want to daysail or make offshore passages. US Sailing lists the schools that participate in the program on their website (see the Resources appendix). From the drop-down menu under Getting Started, click on Find a Place to Sail or Find a Place to Learn for the locations near you. You can find schools that offer US Sailing certification, including the Keelboat Certification System, by selecting Sailor Education from the Education drop-down menu, and then Keelboat Sailing.

A program at a national sailing school might be beyond your budget or require more time than you can give, so it is important to shop around before you commit yourself. In my estimation, in a small group or in a one-on-one teaching situation, a week of half-day lessons will be enough for you to learn the basics. Talk to recent attendees of the school you're considering to get opinions and recommendations.

Learning on Your Own

If attending a formal program at a national sailing school doesn't fit your lifestyle or your budget, you can piece together an independent program of instruction.

Some well-known cruisers learned to sail on their own. Lin Pardey remembers her first sailing experiences as true hands-on trials. "Larry launched me in a dinghy," Lin remembers, "and then hollered, 'Lin, don't jibe; Lin, don't jibe; Lin, duck!' And I learned to sail." Patience Wales's experience was similar. She started sailing on a 12 1/2-foot Herreshoff. After that, she says, "We learned as we went. We went down the Intracoastal. We had all the books, and we talked with a lot of people. We made a lot of mistakes and screwed up a lot. But we never screwed up permanently or in a way that was damaging to either the boat or ourselves."

Look for opportunities to sail on your own or on boats where beginners are welcome. One popular way to learn is to find one or two women who sail and are willing to take you along. If you wander down marina docks on weekends, you might come across a woman skipper who needs an extra crew for the day. In the process, you might even find a sailing mentor who improves her own sailing ability by helping you learn.

Some regional sailing magazines and newsletters have annual crew signups where potential crew are matched up with boats and skippers. These opportunities often are open to beginners. One word of caution: Make sure you don't sign up with a crew looking for someone who is decorative and good at opening beers. You won't learn much about sailing.

Do an online search or check your local Yellow Pages for marinas, sailing clubs, and boat rental operations. These operations frequently offer optional instruction where you can work out your own schedule and ask for instruction as you need it. Your local community college and universities may also offer courses in sailing that are open to the general public.

An excellent way to gain an overall picture of boating is by taking a course through the U.S. Coast Guard Auxiliary or the U.S. Power Squadrons. These classes are taught by experienced volunteers, and they provide basic information on boat handling, nomenclature, boat operation, and regulations. The courses are taught locally and typically charge a small fee.

Both Lin Pardey and Patience Wales learned to sail on small boats when they were in their twenties. Even if you ultimately plan to cruise on a big boat, learning to sail on a small boat—such as a Sunfish, Laser, or Cal 20—equips you with basic sailing skills.

Nancy Payson cruised with her husband and children for seven years on a larger boat before getting the opportunity to learn on a small boat. "The boys really wouldn't let me do very much, and I became the cook," Nancy says of her early cruising days on large boats. "I didn't learn as much as you think one would. Then we did a trailer [sailer trip] for a year and a half. I learned more on that 22-foot boat than [I did on] the big one, and I learned more on that boat because of the reaction time."

Several years after I began sailing, I started sailing a dinghy. The mistakes I had been making on a bigger boat suddenly were magnified, because the small Laser dingy had just one reaction to the things I did wrong—it capsized. After spending some time in the cold water, I learned to pay much closer attention to wind direction and sail trim. As Barbara Marrett says, "I think it is a good idea to learn to sail on your own in a small boat before trying to pilot an expensive, intimidating cruising boat on the ocean."

Working knowledge of the mechanical and electrical systems on a large cruising boat is part of cruising skills. You won't gain these skills on a small boat, but you can learn about these onboard systems after you learn basic sailing skills and spend some time on larger cruising boats. Seminars and short courses in diesel mechanics, electronics, safety at sea, and heavy-weather sailing are valuable. They don't replace knowing how to sail, but they should be part of your cruising knowledge. Local clubs, boat shows, the U.S. Power Squadrons, and the U.S. Coast Guard Auxiliary offer educational opportunities in these areas. I recommend looking for programs with a woman instructor. She most likely will be in tune with your needs. Contact information on sailing schools and other programs can be found in the Resources appendix.

Do I Have to Become an Expert?

In every endeavor there are levels of competence. Learning to swim can mean everything from staying afloat to competing in the Olympics. And so it is with sailing: You do not need the skill required to earn a gold medal in the Olympics to get your boat from one place to the next. The goal is to learn how to manage your boat.

What Do I Need to Learn?

When you are comfortable taking the helm and piloting your boat, you are on your way. From that point, the degree of competence you acquire as a sailor is your decision.

Learning to sail alone is critical to your survival. You may plan never to sail alone, but a time may come when you have to. If you never learned to pilot your boat alone, your response could be panic and indecision. But if you know you can sail alone, your underlying confidence will make the difference.

For your own survival and peace of mind, as well as your partner's, I recommend being able to do the following without assistance or direction:

- ☐ Hoist and lower or furl the sails.
- ☐ Trim the sails correctly for the course you want.
- ☐ Steer the boat accurately on a compass course and on an apparent wind course.
- ☐ Turn your boat by tacking and jibing.
- ☐ Recognize what point of sail you are on.
- ☐ Understand the difference between apparent wind and true wind.
- ☐ Know when and how to reduce sail.
- ☐ Start the engine, drive the boat under power, and dock or anchor.

- ☐ Pump water out of the bilge.
- ☐ Check your engine oil.
- ☐ Plot a compass course and navigate from a chart.
- ☐ Use a sextant and do celestial navigation.
- ☐ Use your electronic navigation devices.

The reason for developing your own skills is clear. It will enable you to sail the boat if someone falls in the water. All good sailing schools teach recovery—the important thing is, can you do it? If you are alone because your sailing partner fell overboard, you need to bring the boat back to him and get him on board. There are techniques and equipment designed specifically for this type of rescue. Your security and peace of mind will depend on knowing how to use that equipment.

The mechanical and electrical systems on a cruising boat are integral to life on board. I strongly recommend that you learn the basics of those systems. To assume all women are not mechanically inclined is old fashioned. You drive a car, thread a sewing machine, operate a computer, or parallel park a car. All these tasks require some degree of mechanical skill. You might prefer not to do mechanical things, but I don't believe women are inherently unable to learn the mechanical tasks basic to a boat.

Even if you won't be responsible for these systems all of the time, be sure you learn to purge air from a line, check dipsticks, and charge batteries and monitor their condition. On some boats, partners share tasks equally—each changes oil, replaces pumps, cleans filters, shops, cooks, and washes dishes.

Your ability to do a job without direction is important, and confidence in your ability to do so will be your biggest asset. It will allow you to understand that your environment is not out of your control.

Power

Understanding Power

The uninitiated often equate cruising under power with driving a car; anybody can do it. First, let's take a step back. Cars run on highways, and rarely run aground. There are service stations and garages everywhere. There is AAA to help you out in emergencies. There are highway patrol, police, ambulances, and fire departments patrolling on or located near most roads. There are call boxes or cell phones you can use if you have a problem. Life on the water is *not* just like driving a car.

Thousands of boats travel the Intracoastal Waterway every year; it is as close as we come to a freeway for boats. Uniformed folks or traffic lights do not manage traffic, so you need to abide by the rules on your own. You help folks when you see trouble. You carry large quantities of fuel because you don't get 20 miles to the gallon; you're lucky if you get 2 miles to the gallon. Parallel parking a car is a snap compared to docking or anchoring. If you are tired or sleepy, don't pull over—it's not an option. And remember: *Boats don't have brakes.*

There are good things about powerboats. You depend on fuel rather than wind to move you, so you can actually keep a schedule if you want to. Your speed is not dependent on the amount of wind. If you get tired of sitting, you can walk around and stretch without losing travel time. More internal space allows for more amenities. Cold or rainy weather doesn't keep you from traveling in comfort. Clearly there are reasons for cruising in powerboats.

Where Do I Learn to Operate a Powerboat?

There are several ways to learn, but one recommendation applies to whatever method you select. It is best to learn on your own boat, or a sister ship. Powerboats seem to have many more variations than sailboats. You can learn to sail on a dinghy, and the same principles will apply to all sailboats. The type of hull may vary in sailing, but it has little effect on the basic skills of sailing. Powerboat hulls vary in shape. Powerboats vary in number of engines, type of engines, and type of fuel. Each of those variations is likely to introduce new systems and require additional skills. There are classes to help you learn about engines, plumbing, wiring, and electronics. They are a good introduction to general principles. Taking that information and learning to apply it to your boat will get you started.

Learning how to operate a powerboat is essential to successful cruising. Some of us have had success learning from a spouse or boyfriend whereas others have not. You have to make that decision for yourself. There are options available just about anywhere you find boats. Boating instruction from an established school has worked for many women.

Sally Bee Brown, a contributing editor at *PassageMaker* magazine, said of the learning process, "For many women, I would recommend a woman's hands-on boating course, such as Sea Sense. Although my patient husband taught me seamanship, I do know that doesn't work for a lot of women. I wrote an article on Sea Sense about five years ago and spent a week with them as they trained four women. They did a wonderful job, and since I've kept in contact with the students, I know it worked."

Over the years, I have heard women say that they are more comfortable learning from other women. Other women sharing the same experience offer a sense of support that men don't seem to require. Knowing that other women have learned to operate a powerboat successfully is a great confidence builder.

Your Mate as Your Instructor

The most obvious teacher for most women is the man with whom she shares the boat. Alison Fishel said, "Bill's patient and he doesn't yell." She described how they work together: "I didn't see distance the same way. We practiced a lot with Bill asking, 'How long is that boat, how far away is it?' until he trusted my ability to judge distance." When you are docking and can't see one end of the boat from the other, you have to depend on that second set of eyes.

Ellen Voyles offered insight into why she and many women don't always learn from their partner. "He learns by doing and would say, 'Here, do it,' so the broker showed me how to drive the boat, sort of gave me lessons. At first I was very uncomfortable with the sounds, the smells, and I was sure we were going to sink." Ellen is very capable now and says, "The only time I get nervous about driving is when there's lots of traffic."

Although she doesn't have a regular boating partner, Patti McKenna told me about her observations of others. "My neighbor is the kind that tells his wife and other women, 'You sit and stay, I'll do everything.' When I suggest she can steer, or that she needs to know what to do in case something happens to him, his response is, 'It won't happen.' " Patti said, "When she goes out with me, just like anyone else on the boat, I give her jobs to do." Hopefully this man's ostrich-like behavior can be modified.

A number of women have made the transition from cruising under sail to cruising under power. Katie Hamilton has been back and forth between power and sail. Her perspective is very straightforward. "I learned to feel comfortable being aboard and handling any boat. And after my first day aboard a powerboat, I realized it's so much easier than sailing because it's less complicated. Even I had to admit we did more motorsailing than actual sailing in all our years of cruising under sail."

When I made the transition to power after twenty-five years on the same sailboat, it was difficult. There are still moments when I would give anything for a mast and sail, but now those moments are rare. Learning to operate a boat that is only 5 feet longer than our sailboat but weighs more than twice as much was daunting. I realized that putting the sailboat in the berth was my only powerboat experience. Faced with twin engines each more than twice the size of the sailboat auxiliary, my learning curve was vertical. The first time my husband "walked" the boat to a dock I was hooked. I found several books on powerboat operation. Much of the content was familiar because boats are boats. When I found new information, my husband was faced with twenty questions. He didn't volunteer to teach me, but he is my mentor as I learn.

I agree with Katie about the skills being less complicated, but there were many more systems to be learned. With stabilizers, a 15-kilowatt generator, both 12-volt and 110-volt electrical systems, electric heads, a washer/dryer, an 18.5-cubic-foot refrigerator-freezer, plus miles of teak parquet, energy management is still the hardest subject. Our cruising friends tease me about my floating condo, until I tell them about mopping parquet and the constant fear of blowing up the inverter.

Sally Bee Brown described how she learned powerboating and why. "Our first outing was from Seattle's Lake Union to Anacortes. We only were out a matter of hours before I realized I had made a major mistake—for safety, comfort, good partnership, and pure enjoyment I needed to learn everything I could about boating. I am a person who likes to have some control over my situation and, without knowledge, I had none. During the next ten years, I was in constant learning mode."

Professional Schools

As more women find themselves in powerboats, many of the original women's sailing schools are now offering powerboat instruction. Carol Cuddyer and Patti Moore, both licensed 100-ton captains, operate the Sea Sense school. Carol came late to powerboating but has discovered there is an audience of women wanting to learn.

She says that many women are making the transition to power. They don't want to give up their life on the water. She says about women, "The attraction is the amenities available; the challenge is docking, maneuvering, and systems." She agrees with many female instructors that there is a difference in attitude toward learning. "Most men just jump in and start pushing buttons—a trial-and-error approach—whereas most women want to know what the button will do before they push it."

Fortunately men frequently recognize they should avoid trying to be instructors. Carol pointed out that not all men are good teachers and not all women want to learn from men. "We have many testimonials from grateful men whose wives learned from Sea Sense." She said that women do want to be partners on board because they feel safer, and it's more fun. She asked, "You do know the woman's place is at the helm, right?"

In recent years, US Sailing has expanded its education program to encompass powerboating (from the drop-down menu at its website under Education, select Powerboat Training). As with its Keelboat System, it has a very thorough textbook for students and offers instruction by certified individuals who give on-the-water instruction. Not all of these schools have female instructors or offer women-only instruction, but they offer a well thought out program. Statistics on boating accidents, according to US Sailing, indicate that 84% of serious boating accidents involve operators who have not completed a boating course. Simply getting behind the wheel and starting the engine is not sufficient preparation for being on the water.

Alternative Learning Situations

There are two organizations regularly involved in boater education: The U.S. Power Squadrons and the U.S. Coast Guard Auxiliary offer basic courses to help you learn nautical nomenclature and the Navigation Rules commonly referred to as "the rules of the road." More advanced courses include rescue techniques, chart reading, plotting, and weather. These groups regularly participate in boat shows and post course offerings in marine stores and boatyards.

BoatU.S. is another organization that offers educational opportunities. Membership provides a variety of services, and it maintains a major website to help all boaters.

The Resources appendix has contact information for Sea Sense, which offers on-the-water powerboat instruction to women, taught by women. The bibliography lists several books that offer excellent information about operating and maintaining powerboats.

What Do I Need to Learn?

Just as with sailing, you need a command of basic skills even if you don't really want to run the boat. The reason for this is simple: your safety. If that worst-case scenario happens to you—your partner falls overboard or becomes ill—you have to manage the boat for your sake and his.

These are basic skills you need to have:

- ☐ Start and stop the engine(s).
- ☐ Change gears.
- ☐ Check oil, water, and fuel levels.
- ☐ Check the bilge for indication of fuel or water intrusion.
- ☐ Proper starting techniques: Does your boat require blowers? How much warm-up time?

☐ Docking and undocking techniques.
☐ Anchoring technique.
☐ Use your VHF in an emergency.
☐ Steer the boat accurately to a compass course.
☐ Read a chart and plot your position.

If My Partner Falls Overboard, How Do I Rescue Him?

Prevention is the key to avoiding falling overboard. Wearing a harness with tethers fastened to the boat will keep you both from falling overboard. Insist they be worn. If your partner is not wearing a harness and falls overboard, the first thing to do is deploy life rings and other flotation devices he can hold on to while you bring the boat back to him and get him on board.

In my opinion, the best rescue equipment available is the Lifesling, a combination helicopter lifting sling and floating horseshoe. The basic procedure is to tow the Lifesling behind the boat and position the boat so your partner can reach the device. Once he has the Lifesling in his grasp, stop the boat, pull the Lifesling to the boat (don't tow the Lifesling while the person is wearing it), and follow the manufacturer's instructions for hoisting him aboard.

We often talk through a process, thinking that is sufficient as "practice." But the following story shows just how mistaken that can be. One warm day, in warm water, we and another couple tested the theory that it would be possible to hang on to a towed line if the boat wasn't moving too fast, about 4.5 knots. We were very *wrong*. Both of the men could hang on to the line, with effort, at about 3 knots. We two women could barely hang on at 2 knots. We were using a heavy braided line with a big knot and a fender on the end. What a revelation that test was.

There are many aspects to executing a proper man-overboard procedure. It is important for you and your partner to understand this procedure and practice rescues together. You will need to be confident about your ability to rescue a man overboard. Take advantage of safety demonstrations and courses.

How Can I Go Cruising When I Always Get Seasick?

Seasickness has several causes. Unless yours is caused by an inner ear malfunction, which affects your equilibrium, there is a good chance you can overcome seasickness.

Worry and fear frequently manifest themselves in the symptoms of seasickness. Overcoming fear by gaining experience and skill can help.

The most common form of seasickness occurs when your body is adapting to being at sea. Day cruising and weekend trips may not give your body enough time to make that adjustment. With time, your body learns a new set of perceptions and reactions so you won't suffer from seasickness. After many years of cruising, there are still times when I get seasick after being ashore for several weeks or living in a marina for an extended period of time. My body needs to relearn responses that have been unused for some time. See Chapter 7 for more on seasickness.

How Do I Keep the Boat from Heeling?

A sailboat moves because wind puts pressure on the sails. That pressure makes the boat lean or heel. A small amount of heel is normal in efficient sailing; up to 25 degrees is comfortable and efficient for most boats. To make the boat heel less, it is necessary to reduce the wind pressure on the sails. For example, you can achieve this by releasing the *sheets* (lines fastened to the free corner of the sail) so the sail "spills" some of the wind pressure. On certain points of sail, such as when you are sailing downwind and the wind is pushing your boat from behind, your boat will heel less and feel more comfortable.

A powerboat should not heel. It doesn't have sails, so the wind pressure is absent. However, we would be remiss in not describing *windage*. Look at the profile of a powerboat compared to a sailboat. Most powerboats are designed to have more amenities, so they sit well above the water. Most sailboats have very low profiles in comparison. The sails rise above the profile to provide the foil for the wind. In extreme winds, your powerboat will be difficult to operate because the profile will expose a solid surface to the wind. That profile is not adjustable for wind conditions as sails are. The solid surface of a powerboat will take the force of the wind and will need the power of its engine(s) to overcome the windage.

How Do I Live in Such a Confined Space?

Comparing the living space in a house to the space on a boat certainly makes a boat seem confined. Reducing your possessions, both personal and practical, will simplify life and take up less space. A well-designed boat with good stowage and plenty of light does not feel confined to me. But a feeling of confinement is not just physical—it has to do with attitude.

Living in close quarters, 24 hours a day, means learning to respect each other's needs for quiet and privacy. Minor annoyances must be dealt with so they don't become major issues. The cubic yardage of your boat will never be adequate without a give-and-take attitude and mutual respect.

How Do I Manage the Boat on Long Voyages?

The organization you impose at sea is called a *watch system*. For day trips you may not use a watch system, but as you progress to days of consecutive cruising and overnight passages, a watch system becomes essential.

When you devise a watch system, you and your partner divide the day up into blocks of time. You each will be responsible for one block of time, alternating watches so when one person is on watch the other person can rest. You can divide the day into 3-hour watches, 4-hour watches, or in any configuration that suits you. It's a good idea to consider who likes to stay up late and who likes to get up early when devising your watch system. See Chapter 14 for more information on watch systems.

What Scares You Most about Voyaging?

What scares me most is not being prepared for all the things that could happen on a voyage. In the past, ignorance has been the prime factor in my being scared. With each passage, I find preparation is still the most important ingredient in making me comfortable.

The boat needs to be provisioned, and all systems need to be in running order. The route, with alternatives in the event of bad weather, needs to be discussed and agreed upon. An overall picture of the passage, including how long it will take and what to expect in terms of weather and sea conditions, is essential for me. I don't have a crystal ball, but it's on my wish list.

How Many Storms Have You Encountered at Sea?

Fewer than I have living on land! We plan our route using *pilot charts* (charts of average weather trends for a given geographical area) so we are cruising to places where the weather is pleasant and the water is warm. We have encountered bad weather, including huge seas and winds in excess of 65 knots that lasted several days. It was uncomfortable, and I was frightened. Once we were in those conditions, my husband made it clear that we would just have to keep going. His advice sounded so simple and sensible: I just concentrated on getting through the weather. Looking back, I realize that was my only option. I trusted the boat to see me through.

When we first purchased the trawler, we found that even minor sea conditions overwhelmed the fuel system. We had the tanks cleaned and the fuel polished only to discover that the sludge in the bottom of the tanks had not been removed. We could not bring her across the Gulf of Mexico from Florida to the Panama Canal like that, so we shipped her from Fort Lauderdale to Ensenada, Mexico.

She arrived in Ensenada and was off-loaded in heavy storm conditions. Her planks had dried out and opened up during the two weeks on the ship, and she nearly sank when we tried to refloat her. Fortunately, Jim had modified the engines to also function as bilge pumps, and they kept her afloat until we could get her into a boatyard. After drying and recaulking the planking, we decided to leave for California.

The storm had subsided but the seas were still rough and confused. We managed to get 8 miles from Ensenada before the fuel system became clogged with sludge loosened by the rough conditions. We radioed Ensenada and were towed back to the harbor. Unless Jim could solve the fuel problems, we would have to wait for flat seas . . . or be towed the 600 miles to California! He constructed a temporary fuel polishing system so we could pump the fuel from the tanks into clean plastic barrels in the cockpit. From there, the fuel was pumped back through the fuel manifolds to the engines. It took nearly a week to build the temporary system, and another three weeks to get from Mexico to San Francisco Bay. The sludge could not be completely removed without tearing up the bottom, which we did once we got to San Francisco.

How Often Do You Go Home?

Our budget on the sailboat was very limited, so we rarely visited the States. The travel cost, combined with the cost of leaving the boat, was expensive for us. You may have more options. On our seven-year circumnavigation, I went back once for two weeks for medical treatment, and my husband and I went back for five days when our youngest daughter got married. When we left the boat, we used the time to explore our location rather than go to the States. We could leave the boat at anchor with someone we trusted to watch over her and care for our cat. Our children, siblings, and friends could travel and come to visit and cruise with us for several weeks at a time.

4

A BOAT
FOR JUST
THE TWO OF US

SELECTING THE RIGHT BOAT is a major factor in determining how happy you will be cruising.

There is plenty of room for different opinions on what length your boat should be. But the most important thing to keep in mind when selecting a boat is that you are choosing for "just the two of us."

Cruising families and couples who share a boat with others may have different requirements and resources because their permanent crew numbers more than two people. But if you plan to cruise the majority of the time as a couple, your boat should be customized for the two of you and where you plan to cruise. You need to be able to manage your vessel and live with it.

The Right Boat for Us: Power or Sail?

Cruising is the goal, but how do you know whether you want to cruise on a sailboat or on a powerboat? Most people make this decision based on their experience or on the boat they already own. Traditionally, cruising was a sailboat domain. Part of the romance and lore of cruising had to do with full sails, the trade winds, and the first of the recreational cruising boats. When Miles Smeeton's first book *(Once Is Enough)* about his sailing voyages with his wife Beryl became popular in the 1960s, the adventure and the reality of cruising appeared to be within reach of ordinary folks. His tales of resolving problems over a freshly brewed cup of tea or setting foot on a remote island inspired us to dream of the cruising life. Nowadays, thousands of people have the dream. Fiberglass boats were more affordable and easier to maintain. When GPS became an everyday gadget, there was no longer the requirement of learning how to use a sextant to find your way on the water (although it's still a good idea). Finally, recreational powerboats built along the lines of the traditional trawler proved they could cross oceans efficiently and safely, and even circumnavigate.

How Do We Decide?

So how do you choose between a sailboat and a powerboat? Marja Vance grew up in the desert and was introduced to boats when she met Stephen, her future husband. In 1979, they started out on that journey of a lifetime, circumnavigating aboard a Cal 2-27. When they completed their trip, they became full-time professional crew. They have moved through a variety of boats and presently are the crew on a 94-foot power yacht. With thousands of miles of experience, they don't find the choice any easier. This is what Marja recently told me:

"Stephen and I are having a bit of a dilemma, because he would very much like to have a power vessel when we eventually retire, since he feels (as do I) that they are easier to operate and handle. Only problem is, if you wish to cross oceans, you need a very big vessel, which we neither want nor could afford. In addition, a 40-foot sailboat and a 40-foot powerboat are two very different vessels—you would have a much bigger 'home' in the powerboat, more room for comforts than a 40-foot sailboat. I, on the other hand, do not want to give up the world of sailing, even though I do recognize the advantages of power, and certainly enjoy living and working aboard this very luxurious vessel. I enjoy crossing oceans, and I am looking forward very much to returning to the canals of Europe, so I feel we need a boat that could do many things, hopefully. That is why I would lean toward a motorsailer."

However, others might argue differently. Linda Fraser told me about her experience with her husband, Andrew. "We bought a

Hans Christian 38, our dream boat. I took a sabbatical, and we were going cruising for six months. We went to Acapulco and back. We spent too much time trying to maintain all of the wood. It took away from the fun. We decided that we wanted more space, and we looked at pilothouse sailboats because we wanted to have some protection [from the elements]. We finally decided that a powerboat made sense because it had more living space; this one (a Nordhavn 46) has a Portuguese bridge [a bulwark in front of the pilothouse], which is safer at sea, and we wanted more comfort. We did look at big sailboats, but they didn't have the amenities."

Linda and Andrew are taller than average so space is an issue. They also cruise with their dogs, who have a much easier time managing getting on and off the powerboat at dock level.

Sometimes we find that we have to make a choice. When my husband and I made the transition to a powerboat after twenty-five years on the same sailboat, it was clearly an issue of necessity. Getting older brought us face to face with our limitations. We had never changed our sailing style. Our boat was built for offshore racing, and we had made changes only to add a few amenities such as refrigeration and an anchor windlass. From our perspective, a boat that had been perfect for over thirty years was still perfect, and we would have to find a new home for her with younger people. Once we had done that, and still believing in wooden boats, we found a Grand Banks Alaskan 53 built in 1974. It was in terrible condition since it had sat unused for years. Dry rot was rampant, and only the paint, varnish, and Bondo seemed to be keeping her afloat, but the price was right. Nearly four years later she is still a work in progress but is structurally and mechanically sound. She can maintain 8 knots day in and day out while we enjoy hot water, make ice cream, and leave the foul-weather gear in the locker.

But amenities are not the whole story. We only have to look at Lin and Larry Pardey to appreciate the joy of cruising under sail. No ocean is too big for *Taleisin*, and the Pardeys don't believe that complexity is necessarily better. Their adventures have always been and continue to be on wooden sailboats, without an engine and electronic gadgetry.

The Right Boat

Finding the right cruising boat takes time, and you need to invest enough time and energy looking at boats to learn what you want, what you need, and what you can live with.

If you live near a marina or a waterfront where boats are kept, start prowling the docks. Ask boatowners questions about their boat and how it suits the kinds of sailing they do. Most owners love to talk about their boat, and many will give curious folks a tour.

A boatyard, where boats are stored in the off-season and maintenance work is done, is also a great place to see what is involved in owning a boat, learn what problems boats develop, and study hull and keel shapes. If you have seen an advertisement for a certain boat, a boatyard is a likely place to see that boat's underbody and any visible problems that may have developed below the waterline.

Visiting a boat show is fun and should be part of your research, but, generally speaking, a boat show is not where you will ultimately buy a boat.

Photos, stories, and advertisements in boating magazines and on boating sites will acquaint you with all types of cruising boats. Some magazines (such as *Cruising World*) list all their boat reviews on their website. Many magazines have classified sections listing boats for sale, with sellers' telephone numbers. Call them to talk about boats and costs. Manufacturers' websites, used boat sites, and owners' associations are other sources of information.

Cruising on charter boats can be good practice, but the boats in large charter fleets are not necessarily examples of good designs for long-term cruisers. Charter boats are designed for short-term use. They are crammed with amenities and maintained by someone else. Check small charter fleets, which may have a variety of boat designs from different manufacturers.

We tell our seminar participants that trying out a boat is essential. When you buy a boat—even a new one—it should be subject to a marine survey and a test sail. A test sail on a sailboat does not mean motoring around for an hour—it means going out and using all the sails in the inventory, with the engine off, to see how the boat handles. If there isn't enough wind when you go out, reschedule.

Another strategy is to find the type of boat you're interested in and get acquainted with someone who owns the same design. Find a boat that needs crew for a passage or a boat that is going to be raced. One couple took our advice one step further. They decided they were interested in a Valiant 40 because it was affordable, had a good interior layout, and was American built. They found three Valiants that were racing to Hawaii, and they called the owners to find out if they needed extra crew to bring the boats home after the race. They found a ride, spent nearly three weeks sailing a Valiant 40 in all types of ocean conditions, and ultimately bought one. They are happy with their choice, and there have been no surprises since they know the design well.

Sail

Most sailors today would probably not find the Pardeys' boat, which is less than 30 feet long, suitable, nor would they start a circumnavigation in a Cal 2-27 like Marja and Stephen Vance did. When we first went cruising twenty-five years ago on a 48-foot boat, we were often the biggest boat in the anchorage; nowadays, 40- to 50-foot sailboats are common. The issue of size on a sailboat is not unlike the recent trend in housing. We are building and buying houses that are substantially bigger than twenty years ago, although there are some people in mini-homes.

A bigger boat can hold more stuff, carry bigger sails, and get places more quickly than a small boat. On the other hand, small boats cost less, are easier for two people to handle, and maintaining them is easier. But having a bigger boat for two people usually means having electric winches, roller furling sails, and a dependable electrical system. Bigger sailboats often have large auxiliary engines with substantial fuel tankage, generators, and bow thrusters to make them easier to manage and keep amenities working. One of the problems we see in the larger boats is maintaining all of the systems. If you are cruising in populated areas, finding skilled help is reasonably easy. In the third world, the parts you need and the skills to make the repairs are often scarce (which is another good reason to know how to make repairs yourself).

For me, the most telling question about sailboat size is, "Can it be sailed by one person?" In the case of cruising, knowing that you can manage the boat alone is the touchstone for how successful and happy you will be as a cruiser.

Different designs sail differently. Our boat was designed for "performance," which really means it was designed for racing. It had a fin keel and a flat bottom, and was quick and easy to sail. Like most sailboats, it was easiest to manage on a reach. The traditional cruising sailboat—referred to as a bluewater boat by some—has a full keel, is generally quite heavy, and is usually slow. It is an uncomfortable ride because it is slow—the slower a boat travels through the water, the more it is subject to the action of the water. A slow boat is like a cork and reacts to every change in the water. A bluewater boat has a heavy, full keel and a short rig to carry less sail area to keep the boat from heeling. This is the opposite of what it takes to move a sailboat through the water. The heavier a boat, the more sail area is required. As a result, many sailboat cruisers and former cruisers who owned bluewater boats will tell you that they motored most of the time because the boat wouldn't sail well. Being novices, many of these people assumed that a bluewater boat would be safer, which resulted in them purchasing boats that were hard to sail successfully. The manufacturers overcame the lack of good sailing design by installing large auxiliary motors. Linda Fraser pointed out that they changed to power after their experience with a bluewater boat. They rarely sailed because the heavy construction and the short rig weren't practical in the light-air sailing conditions they found in Mexico. Along with space and brightwork issues, switching to a trawler for cruising made better sense to them.

Power

In this decade, powerboats are at last considered capable of cruising. Circumnavigations by Nordhavn trawlers in the last few years have launched a serious effort to sell powerboats in a market typically belonging to sailboats. Previously, cruisers usually planned on sailing because it is the traditional method and it is not dependent on diesel. But trawlers have proved that they can go long distances and survive the open sea. Fishing trawlers have been doing this for years, but it took the marketing of pleasure trawlers to show the cruising public it can be done.

Bill Parlatore, editor in chief of *PassageMaker* magazine, points out that trawler owners often are older sailors who want to keep cruising. These converts to powerboating already know where they want to go and what they want to do, and can knowledgeably shop with their specific goals in mind. Depending upon where you want to go, how long you want to be gone, and who is going, there are lots of cruising powerboats you can choose from.

Sailing our 48-foot sailboat with two people was more difficult as we aged. In comparison, operating our 53-foot trawler seems easy. We don't have masts to climb or sails to trim, but we do have to be quick and accurate maneuvering twin engines on a vessel that weighs three times as much as our sailboat. Size is always an issue because bigger boats hold more stuff. Of necessity, a long-range cruising powerboat will be bigger because it needs to carry large quantities of fuel. A 50-foot trawler can travel the same distance as a 100-foot megayacht, but the trawler will be slower and will not need as much fuel. Indeed, with powerboats the issue is more often speed; how long will the trip take? At 2 miles per gallon, our trawler will travel at 8 knots. Our friend has a 75-foot power cruiser that cruises at 18 knots and uses more than 30 gallons per hour. Bigger engines burn more fuel but don't take as long to reach the destination as smaller engines.

For many powerboaters, cruising is about the destination rather than the travel time. They will accept being cramped or pounding through lumpy seas because they are anticipating the goal. We purchased a 30-year-old trawler that was clearly inadequate in terms of amenities. We knew we had hours of work ahead of us to make the boat comfortable. The hot-water heater didn't work, the heads were not functioning, and the staterooms had an odor that made them unusable. We slept in the main cabin for weeks. The boat was originally designed for long-distance travel, but it had not been used for seven or eight years. When it had been used, it served the purpose of the family "car," moving people from one location to another. We changed all that.

The fast boats are still mostly for moving people, but the slower boats now reflect the impact of cruising. Trawler and tugboat designs are now part of the cruising scene. They are comfortable, efficient, and an acceptable alternative to cruising sailboats. A small tugboat can easily do coastal cruising, weather permitting. It is comfortable at anchor, and can use a generator to power the galley, the heads, and the DVD player. It can squeeze into a local marina for the night if you feel the need for a "night out."

Trawlers meet the need to go long distances. Designed for open water, they have bunks designed for sleeping underway, galleys meant to be used for three meals a day, and hot water for showers. Stabilized with a steadying sail or roll-control systems, they offer the opportunity to enjoy 24-hour travel in comfort and safety.

I have taken advantage of an attribute not available on our sailboat. The weight of an appliance or gadget was a serious issue on *Nalu IV*. She was a performance sailboat and filling her with heavy stuff was detrimental to that performance. Our trawler, *MV Nalu*, doesn't mind extra weight. Filling her with water, fuel, marvelous galley toys, and several guests doesn't seem to affect speed or fuel consumption. I no longer need to ask clerks to weigh my selection of a new coffee grinder or teakettle before I purchase it!

A Personal Choice

The right cruising boat ultimately is a personal choice, and we all have different qualities we want to find in a boat. I have outlined five basic points I use when looking at boats.

First, as a long-distance cruiser, you need to feel confident that your boat can take more than you can, which means sound construction. I want a used boat, because many construction faults develop in the first three years of a boat's life. I want a boat built and commissioned by sailors, not day laborers who have no idea what the end product will be.

Second, the design must be a good cruising boat—not one driven by a marketing department trying to sell me upholstery or marble countertops. On a sailboat, I want a staysail, so I can have an extra sail for power or carry a small sail in bad weather. I want a tall rig, so the boat can carry big sails in light-air conditions. I prefer wheel steering that is operated by steering cables, because hydraulic steering has no "feel." A powerboat must have a stabilizing system, must be able to travel 1,000 miles nonstop, and must have twin engines.

Third, the quality of life on board in all conditions must be as comfortable as possible. Bunks must be dry, able to hold me in place in rough conditions, and changed easily. The galley must be workable whether we are going upwind or downwind. On a sailboat, the head must flush on either tack and should not require that valves be turned on and off each time. Every item on the boat must be stowable, from earrings to spare parts (even the captain, occasionally).

Fourth, routine maintenance and repair must be simple. Whether I am changing a halyard or checking the oil, I know that if maintenance isn't easy it won't get done. Varnished brightwork is gorgeous, but I don't want to spend every spare moment sanding. The cost of repairs has to be reasonable. Otherwise, I don't want the system—electronic or otherwise—on the boat.

Finally, I want a boat that is beautiful to look at. Boats that have a boxlike shape to create more interior space are ugly. A boat should look graceful at anchor and underway. When someone asks me, "Which boat is yours?" I want to be able to say, "The pretty one."

Cruising Venue

Whether you cruise in warm or cold climates is a factor in boat selection. A pilothouse is great for cold climates and wet weather. But the same pilothouse may have to be air-conditioned in warm climates. Large, open cockpits make the perfect living room in the warm waters of the Caribbean or the South Pacific. But open cockpits are wet and cold in Alaska and the North Atlantic.

If you have been cruising farther and farther from home and find that your boat is comfortable and safe, stay with the boat you have until you are certain you need a different boat. Buying a new boat is not a guarantee that you will have problem-free cruising. It will take time to get used to a new boat, resolve minor construction and system glitches, and feel secure with your new vessel.

Size

Overall size and interior space are important, but wide-open spaces and size just for the sake of size are not qualities you should look for in a boat. The more amenities you have, the more power you need to use them, and to generate power you need fuel. While a sailboat can cruise with a 150-gallon diesel tank, a powerboat used for cruising may have to carry 1,500 gallons of fuel. Fuel tanks take up a lot of space. A simple formula in thinking about powerboats is, the more things you want on the boat, the bigger the boat needs to be. One engine or two is the first issue. A single engine allows more space for other installations, but you have the worry of no backup engine. Many single-engine boats have a "get home" engine or a generator rigged so that it will operate a small propeller. With twin engines, you have two of everything—from double controls on the bridge console to duplicate fuel manifolds and filter systems—but you have an automatic backup in the event one engine quits.

It takes a big powerboat to carry sufficient fuel to circumnavigate, but it is possible. You need to carry thousands of gallons of fuel to make the longest legs of a circumnavigation. That tankage alone would take you beyond a 40-footer. A small powerboat with a galley, head, and double bunk would be perfect for gunkholing, traveling the Tennessee-Tombigbee Waterway, or plying the Sea of Cortez. It can be moved across the country on a trailer. Size is a simple issue once you decide where you want to cruise.

Jane and Geves Kenny have a 34-foot Tollycraft that they have used for the last few years to cruise the East Coast and the Great Lakes. They had considered selling it since they had cruised most of the areas they wanted to see. However, they thought they had more options by bringing the boat to their home base of San Diego. As Jane put it, "We are sad to leave the fresh water for salt as she is in great shape but feel we have done all of this area and it is again time for change."

Cruisers have plied the oceans of the world in boats of all sizes. We have several friends who have circumnavigated in boats less than 30 feet long. A sailboat 38 to 40 feet in length is an ideal size for a cruising boat. A boat that size is usually big enough to be comfortable and small enough to be manageable. I have in mind specific designs, such as the old Cal 40 or a C&C 38.

Only two of the women I interviewed sailed in boats over 50 feet; over half the women sailed in boats under 40 feet.

Patience Wales sailed with her husband and another couple, and they have cruised bigger boats because there were four adults sailing on board. Nancy Jewhurst and her husband and son cruised full-time on a Traveler 32. Jack and Lura Francis, both fairly tall, circumnavigated on a Westsail 32. Irene Hampshire and her partner raised two sons on a 33-foot boat. Lin and Larry Pardey's boat is under 30 feet, and Barbara Marrett cruised on a 31-foot boat.

Nancy Bischoff sailed on a Tayana 37 with her 6-foot 6-inch husband and two sons for ten years. They planned the boat around the family's needs when the boys were young, but the design still works for them today. Each boy had his own aft cabin, giving him privacy and room for his possessions. The parents found their privacy in a forward cabin. Crammed between the fore and aft cabins are the head, main saloon, and galley. Both boys actively pursued music and performed at the drop of an anchor. Space was at a premium with drum set, keyboard, bass guitar, and amplifier on the boat—as well as schoolbooks, boogie boards, snorkel gear, and fishing tackle. They were a two-dinghy family, since the boys had an active social life.

Some women might find the amount of space on a boat too tight for their taste. But Nancy Bischoff found the physical closeness of a cruising boat a unique plus, especially where children were involved. (When her youngest son sailed on our boat for two weeks, however, I told him to stow his gear in the forward cabin. Moments later he hollered, "Empty drawers! I've never seen empty drawers!")

Some sailors view size as a safety feature. Certainly, boats under 20 feet can seem tiny in big seas. But crew from aircraft carriers talk about being overwhelmed by big seas, so size may be more of a psychological factor than a safety one. Proper design and solid construction are the most important safety factors on your boat.

Boat Motion

If sailing will be your means of locomotion, the sailing characteristics of a boat clearly are important.

Older designs—with full keels, short masts, and round bottoms—may be more traditional, but they are slow to respond. They go upwind slowly, don't crash into the seas, and ride an anchor beautifully. They are comfortable sailing off the wind but tend to roll when sailed directly downwind.

Newer designs with fin keels and flat bottoms are quick to respond and typically are quick sailing off the wind. Many designs of this type, however, pound if they go upwind too quickly in big seas.

Many cruising boats compensate for poor sailing characteristics with a large fuel capacity and big engines. This is a "chicken and egg" problem. Typically, the more fuel you carry, the heavier you are, and the harder it is to sail. Therefore, you will need more fuel because you may be spending more time motoring from port to port. Dependence on fuel limits how far you can sail and will tap your cruising budget.

The selection of a powerboat after years of sailing had an additional issue for me. I had learned the feel of our sailboat so completely that I didn't need to look out to know what the sea, wind, or weather conditions were. Trimmed properly, she had a groove that made even storm conditions workable. The motion of a powerboat is different.

A powerboat moves independently; it doesn't need to be compatible with the wind and sea. Unfortunately, this means that we drive them without much regard to anything else. There is rolling motion inherent in most boat designs—power or sail. Without the steadying effect of a sail, the powerboat rolls from side to side and bounces up and down. The result is a corkscrew action that I found very uncomfortable. I really had to work through this problem. Operating the stabilizers made a big difference. Before we solved our fuel problem, we didn't use the stabilizers very much. There was an immense difference when we were able to operate them without fretting about fuel use.

Cruising on waterways, lakes, and rivers usually offers calm waters. Wind and other boaters can make for a "bumpy" ride, but you can alter your course and speed to improve the motion of the boat. By adding stabilizers to a powerboat, you can minimize some of the "bumps." With trawlers, adding stabilizers, a stabilizing sail, and flopper stoppers reduces much of the rolling motion inherent in a powerboat whether you are underway or at anchor. (*Flopper stoppers* limit rolling when a boat is at anchor. We use hinged panels that drop into the water folded; when the boat rolls, the panels open flat and stop further rolling.)

A related issue is using gear and amenities on a moving powerboat. Sailboats don't usually have upright household refrigerators, couches, chairs, or stationary stoves. The built-in lockers, bunks, and the gimballed stove (installed so that it swings on pins to maintain a level position as the boat heels) allow you to function with the boat underway. Powerboat interiors typically are designed for use when you reach your destination. Stoves run athwartships (side to side); large, household refrigerators open from the front; and beds don't have lee cloths or bundle boards. Powerboat interiors are designed to resemble a house; sailboat interiors are designed to fit the boat design.

Cruising on a powerboat is comfortable, but it requires adjustment and adaptation if you are changing from sail to power.

Living Space

Life on a cruising boat has a basic irony. The comforts that work well at the dock often don't work at sea.

For example, wide-open spaces are fine at the dock. Underway, however, you need to move through the boat and get a firm handhold every inch of the way. There are ways to add handholds and create visual space. Prioritize the features you want based on how you plan to use your boat.

Some newer boats offer conveniences such as double beds you can walk around and top-loading and front-opening refrigerators. At the dock, the boat doesn't rock so you don't have to worry about falling out of bed. A front-opening refrigerator also spills out the cold air each time you open the door, but when you're plugged into shore power at the dock you don't need to worry about conserving electricity.

Basic to your overall comfort belowdecks are the length and width of bunks, the height of work surfaces, the depth of the icebox, the placement of the head, and the size and number of lockers and adequacy of stowage.

Bunks

I find the ideal situation is having two separate sleeping areas: a comfortable double bunk and a workable pilot berth that you and your mate can share at sea.

You'll sleep in the double bunk at the dock or at anchor. It may be a forepeak arrangement, a double quarter berth, or an aft cabin. If there are only two people living on board the majority of the time, it may not be necessary to have a separate cabin. The pilot berth is a single bunk where you will sleep when at sea, regardless of the sea conditions. The berth should be built with high sides so its trough-like shape keeps you secure. A single quarter berth or a dinette berth with a lee cloth also serves as a good sea berth. Since you and your mate will be on opposite watches, only one sea berth is necessary.

The bunks need to be long enough so you can stretch out comfortably, be wide enough to accommodate your hip width, and have overhead clearance so you can roll over or get out easily. When you are considering a boat, climb into the bunks and stretch out. Note how easy or difficult it is to get in and out of them. Remember, you will spend lots of time in your bunk, and altering a berth is not easy to do.

The Galley

Depending on how tall you are, the height of countertops and overhead lockers in the galley can present a problem. Our sailboat, originally built for a tall man (6 feet 4 inches), would have been totally unsatisfactory if I were shorter. Our refrigerator was top loading, and I could barely manage to reach items in the bottom of the box. When it was time to clean the refrigerator, we joked about who would hold whose ankles to reach the deep recesses.

The opposite situation is harder to manage. If you are tall, raising counters to a comfortable height requires major reconstruction. Or if you don't have sufficient headroom to stand upright when you work in the galley, that area quickly becomes a place to avoid.

The galley needs to be roomy enough to accommodate both you and your mate and functional both at anchor and underway. If you plan to make any kind of passage, the stove should be gimballed. You need to be able to reach items in the galley easily, particularly if you are cooking while wearing a safety harness. For long-distance cruisers, propane stoves are the standard and propane is the fuel of choice. Kerosene and clean alcohol are becoming harder to find in many countries. Diesel is great in cold climates, but it's too hot for the tropics. Microwaves and electric stoves are fine if you can generate electricity on board or plug into shore power at a dock. Compressed natural gas (CNG) is used on charter boats. But if you plan to cook frequently on your own boat, it is costly and inefficient.

A sailboat galley should be constructed to be seaworthy. Top-loading refrigerators and iceboxes retain the cold better, keep contents from spilling out, and are more efficient than front-loading units. The ideal refrigerator has both a top-loading and a front-opening capacity so you can use one opening underway and the other at the dock. Freezers and refrigerators require electricity and may require repair. If you are going to be far from skilled refrigeration repair, an icebox may be easier to live with.

Pressurized water is a great convenience when electricity and water are readily available. For long-distance cruising, manual pumps conserve electricity and water. For ocean cruising, saltwater pumps in the galley and head will stretch your freshwater supply. On our sailboat, I cooked with a saltwater/freshwater combination on long passages. We washed dishes and pans in salt water; we rinsed tableware and metal pans with fresh water and everything else with salt water. This way, I didn't use salt in my cooking. We eventually supplemented the sailboat's 55-gallon water tank with a watermaker. Our trawler has a 450-gallon water tank, so water usage is not a problem.

One of our major projects on the Grand Banks was renovating the galley. Although the boat was more than thirty years old, the galley seemed to have received little use or attention. A previous owner had removed the U-shaped counter and put it along the port side. This open L-shape gave the impression of great space, but the overhead cabinet had not been removed from the U-shaped galley, so anyone taller than 5 feet 5 inches usually walked headfirst into this cupboard several times. I discovered that the counters were too high, there was nothing to hold on to or clip in to, and the lovely teak cabinet doors disguised the fact that lockers were so tiny one trip to the supermarket put us into overflow mode.

We restored the galley to its original U-shape. We replaced the tiny electric cooktop with a propane cooktop and wall oven and replaced the original side-by-side household refrigerator with a refrigerator with a freezer on the bottom. The old teak doors fitted over new cupboards, and drawers on rollers have teak fronts made from the old teak we tore out. The countertop on the restored U-shaped galley was lowered a couple of inches. The final decadent touch came when Jim agreed to install a Fisher & Paykel dishwasher.

The new galley is convenient and ready for sea in short order. Shock cords secure glasses in the wine rack. Cupboards have double sliding bolts. The refrigerator has a latch that drops down over the main door. Underway we use the small dinette on the bridge for meals so we can eat together.

The Head

On boats, the term *head* refers to the toilet and generally replaces the word *bathroom*. It is hard to tell whether the location of the head is satisfactory when a boat is docked at a marina or stored in a cradle at a boatyard. When you take a boat on a test sail, using the head will quickly tell you whether it is going to be adequate.

Is the head accessible from the cockpit? The farther forward the head is, the less comfortable it will be at sea. Can you sit on it comfortably without falling off? Can you pump it (or flush it) according to the instructions? Is there enough room in the head for you to get in and out of foul-weather gear?

Many boats have showers as part of the head. If you have enough space and an ample water supply, showers are a nice convenience. Many cruisers in warm climates, however, find outside showers satisfactory. They bathe in salt water and use the shower for a final rinse. A frequently used shower belowdecks is subject to mold and mildew; you must have an excellent ventilation system. The shower should also have a separate bilge so shower water does not run into the common bilge. This runoff can create an odor, and hair in the runoff can clog your main bilge pump.

We had two heads on our sailboat, *Nalu IV*. Both were equipped with Skipper model toilets manufactured by Wilcox Crittenden. These heads were used continually for twenty-five years. Our trawler has two heads. One is the same Wilcox Crittenden Skipper model and the other is an electric toilet. Because it is electric, we use it when we plug in at a marina. It can operate on the inverter system as well. Jim plumbed it to flush with raw water or fresh water to reduce crystal buildup in the hoses. Both heads are connected to the holding tank, but we open them for use at sea.

The best boat plumbing is expensive. But remember that women depend on having a functioning head on board.

Adequate Stowage

A boat's interior space is truly livable when there is adequate stowage. When you live on board full-time, you find that everything needs a place to be stowed. At first glance, a boat may seem to have plenty of space. But that space can shrink dramatically, depending on where you plan to cruise and how long you plan to be on board.

Think about stowing enough food for a few months. Where will you put your wet foul-weather gear when you come off watch? Books, games, videos, and writing projects all need a place, as do sewing machines, spare parts, tools, bed and bath linens, and dirty clothes.

If you really like a boat, and it is one you own or one you are contemplating buying, check all the places designed for stowage and then think about what stowage you can create. Can you turn a spare bunk into lockers and shelves? Can you open up some liner space (fiberglass boats usually have an inner liner) to make more room for stowage? Can you add space on the insides of locker doors by adding cloth pockets or plastic boxes?

Sailboat Gear

When selecting boat gear, take into account men's and women's differences in physical characteristics. Women are more likely to have well-developed lower body muscles, while men often have more-developed upper body muscles. Training and conditioning can develop and improve muscle groups. But training may not be something you can do or want to do.

A man may be able to use arm and shoulder strength to turn a winch; a woman may find standing over the winch and using both hands is better for her. Winches located on the cabintop under the dodger will be hard for many women to operate. Relocate winches so they can be operated easily.

The size of the winch is important. If increasing a jib or halyard winch to the next size means that either partner can use it equally effectively, it makes sense to invest in a bigger winch. Increasing the mechanical ratio on the outhaul, mainsheet, and traveler, for example, will make both partners equally able to do the task.

Many sailboats have roller furling sails that don't have to be stowed, eliminating the need to hoist, lower, and fold sails. However, many sailors prefer to have the option of switching to different sails. Remember, your sail inventory needs to be manageable, particularly for heavy weather. Both partners should be able to raise, lower, or trim the sails. Our storm staysail was made of heavy, 11-ounce Dacron and measured barely 90 square feet; I could manage the sail in heavy weather without assistance.

One way some couples solve sail handling is to have a split-rig boat: a schooner, yawl, or ketch. With two masts, there are more sails. Those sails can be smaller and still provide the same power as a sloop- or cutter-rigged boat.

A boat is designed to sail carrying a certain quantity of sail area. If you use less than the design calls for, the boat's performance will be affected. Be sure your sail inventory will provide maximum power for your boat.

It is essential for cruising couples to have some type of self-steering system. If there are only two people on board and you have to hand steer the boat every minute of every day, you will be exhausted.

There are two types of self-steering systems available. Many cruisers install both aboard their boats.

Wind vanes are mechanical devices that steer your sailboat according to wind direction. The wind vane can be trimmed to keep the boat at a constant angle to the wind. On long ocean passages where prevailing winds vary little, the wind vane is a quiet, effective device.

Both sail- and powerboats can have autopilots, which are electrical devices that steer to a compass course. Determine what direction you want to go, set the autopilot, and the pilot maintains your course. If the wind changes on a sailboat, you need to trim the sails. Some automatic systems have a separate sensor that will respond if wind direction changes. However, the automatic system cannot work on both a compass and a wind sensor at the same time.

Your personal preferences, the size of your boat, your intended cruising grounds, and your budget will all play a part in determining what systems you install. Be sure that you understand how to operate the systems and can do simple troubleshooting.

Safety Gear

Rescuing a person who falls overboard is extremely difficult. The first rule is to wear safety gear that will keep you on board. If you are alone on deck, wear a harness with a tether that fastens to the boat. When your partner is on deck alone, insist that he wear a harness at all times. If he objects, point out who would have to perform the rescue.

Many new types of harnesses are available. Find one that fits you comfortably and will not injure you if you fall. Chest harnesses are normally designed to fit men; be sure you try on any harness before you buy it. Note the length of the tether that comes with a harness. An 8-foot tether on a small boat may let you land in the water. You would be better off with a 4- or 5-foot tether. We use both lengths. The shorter one, attached to the static line on the side decks, is good for moving about the boat. We use the longer one, attached to the boat on the centerline, when performing a particular task.

The Lifesling is an essential item for all cruising couples. It was developed by the nonprofit Sailing Foundation of Seattle, and all royalties from the sale of the Lifesling are returned to the foundation. It provides 20 pounds of flotation, 150 feet of floating line, and a means of assisting the victim back aboard with a halyard and winch. It is the only reliable, workable device on the market for shorthanded rescue of a man overboard, and it is the only one that will allow a small person to rescue a bigger person. As good as the Lifesling is, however, it will not work unless you practice with it and both partners are confident in using it.

A simple factor in safety is *freeboard* (the distance from the waterline to the upper deck level). It is harder to rescue a person from the water if you have 7 feet of freeboard compared to only 4 feet of freeboard. The high freeboard may make your interior space bigger, but, in my opinion, that extra space is not worth risking a difficult man-overboard rescue.

Every cruising boat should carry emergency equipment: an EPIRB (emergency position-indicating radiobeacon), a flare gun, a life raft, man-overboard gear, and a radio.

No one should cruise without an EPIRB; it is imperative especially for ocean passages. When you activate the EPIRB, it sends a signal to orbiting satellites, which relay the signal to land-based stations. Those stations relay the information to NOAA, which in turn notifies the appropriate search-and-rescue agency, generally the Coast Guard in the United States. The signal alerts the rescuers to the type of boat, name of owners, and who to notify in an emergency. The signal can be forwarded to a ground station without the satellite having the ground station in sight.

Flare guns are used to signal other vessels when you need help or need to be located. Usually, boats carry two types of flares, both of which can be accommodated by the flare gun. Smoke flares are of short duration and are used for signaling. Parachute flares stay aloft and can be seen at a greater distance and for a longer period of time, necessary for rescue situations. Flares deteriorate over time, so be sure to check their expiration dates before they're stowed for a long passage.

Life rafts are essential. Some cruisers believe their shore dinghy is sufficient. Others (even more foolishly, in my opinion) think that extra flotation in their boat makes it a substitute for a life raft. A life raft is only for emergencies, such as sinking or fire, that require abandoning the boat. It is stored in a canister or valise on or near the deck, and will inflate automatically when the emergency line is pulled. The life raft is designed to carry a specific number of people and to withstand crisis conditions. Most life rafts come with emergency gear stowed inside, but it is a good idea to bring a separate bag with essentials such as spare eyeglasses, daily medications, and a handheld radio, among other things. (You can learn more about this by reading Tony Farrington's book *Rescue in the Pacific*—see the bibliography.)

Radios are discussed in several places in this book, including Chapters 9 and 10. In emergencies, a handheld VHF radio that broadcasts and receives only for line-of-sight distances is important for communicating with rescuers or fellow cruisers who might offer assistance. A single-sideband (SSB) radio or a ham radio can be used to call for help on emergency frequencies that are noted in radio manuals or on ham nets operating in your area. In life-threatening situations the term *Mayday* is used to call for help. Other emergencies (illness, broken mast, etc.) are identified by the term *Pan-Pan.*

Safety gear on board is only of value if you know how to use it. Seek out demonstrations and learning opportunities.

Upkeep

All boats require upkeep, and you will definitely spend money on your boat after you buy it. These expenditures include the costs of maintaining the boat, gear, and equipment, and may include the costs of design modifications.

If you cruise close to home, maintaining your boat will likely be fairly simple. An annual haulout to inspect it and paint the bottom can be a quick weekend job, if you have some experience. The size of your boat will also determine whether the annual haulout is a small expense or a formidable one. Most boatyards charge by the foot for haulouts and *lay days* (days your boat sits in a cradle).

If you cruise to distant ports, your annual haulout and inspection are even more critical. Hauling out in a foreign country to find potential problems and make small repairs may be inconvenient, but it beats having major problems with your boat and equipment once you are offshore or in a port that does not have adequate facilities. Hiring sailmakers, mechanics, or electricians in a foreign port is difficult under the best of circumstances. We have found sailmakers who don't have cloth and with sewing machines that stitch only straight and forward. We have found mechanics who have never seen a diesel engine (even our marinized John Deere tractor engines on our trawler). We had a malfunctioning armature on the alternator repaired by unwinding the old wire and rewinding it with new wire because there were no replacement parts. If you can't make your own repairs, don't assume there will be someone available that you can hire. Flying in a mechanic and spare parts will be costly—in dollars and time.

To keep your life as uncomplicated as possible, consider upkeep carefully when choosing a boat. Make sure that daily upkeep is simple, whether it is scrubbing decks, washing dishes, or cleaning the head. A complicated or difficult task is most often ignored. If you want to cruise in faraway places, learn to repair or do triage on all your boat's systems. Otherwise, you can spend months and many dollars on parts and repair.

Before you buy any boat, new or used, hire an independent marine surveyor to evaluate the boat's construction and gear. Insist on going through the boat with the surveyor, so you can ask questions and understand how he or she assesses the boat.

· There are two national organizations of surveyors (see the Resources appendix) that you can contact for names in your area. Your local boatyard is a good source for recommendations, because they know surveyors' specialties and who is the most thorough. Avoid using surveyors connected to boat brokerages and those who do not have a national affiliation.

Amid the excitement of buying a new or used boat—or changing the boat you have—remember that the ultimate purpose of a boat is to bring you joy, comfort, and security.

$$\boxed{5}$$

FEARING
THE WEATHER
AHEAD

THERE IS AN X-FACTOR in cruising that is unpredictable and uncontrollable: the weather. You can time your cruising route so you will be cruising in waters with a low incidence of storms and hurricanes. But it is a mistake to assume that you will never encounter bad weather.

No matter how highly developed our equipment and skills, total accuracy in weather prediction eludes us. On *Nalu IV,* we were caught in the South Pacific between Bora-Bora and American Samoa in a storm that was developing from a tropical depression to hurricane status. Our anemometer, which measures wind speed, registered 60 knots, and the needle was pegged as far as it would go. We had been in the storm for three days before it showed up on our weather fax.

"What is the worst weather you've ever been in?" is the question I am asked most frequently by people planning to go cruising. I can recall those days vividly.

I remember the storm in the South Pacific that I just mentioned. I remember sailing upwind along the west coast of Australia for eighteen days in winds blowing from 35 to 55 knots; eating, sleeping, and living with the howling wind and sea made me exhausted and miserable. A severe thunderstorm in the Chesapeake Bay was the longest 20 minutes of my life.

In retrospect, however, I can describe those situations in detail only because I have been asked to recount them so often. And I realize that this question about the worst weather I've been in isn't a question about the weather at all. The question is about being afraid of bad weather.

Weren't You Scared?

I have been absolutely terrified on the ocean. I have also been absolutely terrified on land. The part of me that is fearful is always with me, whether I'm driving on the freeway or crossing an ocean.

Running aground, encountering storms, and falling overboard are things we, as cruisers, fear. We think about possible scenarios and consequences. But until we actually experience the unknown, it is out there for us to worry about and to fear. It is normal to fear the unknown, unfamiliar, or uncontrollable. They make us vulnerable.

If you haven't been caught in bad weather, you have a gap in your experience. You may learn by watching movies and reading books and scary magazine articles. Those images fill your mind, and your imagination works overtime. Now you have something to worry about, so you worry.

Listening to the questions women ask me about cruising has brought me to a conclusion: I am not the only woman with an advanced degree in worrying. Lin Pardey notes, "All women are worriers. We have expectations to live up to." Even if you haven't acknowledged it, your capacity for worry exists.

Have you ever worried about how you were going to look at a party? Do you find yourself worrying about joining a new group? Do you worry about a new computer program? Do you worry about what is going to be on sale when you get to the store? It's all right to worry about those things. Some things may be more important than others, but worrying is part of a basic planning process. You want to know how things are going to turn out before they happen, and you want to be prepared. So you fill up your brain with all the "what-ifs."

In that process, you learn there are what-ifs you can take care of. You can prepare for eventualities. Worry pushes you to learn about safety gear, how to reef sails, and how to read weather faxes. In the worrying process you make lists, read, and attempt to plan for every circumstance. Sailing in bad weather, managing a grounded boat, and sailing at night are things you can learn to do. But worry by itself, the kind that does not inspire you to learn how to better handle a potential situation, can be crippling.

Patience Wales describes how fear can play a role in survival. "I've been afraid hundreds of times. I was afraid of not knowing what to do. . . . I still am [afraid] when I don't know what to do. More than anything else, that breaks down into feeling out of control. [But] the thing about fear that's encouraging is that you learn what to be afraid of when you're ocean cruising. . . . I think for cruising there's a kind of smugness as [we] get more and more experience that 'we know what to do.' You need to be particularly afraid of a complacency and a smugness, and the fact that your own experience is any assurance that you're not going to die."

Gathering Information

When you have made all the constructive preparations you can for a potential crisis, move on to the next project. Put your fears about bad weather on hold until you can collect more constructive information and experience. Going to seminars, watching videos or DVDs, and reading books about handling bad weather can be helpful.

In gathering information, Lin Pardey learned an important lesson early on: Discerning between good and bad information is important if you are going to manage fear. "I think fear is fed by radios, talking with inexperienced people, information coming from the outside," says Lin. "We had been cruising for three years and I had never been afraid, except of expectations. When we got to the Canal—watching boats come through, talking to everyone coming through, and talking to two couples who were novices—I nearly walked off the boat. My fear came from other people. Talking to other people scared me. I wasn't listening to Larry or looking at the boat."

Lin is absolutely right about knowing the difference between good and bad advice. I'm not sure there is a way to learn the difference, except through experience. One thing that is a waste of time for me is reading articles or seeing films designed to titillate my imagination. *Dead Calm*, a movie that was popular several years ago, was designed to scare and horrify. Any similarity to the realities of cruising and sailing was accidental, yet many people wanted to see the movie because it was about cruising. Stories without substance don't improve my learning. It is important to ask yourself, what did this person do that was right? Try to evaluate the value of an article, book, or film by looking for the author's biography at the end of the story or reading an editorial review.

Reading analyses of bad weather situations that have happened can be worthwhile. Two excellent books about actual storms are *Fastnet, Force 10* by John Rousmaniere and *Rescue in the Pacific* by Tony Farrington (see the bibliography). There are important lessons to be learned from the storms covered in these books.

Information that is thoughtful, precise, accurate, and—above all—true will help you learn more about the unknown. Avoid basing your judgments on information from unknown sources and war stories.

Learning to Cope

More than forty years ago, Lael Morgan was caught in Hurricane Ginny off Cape May, New Jersey, with her then-husband, Dodge. "We were out in the cockpit for three days, not far enough offshore. We took everything down, put out a sea anchor. I went below. I couldn't function. I prepared to die. I was so pissed because I woke up and hadn't died. I went up into the cockpit, and [my husband] tied me in [so I wouldn't fall overboard] while he went below. I was mad and I had decided to lick it."

Confrontation is the ultimate response to fear, because you face the unknown and get acquainted. Lael's description of her fear being replaced by anger is not unusual, although no one would choose to be caught in a hurricane as a means of overcoming fear. Dawn Riley's attitude is, "The key is to be prepared. Think about it before it happens. The worst is to be an ostrich and just try to ignore the dangers."

Barbara Colborn remembers her first bad weather experience: "We had been close-hauled for several days. Each time a wave pounded the hull it felt like we were being hit by a medium-sized car. Everything was rattling inside, and the boat seemed on the edge of control. I put my head in a pillow and I just screamed. I cried. I prayed, and my husband prayed with me. He said, 'You just have to wait.' So I learned I had to wait." Although Barbara says that she has since been frightened on boats, prayer and experience helped her build a reservoir of confidence to overcome her fear.

Barbara now prefers to stay on deck, she says, "because I'm out in the open and the noises are not as bad on deck as they are below."

Going belowdeck is often a response to fear. We sometimes like to think that if we don't see something, it isn't there. But in my experience, belowdeck is the worst place to be if I'm afraid. I have no idea what is happening, so my imagination and the noises I hear combine to create dreadful scenarios in my mind. There is nothing more frightening to me.

Confront the unknown thing you fear. Don't give in to the urge to go below and hide. Snap your harness tether into a safe pad eye and sit it out. When you have gained some confidence, adjust your tether so you can go forward and look at the rig, the sails, and the water. Steer the boat in this kind of weather. ·

Paula Dinius, who experienced the Queen's Birthday Storm, rode out some of the worst weather imaginable before being forced to abandon their boat. Her faith in the integrity of her boat was paramount to overcoming her fear. "I was afraid of the power of the wind," she says. "After the hurricane, I am a lot less afraid . . . not that I think I can't die, but I trust the boat. . . . After all the things happen that you're afraid of, I'm confident that I [know] what I can do."

Advocating that you go out in a hurricane would be imprudent, and I am not suggesting that you risk your life in order to be happy cruising. Exercise the opportunity to confront the things you are afraid of and put them behind you. You need to know that your boat will take care of you, regardless of how you feel.

Sailing in strong wind is an opportunity to confront the weather and deal with it. An afternoon of "bad" weather may quickly become an afternoon of windy weather. If the wind blows above 20 knots, don't go home immediately. Keep sailing. The next step is to stay out when the wind kicks up more, maybe to 30 knots. If you sail on a sound boat with sails reefed and wearing a life jacket and safety harness, you should be able to manage fine.

As Paula Dinius says, "By living with the boat over time, you get this bond and you get to know [the boat] and what it can do. That's what kept me going farther and staying out longer: confidence in myself and my boat." She attributes her survival in June 1994 to knowing that her boat would take care of her and her injured husband.

Patricia Miller Rains took a very pragmatic approach to her fears. "To conquer a small but lingering fear of drowning, I took a scuba class that taught me to navigate underwater in the open ocean. Now, whenever I'm frightened of the ocean, I spend a few minutes looking realistically at what would be the worst that could happen. After taking every action to stabilize the situation, I mentally rehearse what I'll do to survive it. After that, I just take deep slow breaths and observe the beauty, because in the midst of even the worst storm, there's dramatic beauty."

Powerboats are also susceptible to bad weather, although we may think they are less vulnerable than sailboats. Marja Vance made the point that on a 94-foot powerboat, she hasn't been affected by any bad weather they've encountered—the bigger a boat, the less you feel the weather. The corollary is that the bigger the boat, when you do feel the weather, the bigger the weather is.

Alison Fishel was caught in a hurricane while she, her husband, Bill, and her brother were bringing their new 56-foot trawler to California. The boatbuilding project had started and stopped, had changed yards, and had been problematic overall. This was a shakedown cruise as well as a delivery. She described her feelings. "We were caught in a hurricane offshore of the Carolinas. There were 30-foot seas for 6 or 7 hours and we only made 20 miles. I have blocked the recollection—terror, panic, fear. I was in the pilothouse with my brother next to me, and it was almost a feeling of not being there. I couldn't believe we weren't going over—three times I thought we were going to roll over. Bill said it was a 35-degree roll. It seemed forever but probably lasted 5 to 10 seconds. I kept wondering, 'How many more?' Later we discovered that the entire lazarette was filled with water."

Earlier we pointed out that wind and wave action affect different boats differently. Whether you face bad weather on a sailboat or powerboat, anticipation and preparation are essential.

Learning all you can about the things you fear and how to cope with them allows you to exercise control over yourself and your environment. As Patricia Miller Rains says, "If you allow fear to occupy your attention, it can paralyze you mentally and physically, thereby robbing you of your power and options. Sheer fear has never done anyone any good. But taking intelligent action on your own behalf will rescue you and evaporate fear at the same time."

Several years ago I read *Feel the Fear . . . and Do It Anyway* by Susan Jeffers (see the bibliography) at the suggestion of a friend after we discussed worrying and fear. The author is clearly directing her ideas to a broader audience than I am here. But I found that certain scenarios and responses were familiar, and it helps to realize that fear is common to all of us. Years later, I still say out loud, as one of her techniques suggests, "I can do this!"

Steering Clear of Bad Weather

There may be sophisticated electronic equipment that provides us with weather information, but it is unwise to put your total faith in it. Elaborate, expensive gear and the best possible planning cannot protect you from encountering bad weather. Prepare for the weather and use common sense.

Pilot Charts: A Basic Tool

Part of your preparation is knowing when the prevailing winds are in your favor and knowing what times of the year you can expect storms and difficult sea conditions. Pilot charts can help in your planning. They do not give daily weather information, but they do tell what weather trends to expect for certain geographic areas.

Weather data has been collected over the years and is compiled on pilot charts. Information is grouped by regions: for example, charts are available for the South Pacific, the Indian Ocean, and the South Atlantic. For each area, there is a pilot chart for every month of the year, providing a summary of the average weather conditions. A system of symbols and codes details information about winds, wind direction, days of calm, prevailing currents, wave heights, iceberg intrusion, shipping lanes, tornadoes, and typhoons.

If, for example, you are trying to determine the best time to sail across the Atlantic Ocean from Europe to the Caribbean, the pilot chart for the Atlantic shows which months have hurricane-force winds, currents running in your favor, and winds blowing in a favorable direction.

We like pilot charts because we can visualize a passage, plan our stops, and get an overview of what to anticipate each month. We also carry *Ocean Passages for the World*, published by the United Kingdom Hydrographic Office (see the bibliography). It summarizes the world's passages and ports traditionally used by sailing vessels. We rely on charts first, however, because books condense information we want to see in detail.

Daily weather information is available via weather fax, WWV radio (the international time station), and the studious use of a high-quality barometer. More and more cruisers also use computers and satellite connections to receive weather information. But remember, there is no guarantee that the forecast is accurate.

When Paula Dinius advised land-based radio operators in New Zealand of the extremely high winds she was experiencing in the South Pacific during the Queen's Birthday Storm, they found her report hard to believe: the weather did not coincide with the forecast. It was not until a rescue plane flew overhead and corroborated her findings that broadcasters believed her reports of the weather.

Use pilot charts for long-range cruise planning and purchase the charts that fit your cruising route. (Used pilot charts may be adequate, since information is averaged over many years.) Use onboard electronic weather equipment and learn to read the barometer.

Barometers

In this day of high-tech electronic instruments, most of us ignore or forget the barometer. We look at pilot charts to outline a cruising plan, and then we go to the weather fax to get the forecasts. When coastal cruising, we can also listen to the local weather on our VHF. So why do we need a barometer?

First, the barometer is continuously telling you about the weather. The air pressure rises and falls in a regular pattern. Recording the pressure information on a planned schedule familiarizes you with the pattern. When the weather is changing, you will notice those variations from the norm.

Second, when unstable weather is expected, your barometer will show you it is approaching and how serious it is. Clearly, when you are expecting a low-pressure system, your barometer reading should go down. The normal is 1013.25 millibars, so anything lower indicates low pressure. The pressure in tropical storm fronts often drops close to 1000.

We anchored in Cold Bay on the Alaska Peninsula in late July when our barometer dropped to almost 1000. The next three days we stayed put as the barometer dropped to 993. We might have foolishly assumed that we could anchor overnight and leave in the morning had we not had a barometer. Neither the severity of the weather nor the duration was indicated on our weather fax.

What Do You Do to Prepare for Bad Weather?

Bad weather makes me crazy. I don't like wearing the same smelly clothes and not washing my hair. I hate being jammed into my bunk to sleep. I don't look forward to cleaning up after a seasick cat. After several days in the same soggy clothes, stiff salty hair, and moss-covered teeth, I am not nice. Who would be in those conditions? I look awful, feel frumpy, and would give anything to be anywhere but where I am (chances are my husband has similar feelings—even if he doesn't say so).

A positive way to deal with bad weather is to take control of the situation so that comfort, rather than fear, is the issue.

Equipment

You may use up your entire wardrobe trying to keep dry in a long stretch of bad weather. If your clothing gets wet, change it. Keep your head and hands covered. Maintain body heat to delay the onset of fatigue and help prevent hypothermia. When you go below to eat or rest, strip off outer gear. In short: Take care of yourself.

Good foul-weather gear protects you from the elements. If you day-cruise or cruise only on weekends, you shouldn't need to invest in expensive gear. But if you cruise on a long-term basis or in severe weather, expect to pay several hundred dollars for gear that fits properly and keeps you dry.

Most good foul-weather gear is unisex, which really means it's designed for a man. The BoatU.S. online store (see the Resources appendix) does carry gear made for women. If cruising takes you to higher latitudes, gear that fits is worth it!

When you invest in high-quality ocean-going gear, consider the overall weight of the clothing. My foul-weather gear weighs 10 pounds and is exhausting to wear, but it keeps me dry and warm.

I wear a men's extra-small size for a good fit. Make sure that wrist, ankle, and neck openings can be made watertight. Some manufacturers incorporate nice features, such as fleece-lined pockets and high collars for cold weather. Be sure to find out if the company that manufactured your foul-weather gear will alter it if it does not fit properly.

Overalls under a foul-weather jacket may seem bulky and cumbersome but will protect you when worn without the jacket. And when you sit or bend, there is never a gap at the waist between your jacket and pants that can fill with water.

Try on foul-weather gear with the kind of clothing you intend to wear underneath. The right underlayers can mean the difference between comfort and misery. Synthetic fabrics perform well in cold, wet environments. They can wick moisture away from your skin and insulate by trapping air in the fabric's interlocking knit.

Think about the gear you will wear on your head, hands, and feet. You will find waterproof seaboots, Synchilla hats, and gloves made out of neoprene and synthetic leatherlike fabrics in the wardrobes of cold-water sailors.

Boat shows are good places to research different kinds of gear, since many of the manufacturers and their representatives are in attendance. Ask other cruisers what gear and what combinations of garments and fabrics work for them.

Everyone on board should wear harnesses and tethers during bad weather. On a sailboat there should be pad eyes at the companionway so you can fasten your tether to the boat before entering the cockpit, and another at the steering station. Powerboats should have static lines along the passageways to which you can tether yourself. Your tether should be no more than 4 feet long to ensure that you stay on the boat if you fall.

Discomfort

Preparation is essential for battling the discomfort the weather can cause. If there is no safe harbor close by, you need to get ready. Organize food that can be easily prepared; shorten the watch system so you don't have to spend too long a time at the helm; maintain body heat with warm clothes, including hats and gloves; and drink as much water as you possibly can.

You must eat. You burn fuel rapidly in bad weather, and eating helps prevent fatigue. Hot food at least once a day will do a lot for your morale and your energy level. Even instant hot cereal or soup will taste like a real meal. If you have advance notice of bad weather, cook a pot of something that will keep in a pressure cooker on the stove. A pot of rice with anything thrown in for color and flavor makes a meal. It can be reheated without the pressure cap, and the sealed lid is handy in rough seas. Have a thermos of boiling water on hand for soup mixes, hot chocolate, or instant coffee.

Don't let concern about fat intake dictate your food intake. Frequent snacks of fruit, cookies, or trail mix will help keep your energy up. If you become nauseous in rough weather, try to manage some food intake—even if it's only crackers or dry biscuits.

Standing watch in bad weather requires being on the helm at least part of the time. Concentrating on steering in bad weather is exhausting. The normal 3- or 4-hour watch will be too long. Take shorter spells and periodically try to stand a longer watch so your partner gets some sound sleep.

I admit that I hate drinking lots of water during bad weather because getting undressed to use the toilet is a major event. A rolling boat, zippers, Velcro, and a head without a seat belt all conspire to bruise and batter you. But a full bladder is impossibly uncomfortable, so you have no choice. I tried one of the funnel devices designed to equip a woman like a man, but it was impractical; in bad weather, you don't have that many hands. Drinking water is my least favorite advice—but probably the most important. Dehydration can make you very sick and render you completely useless. Drink water often.

Practice

There are several techniques to employ when the weather gets bad. On a sailboat, reefing sails, heaving-to, and deploying sea anchors and drogues are skills that require practice to perform them with confidence when the time comes.

Reefing a sail means making the sail area smaller. Reefing sails reduces your power aloft, and smaller sails make a boat more manageable in high winds.

Many cruising boats have roller furling sails, a system that allows you to roll a sail up quickly. On our sailboat, we reefed the mainsail and changed to smaller headsails. We never needed to remove our sails completely.

Heaving-to, putting your boat into a holding pattern at sea, is a technique frequently used in heavy weather. It keeps the boat from making progress but allows you time to rest, eat, or make repairs.

Assuming you know how to heave-to without practice is a mistake. Learning before you are in a situation that demands heaving-to is part of your preparation. Each boat has its own peculiar characteristics determined by hull shape, keel, and sail plan. Learn how to heave-to in calmer conditions and gradually practice the technique in more wind and rougher water. Always maintain a watch when you are hove-to.

Drogues and sea anchors typically are used in very bad weather. Depending on the type of boat, drogues and sea anchors will be deployed from the stern or from the bow. Dragging drogues and sea anchors will slow your boat down if reducing your sail area hasn't sufficiently slowed your speed. Sometimes drogues are used to keep a boat with a steering failure on course. They can also be deployed from a powerboat.

Bad weather under power is an issue of steering, and of coping with large waves. Approaching big waves or driving in following seas is a miserable ride. To smooth the ride and reduce your exposure to a roll, steering on the diagonal across the waves does help. You need to pay attention to navigation when you set a zigzag course. You need to keep the propellers in the water and the power on.

On-the-water seminars, videos, and books explain the above techniques in detail. You should practice these procedures and develop the best procedures for your boat. Learning these techniques will allow you to control situations before they control you.

The Silver Lining

Bad weather does have its silver lining. There is nothing so glorious as the first bright morning after a storm when you peel off those stinky clothes, scrub your skin till it glows, gorge on every morsel you can hold in your stomach, and curl up in the sunshine for a nap. When we talk about weather, we can guarantee one thing: It will change. Bad weather fades quickly.

6

PIRATES
AND
PROTECTION

ONE OF THE MAJOR ATTRACTIONS of cruising is visiting exotic places. The opportunity to live in new places, participate in new cultures, and experience new lifestyles can be a heady experience. But the thrill of going to exotic places is often dampened by our fear of those same places, their people, and their practices.

Many Americans have a preoccupation with personal security that dominates their lives. For some, the preoccupation is gained from the media and its sensationalism of violence. For others, it is gained, unfortunately, through personal experience. Violence in an exotic setting can become front-page news. If there is a murder in the Caribbean or piracy in Asia, the media has a new story with which to feed our national paranoia. As a result, we are as afraid of the rest of the world as we are of our own country.

There are some truly dangerous places around the world. There also are places with customs, practices, and poverty levels that we, as visitors, need to be aware of.

Isn't It Dangerous Out There?

I cannot speak for all cruisers. But based on my own experience, my answer is no, cruising is not dangerous. I felt safe on our sailboat, and I feel safe on our trawler and in foreign countries. At the same time, I have had encounters that could have been dangerous in different circumstances.

We were in the new fishing harbor at Melilla, a small Spanish enclave on the north coast of Morocco. Our sailboat was moored stern-to at the dock. We had been befriended by the local fishermen from Spain, who had warned us that the "Moros," the local Moroccan population, were "bad." But they gave us no further details.

During the night, I woke up and went into the galley to get a drink of water. I heard a noise from the aft cabin and assumed it was my husband coming in search of water. When I turned back to our cabin, a small, dark, bearded man wearing a track suit stood at the foot of the companionway ladder. My first thought was to hit him, but I was holding a plastic liter bottle filled with water that would not hurt him in the least. My second thought was to yell loudly enough to wake my husband and our friends in the forepeak.

I hollered my husband's name at the top of my lungs. The man threw his arms over his head and started shaking his head vigorously back and forth. My husband, barely awake, charged out of the bunk and fell headfirst, tripped by the bedsheets wrapped around his feet. The man scampered up the ladder. My husband's body on the floor blocked me from pursuit, and—as we laughingly acknowledged later—our lack of clothing prevented us from chasing the intruder.

I wasn't hurt. I was angry that someone had come aboard without permission. The intruder had run away before getting his due. Fortunately for me, his small size, his defensive stance, and the element of surprise made me feel in control of the situation. A few more inches or pounds on him might have made all the difference in my reaction to the entire incident.

Your reaction to the unexpected can determine what may or may not be a dangerous situation.

I was frightened by local boats while we were anchored in Malaysian waters. A boat came alongside and tied a line to us. Soon another boat came along. We signaled that he wasn't welcome, but he tied up to the boat already tied to us. Within a half-hour, eight boats were strung behind us like cars in a train. Their crews were eating, mending nets, making preparations for sleep, and ignoring us completely. It dawned on us that we had anchored in a regular anchorage spot for the fishing fleet. Our anchor was already down, and they thought it was perfectly sensible to tie off our stern rather than put down their own anchor.

Our immediate response was fright, but as we watched the situation develop, we realized we were not in danger. Similar situations have escalated because cruisers reacted aggressively, sometimes with firearms.

Nancy Bischoff worried about being in Mexican waters when she and her husband left San Diego. "[Although] I was apprehensive," she said, "I didn't see anything in Mexico that made me nervous. I heard stories, but they didn't keep me from cruising. We had a *panga* [Mexican fishing boat] tie up to us while we were underway. They were drunk. They wanted cigarettes. We don't smoke, so they smiled and then took off. It could have turned out differently."

Hearing stories and rumors makes all of us nervous. "It makes you afraid. You feel like you always have to look over your shoulder," says one woman cruiser. "I was worried about going up the Red Sea. We don't carry a gun. [But] we never had any problems."

We had planned to make a quick passage through the Strait of Malacca because of the pirate stories we had heard. But our intended six-day passage turned into a three-month stay. The stories of danger, like many tales told at sea, were embroidered beyond recognition. The story of a reported shooting, at least ten years old at the time, kept surfacing in a manner that made it sound current. But we learned from cruisers who had recently sailed the Strait that no one had encountered any problems.

When you don't have a means to evaluate reports, you have to take them at face value. Some cruisers suggest that such stories keep the beautiful cruising grounds of Southeast Asia relatively pristine and uncrowded.

There Are Some Real Dangers

Pirates are real in Southeast Asia, and the potential for danger does exist there. Large merchant vessels carry cash in their safes, since crew are paid in cash at the end of a voyage. These vessels are the targets of waterborne thieves, and the owners have learned that it is more prudent to allow robberies than resist the boardings. Word passes among the cruisers to avoid the areas where these thieves are known to operate.

But as one cruiser who has sailed many miles in the China Sea explained to us, pirates know they will find money on ships. Small cruising vessels are likely to yield nothing but angry owners and a fight. His opinion was that the pirates were smart enough to know the difference between "a fat hog and a wild cat."

We entered the Philippines as participants in a memorial regatta the government was sponsoring commemorating their centennial of independence from Spain. We sailed the Galleon Route from Acapulco, Mexico, to Manila, Philippines. When we reached Leyte Gulf, a Philippines naval vessel hailed us. They had been assigned to escort the boats in the regatta to our next stop in Cebu. This highly publicized event had not generated concern on our part, but the government felt it was necessary. A couple of weeks later at the Manila Yacht Club, we were awarded a cash prize of $25,000 (U.S.) for winning the regatta. We rode in a cab with two of our crew and an armed guard from the yacht club. When we reached the bank, two more heavily armed guards joined our entourage and escorted us inside to the wire transfer desk. It was quite a show when you consider I was carrying the money in a brown paper bag.

Drug traffic is a source of concern for cruisers in Asia. Again, knowledge passed among cruisers says to avoid congregations of native boats or high-speed craft. If you attempt to anchor in a questionable area or approach a suspicious-looking group of boats, you are courting disaster.

Many potential cruisers have expressed concern about being hijacked by drug runners who want boats. Most of our information about boats being hijacked refers to high-speed boats that can outrun the authorities. Cruising boats generally don't fit that category.

Thieves might think trawlers are desirable if the thieves aren't knowledgeable about design—most cruising trawlers are not "high performance." Similarly, if the perception we mentioned previously about powerboats—that they're just like driving a car—is at work, a powerboat might be seen as easier to operate than a sailboat even if it isn't "fast."

Cruisers must also recognize danger ashore. Many countries cruisers visit have large numbers of extremely poor people. If you flaunt wealth in this environment, you can expect trouble.

Lael Morgan acknowledges the risks they took in the 1960s. "We were both gamblers. We were going to Haiti; they had just hanged an American. People were so poor. We did go to Caracas expecting trouble. We were fired on and then discovered it was a welcoming salute."

Lin Pardey takes a no-nonsense approach to the issue of security. "We've visited sixty-seven countries and been in hundreds of foreign ports, and never felt threatened in any case, except the Philippines. The military explained what to avoid and offered to provide an escort. Sometimes there are areas to avoid."

The United States is often seen as an unsafe place, and some foreign vessels choose not to cruise in U.S. waters. Migael Scherer presents a scary picture of our own country as a cruising ground. Migael has spent nearly all of her cruising years in Puget Sound. In her memoir *Still Loved by the Sun*, she describes recovering from a rape at knifepoint. The incident occurred in broad daylight in a locale familiar to cruisers: a laundromat.

Her feelings of security changed dramatically. "There are jerks on the water like [there are] jerks on land. . . . You can be in a harbor and there's theft. We lock the dinghy to the boat. We lock the hatch when we go to sleep; we lock ourselves in. At anchor, we don't assume we're invulnerable. People think they are invulnerable. I think women have fewer experiences of being in control, and the experience of having [control] taken [away] leaves you powerless. You fear the world."

Still, Migael has not been deterred from cruising. "I, and numerous women who have had my experience, learn to overcome such fear and continue to seek out adventure, just as fear of storms doesn't prevent joy in cruising."

How Do We Protect Ourselves?

Concern about crime is legitimate in the United States. Based on the experiences of most cruisers, the rest of the world doesn't necessarily have the same problem. Still, I believe you should develop good habits from the outset.

Traveling in Company

Flotilla cruising is popular, but it needs to be organized carefully. Irene Hampshire found herself in the middle of a bad situation created by other cruisers. "We got into a group of American cruisers and sailed with them," she says. "We probably should have gotten out, but we didn't. It seemed all right." Her family ended up witnessing a fellow American in their flotilla needlessly murder two fishermen. It took the joy out of cruising in Mexico for her and her family.

Although cruising in company with other boats can offer a sense of security, it turned into a bad experience for Irene—one she will always remember as part of cruising.

We have encountered situations where theft suddenly breaks out among the cruising community. These thefts are frequently "Midnight Marine Supply," not the local people. Yes, I mean that other cruisers in need of a part or specific piece of gear are the perpetrators. I talked with a woman recently who had been the victim of a boat burglary. The Pactor modem used for e-mail communication was stolen from her boat. Nothing else had been touched—money, valuables, or other gear—because the intruder wanted a specific item and knew where to find it. Screen carefully what you say and whom you permit on your boat, regardless of nationality.

If you are sailing in company, it is crucial for you to know and trust the crew on your buddy boat. According to Dawn Riley, "We were in the Bahamas doing an overnight passage, and a large, suspicious-looking fishing trawler approached us. I was on the bow, and they held the boat with grappling hooks and asked for cigarettes. We told them we didn't smoke, but they kept near. Fortunately we were cruising with another boat and called them over the VHF [radio], stating loudly that we were being approached and asked them to answer and flash their masthead light on and off. The trawler must have heard because they immediately took off into the night. Traveling with another boat is always a good idea."

Cruising friends were recently attacked as they left Aden to travel north in the Red Sea. This is an area of the world that has always been a security risk for cruising boats. They were traveling with another boat when locals attempted to board both their vessels. The attackers and our friends were armed. One of the vessels was steel, and it ultimately ran down and sank one of the attacking boats. Our friends and the companion boat got away and finally got some protection from a large commercial ship.

They were fortunate to escape, and some cruisers who heard the story decided that having weapons aboard was the answer for such situations. I think in this case traveling in company—five or six boats at least in that part of the world—would have given the attackers pause in initiating an attack.

Carrying Weapons

On our first long-term cruise, friends concerned about our welfare pressed us to carry weapons on board. We took a handgun and a shotgun. We declared the guns upon arrival in each country and were faced with turning them over to officials, locking them aboard the vessel, or storing them off the boat. Carrying weapons into a foreign country created such problems and paperwork that now we refuse to carry them. Not everyone shares our feelings about firearms, although many agree.

Patricia Miller Rains learned to use a slingshot while cruising solo in Mexico. "Now my husband often keeps a small gun handy at night."

Lin Pardey's reaction to having weapons on board was shared by most of the women I spoke with. "In the rest of world, guns are rarely used, and it's safer," says Lin. "We don't carry weapons. We have had friends killed by their own weapons." A tragedy several years ago verifies this unfortunate fact. A boat in Panama was boarded by convicts. To protect himself, the captain produced a gun. He was disarmed and shot, ultimately dying from the wound.

A Canadian provincial police officer once told us, "In my country, only criminals carry guns." That is the perception, if not the truth, in many countries of the world.

If you decide weapons are necessary for your own security, know how to use them and carry them legally. Attempting to carry undeclared weapons has dire consequences in many countries.

Attention-Getting Goods Aboard

Another potential problem is liquor. Judicious use is one thing, but using alcohol as a trading good can create serious problems. In many Muslim countries, alcohol is illegal or extremely limited, and it is not uncommon for locals to ask for it. In remote villages in Mexico or the Caribbean, fishermen often ask for liquor as payment for shrimp and lobster. In some ports, officials even ask for whiskey as part of the check-in process. If your boat gains the reputation of being a "booze" boat, you can become a mark. Displaying other commodities of value, such as jewelry or cash, also can increase your security risk.

Other Things You Can Do

Remember that as a cruiser—whether you are in your local waters or far from home—you are part of a community that enjoys traveling the world in a simple fashion without fanfare. Unlike the charterer who has a two-week vacation and doesn't have to live with the consequences of inappropriate behavior, your actions can follow you wherever you cruise.

When we began cruising, we contacted the State Department for information on "hot spots" around the world (the website address is http://travel.state.gov). If there is political unrest in a place you want to visit, contact the country's embassy or consulate and talk with them about your plans. We have found that many places that have questionable reputations are wonderful cruising grounds.

Lin Pardey exercises caution to diminish her likelihood of being a target. "We take precautions. We lock the boat. We talk to people about the local area. We have a low-key-appearing boat and no rubber dinghy. We never had a theft, except a bailer from the dinghy. The important thing is to be low key."

Boat appearance can be important to how you will be treated, but a low-key appearance doesn't mean looking neglected. A boat that doesn't show pride in ownership is as likely to be trashed as a fancy boat with lots of accessible toys. Some argue that appearing derelict is an invitation to being stripped of all gear. There certainly are rules about salvage that might justify such thinking.

Just as a boat bristling with antennas, fast tenders, and scuba and fishing gear may attract thieves, an inappropriately dressed cruiser is asking to be noticed. In the United States, we are used to dressing without regard for the opinion of others—particularly in large metropolitan areas. But when cruising, your appearance and behavior can affect your reception and, subsequently, your security.

If you cruise away from home, I believe it's important to exercise restraint. A quick look ashore with binoculars or a glance in a guidebook will show you how locals dress.

Using a phrase book allows you to use a few words of the local language, and it demonstrates that you have made an effort to learn about the culture.

Shopping with an appreciation for local food—instead of demanding peanut butter, frozen vegetables, and microwavable products—makes you a popular visitor rather than an unwelcome stranger. Put-downs of local products as inferior to American standards won't endear you to anyone and may make you a target.

When we started cruising years ago, tattoos were not the fashion. More recently, we have been aware that tattooing is common among Americans. There are cultures, such as Japan, where tattoos have a very negative connotation. A friend and I went to a public bath in Japan, and we were in the women's dressing area. When the other women saw the tattoo on my friend's leg, they moved away from us. A tattoo is frequently a symbol of the criminal element in that country, and the women were afraid of us.

Failing to recognize the local standard of living and practices is a frequent mistake. In the world's large cities, many styles, standards, and types of behavior are acceptable. It is easy to become absorbed into the local scene without calling attention to yourself. In a small town—in the United States, Europe, or the South Seas—your presence is obvious. A new boat in the harbor, a new face in the market, or a different language singles you out as a stranger. To me, it is obvious that wandering through the streets of a poor town wearing gold jewelry, flashy clothes, and carrying wads of cash is unwise. Yet cruisers forget to exercise common sense. The smart cruiser dresses neatly and with restraint, carries minimal cash, and leaves the jewelry at home.

My Own Approach

Looking at my experiences and those of other cruisers has led me to devise my own approach to personal safety.

- ☐ I do not want guns aboard my boat, because they don't make me feel safe. And they can create problems in a foreign country.

- ☐ I am careful in my choice of companion vessels and friends on shore. Just because a vessel carries the same nationality as I do does not mean its crew shares my values or concerns.

- ☐ Stopping at a new port is an endeavor that requires advance preparation—including researching the standard of dress, the area's cultural and religious practices, and the local language.

- ☐ Carrying unnecessary money, wearing jewelry, and wandering unescorted in unknown neighborhoods or after dark is taboo.

- ☐ Trading liquor, ammunition, or drugs with locals is inviting disaster.

I am not willing to give up cruising, but neither am I willing to cower in overcrowded ports because of a fear of "bad guys," whether real or imagined. Common sense, intelligence, and some basic precautions go a long way in protecting your welfare as you visit the exotic ports of the world.

7

IN SICKNESS
AND IN
HEALTH

A CENTURY AGO, doctors prescribed an ocean voyage to cure
many ailments. "The salt air will do you good," they said. If I were
a doctor, I would offer that same prescription: cruising and salt air,
on a regular basis.

Many people living in the fast-paced modern world seem
unduly stressed—by jobs, family problems, and traffic, among other
things. But when you meet real cruisers, that harried expression
is missing. Constantly looking at a watch, talking on the phone,
and checking a daily appointment book are not what cruisers do.
Cruisers are organized, but they are not harried.

Most long-term cruisers say they are the healthiest they have
been in their lives. But that does not mean you won't have to make
an effort to stay healthy and fit. As a cruiser, you have to take a
more proactive approach toward managing your health. Dr. Gail
Bowdish offers sensible advice: "Make lifestyle changes in your
diet, stop smoking, and reduce the risk for yourself. Understand
the risks of cruising, acquire knowledge of what to do, take precautions, and work within your limitations."

Make preparations before you start cruising in terms of your
own medical training and the medical supplies you carry on board.
You and your mate will also need to get complete physical exami-
nations before you leave—to better understand the status of your

health and to take care of problems that can best be handled while you are still at home.

Medical Preparation and Planning

Planning to live without ready access to medical care requires forethought and training. In the United States, we are fortunate to have 911 emergency numbers, large hospitals, and well-qualified medical professionals. We assume that the rest of the world doesn't offer this same quality of care, which is not necessarily the case.

"Medical care is superior cost-wise in most countries, and extremely good," says Lin Pardey. She and her husband paid $310 for his eye surgery in South Africa, which included all costs for doctors and the hospital.

Our experience with medical care in foreign countries has been good. Jim had rotator cuff surgery in Mazatlán, Mexico, and I had knee surgery in Hong Kong. In both cases, our international medical insurance worked very well. We paid a small additional fee—less than $50—for renting arthroscopic equipment in Mexico, and about the same amount for a series of physical therapy sessions for me. We were both fortunate that the attending physicians were fluent in English.

On remote islands and in third world countries, finding a doctor can be difficult. So can finding someone who can speak your language in a medical emergency (a good phrase book should include a few basic phrases on doctors and emergencies). In those situations, you may have to be prepared to attend to your own medical needs. There are several ways to make health problems less worrisome while cruising.

Training

First, acquire some training. Courses in Advanced First Aid, First Responder Courses, and Emergency Medical Technician (EMT) programs offer varying degrees of preparedness. If you have the inclination, the 100+ hours for a basic EMT program may be well worth your while. On the other hand, basic first aid, the Heimlich maneuver, and

CPR may be all you choose to learn. Whatever level you aim for in training, spend time learning how to recognize basic problems and understanding what emergency treatments are required.

Some medical courses are designed specifically for cruisers. A woman who sailed with us had taken an EMT course and a medicine-at-sea course. In her opinion, the four-day cruising course, which was given on a boat, was more valuable. Local clubs, sailing magazines, and online searches are your best resource for locating these courses.

We have two good medical books that are a permanent part of our onboard library and dog-eared from use: *Where There Is No Doctor* by David Werner, and *Advanced First Aid Afloat* by Peter F. Eastman (see the bibliography).

David Werner's book is used by health care workers around the world and by travelers and people living in remote areas. It discusses symptoms and treatments and includes an excellent section called the Green Pages, which covers medications. Peter Eastman's book includes hands-on information for handling situations at sea. It has a recommended medical kit that can be easily modified for your situation.

I took an advanced first-aid course to qualify our boat for an ocean race. My title for the race was "Doc." I was not faced with anything more serious than constipation and a bruised knee, but the experience made me appreciate the need to be prepared when you go offshore. I have always believed that if you are prepared for something, it won't happen.

I have learned how to give shots, close wounds, and remove fishhooks. At times I have been afraid I might hurt the patient, but reminding myself that not doing the required procedure was even more harmful was sufficient motivation to do what I had to.

Medical Kit

Your onboard medical kit may be anything from a basic prepackaged drugstore kit to a large duffel with many separate pouches, depending on where you go and for how long. The effectiveness of your medical kit also depends on your ability to use it.

I made ten small canvas bags with drawstring tops (next time I'll use Velcro for closures on the bags) and labeled each one to cover certain medical situations. Among the labels are kits for common problems, medications, burns, major trauma, etc. The master inventory for each bag is posted in a plastic sleeve on the locker where the bags are stowed.

There are similar, prepackaged medical kits for cruising, with all items for specific problems in labeled zippered pouches, all of which are put into a large sea bag. Search online or check cruising equipment ads and directories in cruising magazines for types and manufacturers of these kits.

Whatever you include in your medical kit, it must be packaged carefully, especially if you sail in a saltwater environment: avoid ferrous metal zippers on kits, seal scalpel blades and scissors in plastic bags, use desiccants to reduce moisture and mildew, and be sure your prescription drugs are current and tightly sealed.

We try to avoid daily rummaging in the first-aid kit by making a few items readily available in the galley, including bandages, aspirin, and Super Glue (cyanoacrylate). We use Super Glue for fixing broken fingernails and quick sealing of cuts (but be sure not to let any glue seep into the wound), as well as inanimate object repair.

You can buy dental kits that a nonprofessional can use to mend broken teeth and lost fillings. New technology in epoxy makes repairs quick and semipermanent. Many cruisers find a toothache the most excruciating pain possible. Painkillers are an essential part of your dental gear. Search online or check sailing/cruising equipment ads and directories in cruising magazines for these kits or ask your own dentist to prepare one for you.

Drugs and medications are available without a prescription in many countries. If you need to take something regularly, such as prednisone, you may find it cheaper locally. This also will keep your supply current, rather than buying a supply at home that will last a couple of years. Antibiotics are readily available in many countries, so you will be able to keep an up-to-date supply on hand.

Many cruisers believe drugs should be kept in locked containers, but I believe emergency items must be readily available, and I have never been required at home or abroad to lock up medications.

Medical Records

Before departing on a cruise, everyone should have a complete medical evaluation. For women, a standard evaluation includes blood and urine tests, a Pap smear, and a mammogram. It is very important that you communicate to your physician where you are going and what you plan to do. Standard treatments and care may not fit your travel plans. Be sure your doctor understands the limitations in health care that you expect to face. In your round of medical visits, be sure to include stops at the optometrist and the dentist.

If you assume the responsibility for onboard medical care, be sure everyone on board provides up-to-date, accurate information, including medical records, prescriptions, test results, and X-rays. I encountered resistance from my husband when I suggested he get a physical exam. He stalled and told me he had one when he went into the army some forty years earlier. Once convinced that I could not perform brain surgery or heart transplants at sea, he agreed that my request was reasonable.

If you wear glasses or contact lenses, take a copy of your prescription and extra sets of prescription glasses and contact lenses with you. If you wear contacts, be sure to take your glasses. Extended exposure to a saltwater environment may cause eye irritation for contact wearers. If you scuba dive or snorkel, a mask fitted with your eyeglass prescription is a nice addition. Life underwater is exciting when the curtain of fuzziness disappears.

Your dentist can give you your most recent X-rays. If you have been postponing a crown or the pulling of a wisdom tooth, have it done before you leave. Waiting to reach a port to see a dentist is hard on you and everyone else aboard.

Cruising to distant countries may require a variety of immunizations. Check the requirements at least two months in advance of departure. If you need several immunizations that are not compatible with one another, it will take several weeks to get through all of the shots. You can find information on international health requirements in the Centers for Disease Control (CDC) publication called the Yellow Book, *Health Information for International Travel.* It is published every two years, and updates are available online. The latest edition is for 2005–6. You can review it and/or order your own copy online from the Traveler's Health page on the CDC website (see the Resources appendix).

The CDC also operates the Travelers' Health Automated Information Line (877-394-8747), which provides information about ordering the Yellow Book and International Certificates of Vaccination, and recorded messages on travel-related topics.

Shots and serums were formerly provided by public health agencies, but increasingly this has become a private sector business. Check with clinics in your community.

Health Insurance

Your regular health insurance may cover you while you cruise. However, many cruisers have found that they won't be covered if they leave the country. If you need to secure new medical insurance before you go cruising, start looking early.

For trips of short duration, travel agencies may offer suggestions on programs typically used by vacationers. These programs, which cover emergencies and travel back to the United States for care, typically are short term with coverage limited from six to twelve months.

I have used carriers, such as Blue Cross Blue Shield, that offer catastrophic coverage. There is a high deductible, which essentially means you cover medical costs as you go. But if you're stricken with a major illness or emergency, the insurance covers you and, in many cases, requires you to return to the United States for care. If you are in good health, this may be the most economical insurance.

Foreign carriers provide health insurance useful to cruisers because the duration of travel or the location of care is not limited. See the Resources appendix for some suggestions; we have had direct experience with the Danish company. It has offered free coverage for children and has been able to work with certain pre-existing conditions. It offers a program that covers you around the world. You have a choice of coverage, but there are cost limits that would not meet typical fees in the United States. This program offers coverage for individuals up to age 75.

The availability and costs of insurance programs change constantly. Stay abreast of health insurance trends and information, some of which may be covered in sailing periodicals and online.

Many cruisers go without insurance and are comfortable with the risk. Your budget and health requirements will dictate the best course for you.

Help and Emergencies

As Dr. Gail Bowdish says, "When it is a true emergency, sail to port and get an ambulance or the fastest transportation to the nearest hospital. Catastrophic events need medical care. These can happen anywhere."

The U.S. Coast Guard does respond to emergency calls if they are within reach. In other countries, obtaining assistance may depend on your ability to communicate your need and on available government services. Merchant vessels and military vessels may offer assistance in some situations. But remember that the reality of cruising is that there is no 911.

Years ago we used a medical advice service that provided help over the radio. That service morphed into a much more sophisticated company called MedAire, which provides assistance for medical emergencies at sea. MedAire offers a program for the private maritime market called MedLink, which, among other services, runs an around-the-clock medical support center. It can receive calls by satcom, telephone (GSM), and radio. First, a communication specialist assesses the problem and then a board-certified physician joins the call. The doctor will help diagnose the condition and make a recommendation to the captain on the next steps. Medical follow-ups with MedLink nurses and communication specialists are done via e-mail.

MedLink also offers various types of web-based medical training, medical kits, and equipment for emergencies and routine care on board vessels. See the website (listed in the Resources appendix) for more information. This type of program may be expensive depending on your budget. However, it may be possible to use such a service in conjunction with a health insurance program.

Resolving issues that concern your health is not easy, but it's necessary for your safety and your peace of mind. Planning ahead to get everything in order is the first step. If you want to take training courses from the Red Cross, a resource like MedLink, or the EMT program at the local community college, it will require time. If you need to find an insurance plan that will cover some specific health issue, it will require research. Building a good medical library and familiarizing yourself with the content is time consuming. Selecting the right medical supplies and the best way to store them on your boat is another issue. Plus, you'll need time to acquire and organize your personal records, medical exams, injections, and medications. But planning now will save you stress and worry later.

Medical Concerns

Seasickness

Debate flourishes on seasickness. There are endless theories about its causes and cure. Bad weather (or worrying about it) can produce seasickness. Stress, worry, and fear can cause nausea, chills, and a range of symptoms typically associated with seasickness.

As Patience Wales said, "Feeling that I don't know what I should do physically, I get seasick. It's out of fear. I know that."

A small portion of the population gets seasick from disorders of the inner ear that affect the equilibrium. No drugs or techniques seem to work. I have great respect for people who suffer from this disorder and continue cruising.

The majority of victims overcome the symptoms of seasickness with remedies ranging from wrist bands that pinpoint certain pressure points to ginger and prescription drugs.

The antiseasickness drugs I find most common are Marezine (cyclizine) and Dramamine (dimenhydrinate). Neither requires a prescription; both make the user sleepy and must be taken in advance of symptom onset. At present, many cruisers who suffer seasickness use Stugeron (cinnarizine). It is popular because it is effective *after* the onset of nausea. It is not available in the United States, but it can be purchased over the counter in many foreign countries. The Transderm Scop (scopolamine patch) is once again available, with a doctor's prescription. It alleviates seasickness without causing drowsiness.

The first time I went boat shopping, I couldn't go belowdeck on a boat tied at the dock. Even the gentle rocking motion, which is normal in any marina, sent me back on deck. Today, if we have been in port for a time and then go out into rough weather, I know that I can't go below for 6 to 8 hours. It takes that long to get my sea legs back. But if the weather is nice when we start out on a passage, going below presents no problem.

My workspace on the sailboat was a quarter berth that converted to a desk. It faced aft and allowed me just enough room to work at the computer. In port or at anchor, the workspace was perfect. But when we were under sail, even after I had my sea legs, I couldn't sit down at the computer without developing the symptoms of seasickness in a matter of minutes. Instead, I sat on the sole next to the companionway ladder, facing forward, with the computer on my lap. On the trawler, I have a small forward-facing desk space.

Your body needs to adjust to sea motion. Steering the boat, watching the horizon, and actively moving with the boat's motion are ways to get your sea legs. Going below and sleeping may solve the problem for some, but it can also prolong it.

Avoid reading or doing other close work. If you begin to yawn or experience chills or sudden warm spells, sit up on deck, watch the horizon, and breathe deeply. If you wait until your stomach is queasy, you may have passed the point of no return. It is not unusual to have the same symptoms on land when you return to shore after being out cruising.

Boat motion can also make you seasick. Rolling back and forth or yawing in light winds is worse for me than heavy weather. Some find that the pitching of a boat, the fore-and-aft motion, makes them sick. Traveling diagonally across the waves can reduce some of this up-and-down motion.

I don't take medication for seasickness because I need to get my sea legs in order to be comfortable, and medication postpones that adjustment for me. If you experience symptoms, don't give up. You need to find out what works for you.

Menstrual Cycle

Menstrual cycles, pregnancy, and menopause are issues all women deal with. With increasing numbers of women sailing, questions about dealing with these life patterns are common. Generally, there is little difference in how you manage these events cruising or on shore.

Dawn Riley faced a rigorous life skippering a boat in the Whitbread Round the World Race. She dispatched of her period in a practical manner. "My solution was to take my [birth control] pills straight through. The doctor said that it was okay for a limited period of time."

Suppressing the menstrual period is an option many women choose if they are only concerned about a short period of time, such as a matter of months. Over the long term, the physical and emotional issues that many women experience have to be dealt with on a more permanent basis.

Premenstrual syndrome (PMS) is a problem many women face. The close quarters of a boat make it important to have the understanding of those around you. If a husband or boyfriend is aware and sympathetic, life is easier on board.

Barbara Colborn devised a way to communicate those times to her husband. "I learned to put a little lightning bolt on the calendar for the days I thought would be really bad. Some months were bad, and I tended to be more nervous and on edge, more prone to some depression. But it was no worse than on land."

What Barbara says may be the most reassuring thing a woman who suffers from PMS can hear: It was no worse when she was cruising.

"Menstrual cycles are never problematic [for me]," reports Patricia Miller Rains. "I use tampons and I take vitamin B-6 whenever my hormones inflame my emotions."

A number of women ask about disposal of napkins or tampons. Unless you are using totally biodegradable brands (read the manufacturer's label), these products should not go overboard. If they are biodegradable, dispose of them only beyond the limits specified by local and international law. (The minimum under the MARPOL treaty is at least 25 miles offshore and never in inland waters.) A double, self-sealing plastic bag will suffice for soiled supplies until you can reach a proper shoreside disposal.

There was a time when sanitary napkins and other supplies were hard to find in more isolated areas. Unless you are going to be in very remote areas for an extended time, a six-month supply should be sufficient. Store supplies in sealed plastic bags or containers.

Pregnancy

In times past, it was suggested that women who were unhappy cruising could save face and go home by becoming pregnant. The pattern was to sell the boat, hop a plane, and have the baby at home. Today, pregnancy does not automatically mean giving up the cruising lifestyle. Some cruising couples look forward to having a family as they travel.

When we were in transit through the Suez Canal en route to Cyprus, we befriended Karen and Mike Riley, who were expecting their first child. Their 24-foot boat had no engine, and they were towed through the canal alongside a sand barge. The trip on the Red Sea had been arduous. When she told me she was pregnant, I asked if she had seen a doctor. "Not yet. I'm only three months along," she replied.

She saw a doctor in Cyprus and continued to sail during the summer. Two weeks before she was due, she stopped at Malta and gave birth to their son. They completed their circumnavigation, bought a bigger boat, and set sail again.

As Dr. Gail Bowdish says, "The risk of miscarriage is greatest in the first twelve weeks; 25% of all pregnancies don't make it past the first trimester. It's a natural consequence, and not all pregnancies are going to survive." In the early stages, she states, nutrition is important, and medical advice is important as the pregnancy progresses. "Contact with a doctor should be established," she says.

We are fortunate now because we can maintain contact by e-mail. Be sure your doctor understands your circumstances and is willing to use e-mail. If you change doctors as you travel, you have the opportunity for the doctors to pass on information, again using e-mail.

The risk of trauma increases during the second trimester. Pay attention to moving about on the boat, since falls can lead to miscarriages. Because cruising is flexible, difficult or long passages should be avoided during this time.

"Premature labor can be caused by dehydration and stress," Gail points out. "Rest and drink plenty of fluids. Consider a shoreside residence approaching the third trimester," she suggests, which will also allow you to establish a relationship with a local physician.

Gail notes that a healthy woman should not be overly concerned about giving birth, especially if it is not her first pregnancy.

Every woman who is pregnant, whether on land or boat, should understand the importance of proper medical care, nutrition, and prenatal care, and know what activities pose risks to pregnancy. Cruising women who have children during their voyages have the same responsibilities as pregnant women on land. The main difference is that a cruising woman has to learn how to fit pregnancy into the unique circumstances of the cruising lifestyle.

Menopause

Many people begin cruising in their late forties and early fifties, the time women are most likely to enter menopause.

I received a letter from my sister filled with concern because I was not taking any hormones during menopause. To appease my conscience, I made an appointment with my doctor. After a lengthy discussion of the pros and cons, he told me he didn't want to prescribe hormones and have me head off to some unknown port where I couldn't stay in touch with him. With no family history of heart disease, cancer, or osteoporosis, I did without hormones.

I did have hot flashes as we sailed through the Southern Ocean, and I practically wore my clothes out taking them off and putting them on again. But there is no way of knowing if my life might have been easier had I taken hormones.

To stay informed and comfortable during menopause, talk with your doctor and other women and stay current on the use of hormones. These days, there is controversy about hormone replacement therapy. Be sure you research it thoroughly before making a decision. For women who will be long-distance cruising, the reassurance of a discussion with a medical professional is invaluable. If you're making long-range cruising plans and are concerned about when menopause is likely to begin, remember that menopause onset is known to be similar among family members.

The major health problem related to menopause is the loss of calcium, leading to osteoporosis. Falling on a boat is dangerous if you are calcium deficient. After menopause, a calcium supplement may prevent further bone loss, since your system is no longer able to make new bone. In early adulthood, you establish your calcium account by a good diet. Later, you draw the calcium from that account just as you draw funds from your retirement savings.

I used to take generic calcium tablets daily, but I don't anymore as calcium is easier to absorb from natural sources. Many calcium-rich foods are available around the world and are easily prepared on board. I eat a lot of yogurt, and I make fresh yogurt when we are underway. Beans, cheeses, and the ultra-high-temperature (UHT) milk that comes in a box are all easily managed on a boat, even without refrigeration.

For some women, menopause and cruising mixed without aggravation. "I was always so busy saving up tampons, and suddenly I had a year's supply, and I realized I was in menopause," Nancy Payson laughed, describing menopause as a nonevent.

"I went through menopause without recognizing it," says Lin Pardey. "I am healthier now, and I took hormonal therapy for a year to alleviate the most annoying problems. Pills were available everywhere."

Skin Protection

Both you and your partner are subject to serious skin problems when you go cruising. According to Gail Bowdish, the damage may have been done long before you took to the water. "Exposure as a child turns up decades later," she says. "The important lesson is to use sunscreen and protective clothing and avoid sunburn at all costs. The burn does the damage to your skin, and a severe burn is more likely to burn again."

I protect myself by using an awning, wearing lightweight cotton clothing to cover my arms and legs, and—of course—applying sunblock. In warm, tropical climates, I often wear long, loose, cotton dresses. A hat with a visor or brim and dark Polaroid sunglasses are part of my regular attire.

Many cruisers continuously exposed to the sun get basal cell cancers. These are not considered life threatening but are aggravating and ugly. The cancer known as a melanoma, which can also develop on the skin, is extremely serious and can be fatal. Any unusual changes in your skin—from patches of dryness to blotchy pigment or tiny bumps—should be examined. If you have a history of keratosis, basal cell cancer, or melanoma, spend time with your dermatologist. Discuss your cruising plans and find out how to best protect yourself.

My husband rarely pays attention to his physical condition unless he is actually in pain or bleeding. While we were living in California, I took a phone message on the boat from his doctor. She refused to leave a message other than to tell my husband to call and schedule another appointment. When he called her, he made a second appointment. I asked why he had to return so soon. He mumbled something about "margins." The rest of the conversation isn't printable. The problem was that one of the many skin removals his doctor did had resulted in detecting a melanoma. Fortunately he received early treatment, and he's fine. The appalling news was that he was unaware of what the diagnosis meant; he was shocked to discover that a minor little colored spot could have ended his life.

If you are determined to be a bronzed cruiser, you can choose from a wide range of products that both color and protect. Despite the fact that sun exposure has damaged my skin, I don't like to look pale. I use a combination cream that blocks the sun and colors my skin. Cosmetic companies have finally realized that sunblock is essential. There are lipsticks, lotions, and shampoos available with sunblock. Read the labels and protect yourself.

Pterygium

Pterygium was not a familiar problem to me in spite of my many years on the water. While in the Philippines, I thought something had lodged on my eyeball. It was a pterygium, a growth caused by dryness from exposure to sunlight and wind. It had started on the lens of my eyeball near the inner edge of the iris. Another one was just beginning in a similar spot on the other eye. In my case, it is slow moving, but it can eventually grow and cover the iris and pupil. It requires surgery to remove it.

Pterygium is very uncomfortable when you allow your eyes to become dry. An ophthalmologist can diagnose and evaluate this condition. I have had no appreciable increase ten years after diagnosis. The dryness returns frequently so I use a liquid to keep the surface of the eyeball from becoming irritated.

Fitness

I am often asked, "How do you get exercise?" On a boat, space for jogging or even simple exercise equipment is precious or nonexistent. "Plan for getting exercise, regular exercise, if you can't get enough on the boat," says Dr. Michelle Simon. An extremely athletic person may find it important to schedule off-the-boat exercise to maintain a normal level of fitness. For others, being on the boat may provide sufficient activity.

The normal motion of the boat and your body's continual effort to counterbalance those movements is around-the-clock exercise. Steering the boat or staying on your feet while cooking requires you to tense and relax your muscles as you synchronize with the boat's motion. Like isometric exercises, this activity goes on at a low level, even while you are asleep.

The Pilates theory of exercise is quite similar to the action of sailing. Gayle Jones, a personal trainer in Gig Harbor, Washington, describes how to incorporate these exercises while cruising:

"The main one is performed on a Pilates Reformer, which uses springs and a bench that slides on rails. The core muscles are worked on every exercise, some are performed supine, some standing (more balance required), and some are performed without the sliding bench, just using springs. I have done both, and the standing exercises would be most appropriate to sailing motion. The Reformer is too cumbersome to take cruising.

"With each form of Pilates, core muscles are emphasized. This is always important to have on a moving sailboat and a great way to prepare for cruising. These exercises can be performed anywhere with just a knowledge of the exercises. Pilates exercises can be done on a mat, hence the name Pilates Mat exercises. You are on a stable surface, but the core muscles are integral in every exercise.

"I use a stability ball with many of my clients (even Tom!) [Gayle's husband], and this gives you an unstable surface to really activate the core muscles. The stability ball would also be easy to take on a boat to keep in shape as you are cruising; you can deflate it if needed."

Learning the Pilates routine at the local health club is time well spent. If you can't take advantage of classes, look for a video, DVD, or an illustrated book on the topic.

Spend time trimming sails, grinding winches, hauling the anchor, and doing other cruising activities on board. The more you actively sail the boat, rather than use an automatic steering system, the more calories you burn. Sitting all day and reading a book while an electronic or mechanical device steers the boat deprives you of exercise and a chance to build your skills. It is not effective watchkeeping, either. You may not feel the exhaustion you feel in the gym or on the tennis court, but aggressively steering the boat will help you maintain body weight and feel rejuvenated.

On our trawler, I have the choice of standing or sitting at the helm. I stand, and do isometric exercises. Also, since the boat has several different levels, climbing stairs and ladders is part of my daily routine.

Yoga, even if you have never tried it, is excellent exercise on a boat. It helps you stretch and tone your body. It will also keep you limber and better prepared for quick movements or short bursts of intense activity. Almost anywhere you can stretch out will provide sufficient space.

Opportunities to maintain your fitness level exist in port, too. Provisioning a boat requires trips ashore. Rowing ashore is great exercise. Walking from shore to the store is very different from the weekly trip to the supermarket in the car. If you are in a country where outdoor markets are the rule, shopping can be an almost daily activity that requires walking and carrying bags or backpacks. Natural activities such as these don't put stress on your system, but they do burn calories.

When anchored, you can exercise while doing many activities. Swimming, snorkeling, and diving exercise major muscle groups and provide cardiovascular conditioning. Scrubbing the bottom of your boat may be something you've never done, but it is both excellent exercise and a productive task.

We started carrying bicycles on board in Japan; bikes provide transportation and good exercise. I've seen cruisers with inline skates, but there is a limit to their usefulness on dirt roads. Sailboards and kayaks are popular among cruisers with the space to carry them, and we have seen cruisers who bring tennis rackets and golf clubs. We have joined cruisers on the beach for Frisbee, volleyball, cricket, and bowling.

There is a temptation when cruising to socialize sitting down, with your elbow bent. Foods and beverages, mixed with the camaraderie of your neighbors, are tempting. But the result can be clothes that soon fit more snugly. I use how my clothes fit as my measure of my weight.

If you maintain a reasonable calorie and fat intake and make an effort to take advantage of the activities that cruising offers, you should stay fit. If you are sedentary aboard and ashore and neglect to manage your calorie and fat intake, you may have a problem.

8

CHILDREN AND PETS
ON BOARD

I HAVE COME TO BELIEVE that children who grow up cruising
are the best children in the world in terms of their behavior, education, and appreciation of the environment. If I could do it over,
I would raise my children aboard while cruising. But not having
been a cruiser when my children were young, I can only report
what cruising parents have told me.

We know cruisers who started families during their cruise and
raised their newborns aboard. We have seen toddlers and school-
age children who love cruising. We have watched adolescents blos-
som in the heady atmosphere of cruising.

There are parents who feel a boat is no place for their children,
and there are parents who believe there is no other place for their
children. If you choose to cruise as a family, you and your children
must be happy with the decision and enjoy the endeavor together.

Nancy Payson believes cruising gave her children something
that land life did not. "Two of my children were having problems,"
she says. "One had a run-in with the law, and the other was on drugs.
They came and asked if they could go on the trip with us. They grew
and matured. I really thank living on the boat for giving them the
knowledge of their own self-worth. . . . They knew when they were
on watch they were responsible for the rest of our lives. . . . They all
learned things they never would have learned [on land]. They grew
up with self-assurance and a strong sense of responsibility."

Nancy Jewhurst and Nancy Bischoff offer advice and information about their child-rearing experiences. Nancy Jewhurst took her son, Kyle, then 4 years old, on a six-month test cruise to learn if she, her husband, and her son wanted to make cruising their lifestyle. The voyage was successful, and they returned to cruising when Kyle turned 9. Nancy Bischoff spent ten years raising her two sons aboard.

Whether you live on land or on a boat, raising children is not a simple matter. Wherever a child is raised, that child still has needs and problems at every stage of life that parents need to confront.

Infants and Toddlers

Some couples don't want to postpone starting a family or going cruising, so they combine the two pursuits. Still, babies in the cruising world are few and far between. But we have the pleasure of knowing several couples who have conceived and delivered their children while cruising.

A Canadian couple we met chose to have their baby in Mexico. They selected a hospital and doctor in the Guaymas area, which is near the port of San Carlos. Just before the baby was due, the about-to-be grandparents flew to Mexico to be there for the event, and the entire family was present for the arrival of a baby girl. The proud father was impressed with the quality of health care and the modest cost. Doctor, hospitalization, and housing for the visiting families was less than $500.

The Rileys had their baby in Malta. One consideration for expectant mothers is good communication with caregivers. In Malta, the entire staff spoke English. The Rileys also found that the quality of health care was far better and less costly than anticipated.

Caring for an infant, especially your first, can be very stressful. Not everyone is predisposed to deal with a tiny infant 24 hours a day. Depression, fatigue, and insomnia are common reactions. If you plan to have children while cruising, be sure you have some alternatives in case you encounter physical or emotional problems when caring for your newborn. A shoreside residence or someone to help you with onboard care are two ways to make the experience easier.

If you have young children who will be going along on a family cruise, think about ways to ease the adjustment for all of you. Take test cruises together. Start with daytrips and gradually make trips longer and longer. Use these trips as a way to realistically assess whether sailing with small children is for you and to learn what you need to do to make it work better.

Children love routine. When you move on board, try to continue some of the same rituals and schedules that you established on land. Maintain the same bedtime rituals, for example. Bring bedding from home and make room for that favorite teddy bear.

Preparing Your Boat

Cruisers planning to start families while cruising need to make sure they have adequate space on board and all the necessary paraphernalia.

A secure place for the baby while underway is essential. Newborn carriers that fit into cars have worked on some boats as a secure spot to place a baby. We have seen infant car seats suspended from the overhead that rock gently to soothe a cranky baby. Depending on the layout of your boat, you may be able to convert a pilot berth with lee cloths and netting.

As babies learn to crawl and walk, you discover hazards that you have never seen before. You will need to adequately childproof your boat. Go through your boat the same way you would go through a house. Get down to your child's level and look for dangerous areas. Your aim is to both protect your child from your boat and protect your boat from your child. Pad sharp edges that could injure a child. You can also round off some edges with sandpaper. Put safety covers on shore-power electrical outlets, keep tools and sharp instruments out of reach, and stow poisons and medicines in locked compartments. Make sure cupboard latches can't be opened by children.

Know which controls on board are in your child's reach. Can she reach stove knobs, seacocks, or the engine ignition key?

Remember that bodies and objects can move on a pitching boat. Are there any exposed engine parts that your child could fall against while the engine is still hot? Are there any objects that could fly free and injure her?

Netting strung through the lifelines to prevent little ones from slipping overboard is a must. Netting is not, however, a substitute for parental supervision.

It is important that your child learns to hold on as she moves through the boat. A young couple told us that the first words their 1-year-old comprehended were "Hang on!" Make sure there are enough handholds.

Safety Issues

Safety training should be part of every cruising child's upbringing. Provide each child with a life jacket that fits properly. Is there a crotch strap to keep the jacket from slipping over the head? Is there a handle you can grab to ensure speedy retrieval if your child falls? Is there a flotation collar for head support?

Whether you are riding in your dinghy, loading at the dock, or standing on deck, every child should wear a life jacket; it should be taken off only when your child goes belowdeck.

When your child becomes mobile, she should wear a safety harness similar to yours. Most harnesses are capable of some size adjustment, but you can have extra-small ones made by your sail- or canvas-maker.

Think carefully about the safety rules you plan to establish on board. Be consistent and enforce them—both with your own children and visiting children. Make sure all adults on board know the rules and understand that they are to be enforced at all times.

Health Concerns

Keeping an infant or toddler clean is difficult in the best circumstances. Keeping a child's busy hands out of her mouth is always a concern, especially when you are traveling in places with muddy streets, minimal sanitation, and diseases.

One cruising mother told me the meat cases in the market were her son's favorite. The glass was so cold, and he liked to rub his face along the cool glass that was just about 18 inches off the ground!

Infants and toddlers are small enough to be bathed in a plastic tub or bucket. Cruising adults can manage with saltwater baths and freshwater rinses, but young skin is sensitive, and salt water may be too harsh. You may need a watermaker or additional water storage. Prepackaged baby wipes are great for cleanliness along the way, but their availability depends on your cruising venue.

Make sure your children receive all the necessary immunizations as soon as they are old enough. Clinics and hospitals in foreign countries offer the same types of immunizations that you would get at home. Be sure to select a clean health facility that uses current serums and sterilizes equipment properly or uses disposable equipment. Keep a record of immunizations received, especially if you are on the move.

If you already have young children, discuss your cruising plans with your pediatrician before you leave. Find out the best way to handle standard infant shots, what medicines in what dosages to carry, and how to handle the sudden fevers little ones develop. If you expect to be in remote places, make sure the doctor has a clear picture of the limitations in available health care. Ask the doctor for recommendations of medical books geared to children's ailments.

Babies and young children exposed to the sun need sunblock, a hat, and clothing that covers them. It is tempting in warm climates to let babies and toddlers go without clothing. But even if your child is sitting under an awning, the sun reflecting off the water can still reach him and cause sunburn. Skin that is burned, particularly at an early age, is more susceptible to problems later and must be protected. As children grow older and become more active, it becomes harder to manage the discipline of skin protection. In Australia, we first saw bodysuits in use, which provide excellent coverage.

Don't forget about sunglasses for your children. You can have good-quality children's glasses made up in durable frames. A way to attach them to your child is important; neoprene holders work best.

Diapers

The space an infant occupies is minimal compared to the space required for his baby gear. The disposable diaper has become a convenient standard on land. Disposables and pull-ups are often used for several years. But storing and disposing of these diapers while cruising presents some problems.

Most new mothers prefer the convenience of disposable diapers to washing cloth diapers. Cloth diapers are viewed as a backup, acceptable only if there is no other choice. Two people I spoke with chose cloth diapers because of cost. In sunny climates with good access to water, managing diaper laundry was not a problem for either of them.

However, discarding disposable diapers can be a problem. Most cruising mothers dispose of diapers with the rest of their garbage when they arrive in port. If the diaper is so messy they can't live with it until they reach land, they rinse the diaper overboard or in the head before putting it in the trash. Unfortunately, there are many ports where garbage is collected on land and simply dumped back into the sea. Faced with this alternative, I would opt for laundering diapers.

The Rileys cruised on a 24-foot boat with their newborn. They did not have the luxury of space for disposables, so Karen hand-washed cloth diapers and hung them to dry in the rigging. I'm not sure how satisfactory this arrangement was for her—but I know her baby was rapidly potty-trained.

Food

Food is not a problem for breastfeeding infants. Breastfeeding children up to 5 years old is practiced by some women. But toddlers ready for solid food and regular milk may present more of a problem, especially if you are in remote areas or on a long passage.

UHT milk is available in most of the world, even in remote locations (although it is not easily found in the United States). Typically packaged in liter boxes (smaller boxes are sometimes available), this milk has a shelf life of several months. Once open, it can be kept in the refrigerator for three to four days. If you don't have refrigeration, you can use the remainder of the open milk to cook or make yogurt.

Powdered milk and powdered formulas are easily stored, but you will need sufficient water for mixing. If you are leaving the country, check on the availability of formula mixes (both dry and canned). Commercial baby food is readily available in most larger towns, even in the third world. Remote fishing villages and islands with limited supply sources are not likely to have the precooked and pureed foods. You may need to resort to old-fashioned ways, such as cooking food and mashing it to make baby food. Vitamins for kids can be found in pharmacies around the world.

Your water supply on board needs to be safe for the whole family. Potable water from shore and water from the watermaker can work fine. When you go ashore for outings, be sure to take water. Nursing mothers, babies, and toddlers need plenty of water to prevent dehydration.

Social Life

Socialization for preschool youngsters, whether at home or away cruising, is often adult oriented, and living on board in a small space with your infant can yield fantastic results.

Nancy Bischoff believes that living in close physical proximity as a family is one of the benefits of cruising. "When we house-sat for three or four days," she says, "I couldn't believe how separated our family was. There's so much space. We were out of touch. . . . Raising a family on a boat? It's a wonderful lifestyle. I wouldn't change it. It brings the family together."

The closeness that results from living in a small space will give you the chance to know your child more completely and share more of yourself. The most obvious result among cruising children is the verbal skills they typically command at an early age. Without a continual schedule of television, babysitters, and parents who are always away working, interaction between parents and children is continuous. You will equip your child with the ability to communicate well.

Still, I believe 24 hours a day with a baby or toddler has to be broken up while you are cruising—just the way it is on land. Babysitters are often available. We have been in fleets where an opportunity to practice grandparenting for the afternoon was a real treat.

Carry on board a variety of activities and games that your children can grow into. Even for young children, simple games and reading are important for early education and socialization. Keep in mind that books in English are more expensive around the world than they are at home.

Don't forget to pack the ingredients for celebrations: birthday balloons and Christmas stockings. Parties are enjoyed by all, and they create an event to anticipate and a memory to savor.

School-Age Children

It is important to understand the day-to-day needs of school-age children. When Nancy Jewhurst took her 4-year-old son Kyle on a six-month cruise, she left prepared. With assistance from the local library, she was able to fill the boat with books—enough so Kyle had one new book each week. She purchased the Calvert home-study kindergarten course. Out of the 160 lessons in the Calvert course, Nancy and her son completed 19 lessons. "We just didn't have time, and he certainly wasn't bored!" she says.

Education Underway

Even though cruising is often considered an education unto itself, it is important to keep up with formal education while you are cruising.

The home-study programs mentioned most by cruisers are offered by Calvert Education Services, which provides programs for kindergarten through grade eight. The school was founded in 1906 and is based in Hunt Valley, Maryland. Its programs are accepted by most school systems. (See the Resources appendix for contact information.)

Irene Hampshire was satisfied with the home-study program offered by the public school system in Oceanside, California. Her son,

Shawn, was in the program from kindergarten. "When we were away on trips, I turned in work samples and I filled out a report card. When we were [on land], we met with the teacher every three months." Homeschooling has become an option that many communities offer, often without tuition or other fees if you are a resident.

Both Irene and Nancy Jewhurst devoted time each day to act as the teacher. Most cruisers who teach their children aboard set aside specific hours and days for school. Successful homeschooling requires the discipline to maintain the routine.

We discovered that everyone observes the standard school holidays and vacation periods, just as they would in a regular school program. (I suspect the parents are just as enthusiastic as their children about holidays.)

There is a growing movement in home study coordinated by public school systems. Your local school district office is an excellent place to begin your research.

Health and Safety for Kids On the Go

Health and safety for school-age children depend on teaching good safety practices early on. Establish rules and be consistent in enforcing them.

Safety is especially important, because children are in or near the water all the time. Irene Hampshire, who raised two boys aboard, says, "Falling in the water was not my big concern. It was hitting their heads against the dock or boat and being hit by other boats when they were in the water." Life jackets and safety harnesses are standard, everyday gear for many children. Enforce the habit of using these safety aids.

Bumps, bruises, and lacerations are normal with school-age children whether they are on land or on water. You may have to expand your first-aid kit's inventory of ice packs, adhesive strips, antiseptic, and disinfectant.

Without everyday exposure to lots of other children, the rate of picking up diseases and germs from other children lowers. Still, kids do come in contact with each other and share their germs.

According to one cruising nurse, cruising kids regularly pick up head lice from each other. She finds that kids play together and share clothes, and the bugs sometimes get passed along. Rather than discourage interaction among the children, she passes out tubes of shampoo for controlling head lice.

Also, making sure hands and clothes are washed is standard for the welfare of the entire family.

Food for Growing Children

Most cruising parents find that a simple diet works for the entire family. They use fresh fruits and vegetables and introduce new or unusual items as they travel. "The kids were not picky about food," says Gail Amesbury. "We [bought] local food, ate with local people, and it opened up a different environment."

"Whatever we ate was what we served to Kyle," says Nancy Jewhurst. "If he didn't like it, then he waited till the next meal. There was usually something in a meal that he liked. A lot of what we ate was fairly simple, especially underway. Things like Dinty Moore and macaroni and cheese."

With this age group as well, mothers report that UHT milk is ideal. Powdered milk is a hard sell with most children because it is lumpy, and in many places local fresh milk sours quickly.

Soft drinks and sweet juices are generally available in most countries. In recent years, juices have been packaged in liter boxes similar to the boxes used in UHT milk packaging. This offers a distinct advantage since like-sized containers are much easier to stow.

Cruisers who do not have refrigeration on board can encounter problems keeping fresh meat, fish, and cheese for any period of time. Unless you are embarking on a long offshore passage, the regular trips to the local markets you will have to make are entertaining and educational for children.

Fishing is fun for children on long passages—and the activity keeps fresh food on the table.

Quarters for the Kids

Space requirements for school-age children can change weekly. Nancy Jewhurst remembers how, at age 4, her son Kyle and his toys, books, and most of his clothes fit into a quarter berth that was 6 feet long.

At age 9, Kyle packed even more belongings into that same quarter berth. "He had a big plastic storage box at the foot of his bed, and he couldn't stretch his legs out. But he claimed that he slept with his legs scrunched up anyway, so it was okay. He didn't want to give up anything—and yet we had to."

In addition to the box at the foot of his berth, Kyle had three net bins against the hull in his bunk. They stuck out about 8 inches. One bin was for his clothes, one was for his toys, and one was filled with books. "It was a real struggle trying to get him to give up some of those things to make room for his feet," Nancy says. "He just grew."

A bunk big enough for both sleeping and playing seems to be the most common solution for growing children. A quarter berth is often allocated to a single child; it is like a small cave where a child can set up housekeeping. We have friends living on a Bristol 35; their 9-year-old son has the quarter berth, and their 11-year-old daughter has the forepeak. Mom and Dad have a double bunk in the main cabin.

Getting Along

Before they set off, many cruisers express concern about their children's socialization, which normally begins on land when children start school. Once underway, however, few cruisers seem to remain concerned about their children's socialization.

I think the pressure for socialization and to be accepted by a peer group diminishes greatly in the cruising community. A cruising child sees himself less as a separate entity and more as a responsible part of a family group. Individuality is encouraged, because children are respected, given meaningful tasks, and offered the opportunity to be equals.

Cruising children always enjoy meeting kids their own age. "The kids interact no matter what their ages, but in order for them to truly have a lot of fun, the age has got to be somewhere around their own age," observes Nancy Jewhurst. Looking back at Kyle's childhood, Nancy takes a very objective view of his experience: "Cruising as an only child can be lonely. There are not always other children in an anchorage, and even if there are, if they have different interests or are of very different ages they may not be interested in socializing. This is one of the main reasons we stopped cruising when Kyle was 12. Socialization and friends you can grow up with and share with are so important. A sense of community is very important. People certainly adapt, as many children of families that move often can tell you, but I believe the constant moving that is a part of cruising makes it difficult for a child to make and keep good friends.

"Kyle finished high school as tenth in his class and received many awards for his academic excellence. He now attends UCLA," reports Nancy.

Gail Amesbury believes the issue becomes more crucial in teenage years. "After 13, they desperately need to be with children their own age. We've personally found that with any children we met, when we got them together, the liveaboard children didn't know how to play team games or mix with more than two or three children. They didn't know how to take turns at doing things. I firmly believe they need to be in the environment to prepare them for coping with society."

There is no guarantee other boats in any given port will have children aboard. It seems that more young people are cruising today, but many of them don't have children. Contact with adults is the norm for cruising kids, and they quickly learn to carry on conversations—regardless of age differences. For Nancy Bischoff, a less traditional upbringing outside normal social structures is a plus for cruising children. "Getting [our children] out of the mainstream was the best gift we could give them," she says.

Irene Hampshire didn't worry about socialization. "As far as 'socialization,' it came from an assortment of ages, not just their own age group. We were in Nawiliwili Harbor on Kauai once when a huge storm dropped tons of rain on us for 24 hours. There were other kids on boats in the harbor, and they all (all ages) banded together and went from boat to boat looking for something to do. One boat would put a video on for them, then kick them out when it was over, and on to the next boat for something to eat, and then on to the next to play games, etc. Finally, when they ran out of boats, someone donated a sail and tacked it up as an awning on land!"

Gail Amesbury offers a comment about socializing that strikes home for many cruising parents. "Cruising is a social life, and there are so very few children. If you're invited for drinks, there are no children. And most people don't enjoy the children being there."

Whether you are cruising or living on land, there are people who do not like to have children around. Entertaining or being entertained by those people when you have children is difficult. But I find that most cruising children are adaptable. I have seen them sit quietly and read, write, or play games while their parents chat without interruption. Those kids are always welcome on my boat.

Adolescents

Most of the controversy about children aboard centers on teenagers. Opinions range and are sometimes confusing. The key issues with liveaboard adolescents are their need for space and privacy on board and their education.

Health and Safety for Teens

Health and safety concerns are minimal with this age group. The issues of AIDS and other sexually transmitted diseases are discussed by cruising parents, just as they are discussed by parents in many places.

The likelihood of injury is always a concern. As Nancy Bischoff said, "They could be 40, and I'd still worry." Her sons are 16 and 20 years old.

Food ceases to be a problem. Most kids have learned to eat a wide variety of foods by this age. The occasional need to binge on hamburgers, French fries, pizza, and ice cream seems to be universal among young adults.

A Place of Their Own

Families with teenagers on board do face space issues. "Privacy is hard with two boys on a 33-foot boat," says Irene Hampshire. She has managed over the years. But now the boys need their privacy as much as their parents do.

"Erik lived with us until he was 21 and the sailboat became too small for the four of us. So Jon and I bought a Grand Banks 36, moved it in next to the sailboat and along with our youngest son, Shawn, moved into it, leaving Erik behind on the sailboat (it was time for Jon and me to leave home!). Now that Erik is 28, he has moved into a house with his girlfriend on land. We promptly sold the sailboat. . . . Now that Shawn is 21 and still living with us, I am thinking of the next home-leaving!"

Nancy Bischoff found the living space on her boat adequate when they cruised with their kids. But a guitar, electronic keyboard, drum set, and amplifying system, which the family played as a hobby, took up any extra room. On her 37-foot boat, four adult-sized people shared very cramped space in order to keep their pastime alive. The pleasure it gave to the family, and to the people who heard them perform, was their reward for the inconvenience.

Most cruising boats with teenagers aboard that we encounter are in the 40-foot-plus range. At that size, it usually is possible for everyone to have his or her own quarters and privacy. Houses become cramped too, but stretching a boat to accommodate a growing family may mean a major renovation of space or buying a bigger boat.

High School and Beyond

Schooling presents diverse dilemmas and solutions. The main concern seems to be the need to prepare children for college.

Irene Hampshire is still enthusiastic about homeschooling. "The schooling went well; both kids entered junior college while still of high school age. Erik got an Associate of Arts degree and then decided that he had had enough of school. Shawn is still working on his degree and wants to get his teaching certificate. They have had an international education from the traveling that we do, meeting people from all over the world. In addition, being home-schooled, the kids became more a part of the community and actually knew more people and came in contact with more people than the kids in school all day. Shawn especially has no problem with socialization, but his friends are of all ages."

Gail Amesbury's three children attended boarding schools in England while she and her husband cruised. "It was a financial drain to keep them there," she says. "It took away resources quicker than we imagined. Not only school fees, but every six weeks they had a vacation, and they flew out to where we were. The airflights were such a tremendous expense all the time."

Gail's son Simon was going to college, so his situation would not have been different if Gail and her husband were land based. Gail recognizes that her son Jon-Paul, then age 14, could have been educated on board. "But at 14, I don't think we could have coped with the level of education," she says. "We could have educated Rebecca on the boat, but I feel there is an ideal age to be liveaboards and benefit by it between 6 and 13. Girls, especially, need the companionship of a close friend to talk to and to mix in groups."

Nancy Bischoff used the high school program offered by Brigham Young University for her younger son. "His high school recommended and accepted this program. We talked to his counselor. He took courses, and my husband tutored him. He did geometry, American literature, and psychology. We spent 2 to 3 hours in the morning. He got help with geometry, and he did [the other courses] on his own. He wanted to do his senior year back home. We did his junior year over two years, and he graduated a year later. We hoped it would become less important [to return home for school] so we could stay out longer."

But the Bischoffs kept the promise to their boys and returned to Seattle. "After our family returned home from our first cruise (from Seattle to Mexico, Central America, the Panama Canal, the Western Caribbean, and New Orleans), both Kurt and I went back to work, and our boys went back to school. Korum, our oldest, finished programs in both music and graphic design. He soon got jobs as both a drum teacher and a graphic artist for a Seattle music production company. A few years later, he married his high school sweetheart and, almost three years ago, helped produce our first grandchild.

"Jherek, our younger son, also attended college for a while before dropping out to devote *all* of his time to music. He spends all his time composing, recording, and performing music, and he has managed to continue to feed his wanderlust by touring the United States and Europe multiple times every year.

"When my husband and I contemplated leaving for another cruise in 2003, one of our primary concerns was how we would enjoy cruising without the kids, as having children along with us provided a great family experience and the kids forced us into many situations that we probably wouldn't have gotten into without them. We were also concerned because, just as we were untying the docklines, we were told that we would become grandparents within the year.

"What I discovered early on in the second cruise is that, while I missed our children a lot, I was able to devote more time to personal pursuits, like reading, needlework, and interacting with other adults—both fellow cruisers and natives of whatever country we were visiting. My husband and I had a wonderful time on our second cruise and, if we had an income that would allow us to fly home twice a year to visit the kids and grandson, we'd probably still be out there cruising. However, we aren't retired, the money was starting to get low, and we were really missing the family. We *do* really miss the cruising lifestyle and, in particular, the close relationships we had with the friendly locals of Tonga, Fiji, and Vanuatu. Cruising has definitely changed the way we view the world. Who knows, maybe someday we'll head out a *third* time!"

Irene Hampshire's older son Erik finished the homeschooling program at the tenth-grade level. There was no provision for the last two years, so Erik began taking courses at a junior college. In order to qualify for college at age 16, he took an equivalency test and passed with flying colors. Now Erik is an excellent sailor, with a full-blown career in the racing world. He still works on boats with his dad. Shawn is becoming an artist, specializing in ceramics and (of all things on a boat) glassblowing.

We spent some time with the Rileys just as Falcon was entering high school in Maryland. He was attending formalized school for the first time. This was our most recent update:

"I think the baby has grown into an incredibly self-reliant young man, intuitive and polite. He has an ease and confidence about him that lets him talk to adults as easily as he talks with his peers. How much of his success is due to growing up on a boat while sailing around the world and/or how much is innate, who can tell. He didn't grow up with drug dealers as peers, the TV set as a friend, or chemicals in his food. He grew up healthy, wanting to spend more time outside doing things like sailing dinghies, building forts on deserted islands, and hunting for our dinner while snorkeling for hours. Being active for Falcon was an important attribute he looked for in friends.

"Cruising with my son allowed him to live a worldview. He could see people interact with one another, live with different ethnic groups, and learn about cultural differences. He was given everything he needed to grow, make choices, and succeed.

"Our lives were simple; our needs few. We had time to spend laughing, teaching, and learning with each other. I don't think any other lifestyle could have afforded me this pleasure. I would have been torn between work and time with my son. This lifestyle allowed both my husband and me a 24/7 relationship with Falcon. It became a tight unit I wouldn't give up for anything."

The *Independent Study Catalog*, published by Peterson's Guides, lists high school–level programs. The Internet has numerous listings so preselecting websites from the catalog may make your search more productive. See the Resources appendix for a few suggestions.

One discussion about educating children sticks in my mind. Several mothers were talking during a break at one of our cruising seminars, concerned about their children qualifying for college. But in the discussion, they made several assumptions: first, that their children would go to college; second, that formal education would have more value than cruising.

The issue of formal education versus life experience is one that will be debated forever. Your resolution of the issue depends on your value system.

Pets
Felix and Fido

Pet status has improved from getting a cat or dog because the kids want one to in many cases having a cat or dog in lieu of kids. Couples choose not to have children or perhaps can't have children, and the substitute is a pet. Linda Fraser's two dogs are "the boys," who are treated with exceptional care and affection. They are provided with toys, equipment, and furniture; they travel everywhere with their human parents. They have specific spaces on the boat and feel very much at home. The very fact that dogs and cats have such an elevated status has spurred the development of innovative products and improved health care for pets. They are as ubiquitous as their humans are. The daysail, weekend outing, or family vacation on the boat includes the family pet.

Couples or families planning on long-term cruising with their pets have a more complicated set of issues. We used to see the occasional cat or dog aboard long-distance cruising boats. Often they were pets that had been picked up along the way. Many pets were strays that had found homes with softhearted cruisers. Our first seagoing cat was one of three kittens dumped at the marina in Larnaca, Cyprus. The three were picked up by a fellow who realized later that three is indeed a crowd. We agreed to take this tiny black creature aboard. We named our kitten Zorba because he was from Greek Cyprus. We learned the hard way that pets create their own set of problems.

Can We Take Them?

We discourage taking birds or mammals other than cats and dogs. While some countries might accept them, it will be difficult to bring them back into the United States (if that is your home port). The U.S. Department of Agriculture is very aggressive about preventing diseases being introduced here by birds or nondomestic animals. More than once we have heard U.S. cruisers complain about extended quarantine for a U.S.-bred bird. Our vet tells us that bird diseases are a problem and bird care is complicated. It isn't easy to manage, although some people love their birds and won't leave them behind.

There are no international rules that govern whether you can take a pet cruising. Each country has its own policy where pets are concerned. There are three basic rules that we encourage people to follow whether they are going out for a weekend to their favorite gunkhole or headed to foreign waters:

First, neuter or spay your pet. Local animals will make your life miserable if you have a pet in heat aboard. Any contact with the local pet population can be a health risk for your pet. It can also negate any quarantine your pet might have already had.

Second, make sure your pet is current on all shots and vaccinations. You need to carry proof that your pet has had all necessary immunizations. In most countries, you can find veterinarians who can give shots and do exams. The level of care and cleanliness of facilities varies greatly. Many vets don't have small-animal experience; their practice is with agricultural animals.

The third rule is to "chip" your pet by having your vet implant a microchip with a hypodermic under the loose skin in the back of the neck. It has a unique code readable by a special scanner available at veterinarians and animal shelters. There are several scanning systems available worldwide. Scanners can identify the code used so whatever the system for your pet, there is a means to read it. That code identifies the owner of the pet. Check with your vet even if you don't plan to cruise immediately. The microchip can save you from lots of heartache at home or abroad if your pet gets lost.

Special Considerations

Food

Any U.S. or foreign port where you find supermarkets will carry familiar brands of pet food. If your pet is on a prescription diet, you need to stock up in advance and carry the prescription so you can buy refills in local pet hospitals.

The long-term, long-distance cruiser needs to be resourceful where pet food is concerned. Dogs can be fed food very similar to what we eat: vegetables, pasta, rice, meat, and fish (meat and fish need to be cooked and deboned). Check with your vet for recipes and any supplements you might need.

Cats are sometimes regarded as finicky eaters. However, we have discovered that boat cats have broad tastes. We carry large quantities of dried cat food and supplement it with occasional treats of cooked fish, poultry, or meat. The dried food helps keep feline teeth and gums in good shape. Again, be sure to check with your vet for recipes and supplements.

If you decide to stockpile dry food for your pet, store it in vermin-proof containers. We have seen all sorts of large plastic pails, garbage cans, and boxes filled with a variety of pet food. Don't keep original boxes or bags on board because they harbor cockroach eggs. The dry food won't be dry for long if allowed to absorb moisture from the air. Mice, rats, and cockroaches will destroy your stockpile if you use anything short of heavy-duty plastic sealable containers.

Health and Safety Issues

We are frequently asked questions about the age of pets when people are contemplating cruising. Age and health issues do seem to go hand-in-paw. Train and supervise boat pets just as you would do with children. They are very adaptable and bounce back rapidly from bad weather or minor illness. They need to get sea legs in order to avoid seasickness. They need a safe and comfortable place to rest. They also need elimination training to avoid constipation.

The bibliography of my book *Cruising with Your Four-Footed Friends* lists some references on elimination training of pets. Litter boxes and newspaper are okay for short trips. Buying cat litter or taking dogs ashore is not always possible. Training your cat to use a toilet or your dog to eliminate on command are alternatives to consider.

How old is too old? This is a familiar question. Mobility is the issue and the answer. As long as a cat can climb to safety and move quickly enough to avoid danger, then cruising should not be a hardship. If your cat has developed infirmities that do affect agility, it would be my choice to forgo taking the cat cruising. Cats need their claws for survival, so don't declaw them.

Certain breeds of dogs do very well aboard, regardless of age. Large dogs, particularly those prone to hip problems, present a problem as they approach age 10. Customized ramps for getting in and out of the cockpit or cabin make climbing easier. However, this problem is progressive and is increasingly painful, and you will want to keep it in mind in your planning. Getting in and out of a dinghy, even if you have low freeboard, is problematic as pets age.

There needs to be a pet-overboard (POB) drill so you know how to retrieve a cat or dog that has gone swimming. Pets need to have a well-fitted personal flotation device (PFD). Ruff Wear makes excellent jackets for the smallest dog up to jackets for full-grown mastiffs at 178 pounds. Dogs should wear them all the time on board except when belowdecks. We believe that cats should have the PFD on only when they are supposed to leave the boat because it interferes with agility. Our cat-retrieval system is to hang out a towel, rug, or very thick line so the cat can climb on board. Our swimming cats have learned very quickly.

Plan a first-aid kit for your pet with the aid of your vet and learn how to use it.

Paperwork

Again, long-term and long-distance cruising requires extra work if you plan to take along your cat or dog. Quarantine requirements are lessening each year. There are still requirements as of this writing in New Zealand, Australia, and Hawaii. The latter has reduced the length of quarantine if the pet meets certain requirements. It isn't clear, since the new rules were written for the benefit of air travelers, whether pets arriving by boat can stay in quarantine for just a 24- to 72-hour period.

In Europe, likewise, the requirement for quarantine has been dropped if the pet is on a commercial carrier. What regulations exist are the same throughout the European Union.

Some dog breeds are excluded by some countries. Among the unwelcome are the pit bull, Presa Canario, and Akita. Some dogs are excluded that have wolf or similar nondomestic blood within the last four generations. Do your homework on this subject well in advance of departing.

Your vet at home can get you started with record keeping. Record the rabies vaccinations along with the name of the vaccine used and the date. Some veterinarians may still have the international health form. To validate your pet's immunization record, some countries require certification through your state department of agriculture.

Do not allow your pet off the boat except on a leash or in a carrier. We have seen cruisers who believe that cats should roam. This is not acceptable for several reasons. Cats don't know that they are trespassing when they climb onto someone else's boat. More than once a cat has hidden away on a strange boat and been trapped. They can die of starvation or be discovered at sea and dumped. Not all cats are lovers, and if they fight with local cats or bring local cats aboard, contamination is likely. If your cat is serving an onboard quarantine, allowing the pet to leave the boat is grounds for a fine, forfeiting a bond, and destroying your pet in some countries.

There are several books listed in the bibliography of *Cruising with Your Four-Footed Friends* that you may want if you plan to take your cat or dog cruising.

9

FOLKS
AT HOME

LEAVING HOME TO GO CRUISING can be a relief and a liberation. It can also be a guilt-ridden experience. Separating from family and friends is part of cruising. That separation can be difficult, or you can work to make it manageable.

It is most important to prepare family and close friends for your departure. Réanne Hemingway-Douglass stresses the importance of family coming to terms with your decision to cruise. "Your family has to be able to understand what you're doing," she says. "You must get their support. You can sit down with them and say, 'This is very important to us. This is what we are going to do.' "

Preparation

As a first-time cruiser, you may or may not have a clear picture of what you're getting into. You've read books, equipped your boat, taken classes, and tapped every resource to get an idea of what lies ahead. In the meantime, your family has watched scary movies, read hair-raising stories in newspapers, and watched search-and-rescue shows on television. Your parents, children, and close friends may be certain that every kind of disaster possible will befall you. Your adventure is as clear to them as a trip to the moon.

"My father kept sending us clippings about bad things that happened at sea, but my mother was very supportive," says Réanne Hemingway-Douglass. I believe Réanne communicated to her mother the significance of her plans, and she left with her mother's blessing. If both parents had sent disaster clippings, perhaps Réanne would not have made the trip.

Ten years later Réanne told me the rest of the story. "Although my mother was supportive about our trip, she suffered more than I ever imagined she could when we were reported 'lost at sea.' Long after she died, I found a note she'd written to her youngest sister describing her absolute desperation—this from a woman who always kept her negative feelings hidden."

It is important to offset the feelings of abandonment and fear that families often have when loved ones go cruising for extended periods. The fears they harbor are not going to vanish. The farther from home you go, the more reassurance they may need.

Educate family and friends about what you are doing and include them in your planning process. Just as you prepare yourself with information and proper gear, you also need to explain to loved ones the steps you are taking. Pretending that nothing bad can happen while you are cruising is a disservice to you and your loved ones. Helping families and friends understand how you plan to manage the risks of cruising will make them feel more secure about your leaving.

Displaying a practical attitude about your plans goes a long way. If you have been gradually making longer cruises and trying different venues to expand your knowledge and experience, each of those voyages can be reviewed with your family to impress upon them what you are learning. Take pictures and keep a log.

Bring your family on board your boat. Show them your life jackets and safety harnesses. Have them try on the gear you will use. Let them inspect your life raft. Explain how your EPIRB works. Whenever possible, take your family for short rides.

Age, infirmity, and distance may prevent you from having your family visit the boat or go cruising with you, but they can participate and support your plans in other ways. There are many things you need to accomplish before going cruising, particularly if you will be gone for a few years. Enlist your family's assistance in your projects, and more hands will make your list shrink quickly.

Everything from fishing lures to pots and pans, books, flags, and cosmetics will be on your list of things to research and buy. Ask someone to research which lures are best for catching certain fish. It may be better to make flags than buy them; one family member can take on a flag-making project. Involving family in new ideas and projects strengthens their sense of participation. My family helped me find the one item I dearly needed: a hand-crank clothes wringer. I never would have found the hardware store in Ohio that sold them.

Family can help by researching your itinerary and compiling information about sightseeing, history, and languages. Knowing more about the places you will be visiting will help them share your cruise. They are doing you a service and, at the same time, preparing themselves for your absence.

Communicating after You Leave

During short-term absences, regular communication while you cruise is the best way to keep your family happy. Calling from local ports or your cellular phone is easy when you are cruising in the States. As you cruise farther afield to foreign ports, telephones will not be as accessible. (In the next chapter, I cover other modes of communicating during your cruise.)

If it is important to your family to be in regular communication with you, try to work out a reasonable schedule to reassure them. But make it a schedule that does not become a burden on you. I would caution you against setting up specific days and times to call home. One of the joys of cruising is your freedom and independence. Having to make a phone call at a specific time puts you on a schedule. And if you miss that promised call or can't get to a telephone at the designated time, your family may become worried or upset.

As an example, we were crossing the North Pacific and had occasional contact by SSB with friends from Australia. One day our conversation with them was cut short because a storm front was overtaking us. We tried to call them later but couldn't get through.

A few days later, we tried to reach them again. A booming voice responded to our hail; it was the U.S. Coast Guard. Our friends had become concerned about us and had asked the USCG to keep an eye out for us. A plane circling overhead had spotted us and then heard our hail. We told them we were fine and expected to be in Dutch Harbor very soon. When we did arrive, we were greeted several times with, "Oh, we heard you were lost at sea."

Our friends' request to the Coast Guard to keep "an eye out" had grown into a major calamity. Unfortunately, a local San Francisco boating magazine had picked up the "lost" story and had run it in their electronic version. To make matters worse, our eldest child saw the story on the Internet. So in an attempt to do a good turn, our friends created serious concern in our family.

This situation illustrates how schedules, incorrect information, and the best of intentions can backfire.

Your Feelings

Friends and family are not the only ones who will find your leaving difficult. Saying good-bye and starting a whole new life takes adjustment on your part. When Gail Amesbury went cruising, she sold her home in England and left her children in boarding schools. Initially, the magnitude of leaving home did not sink in for her "because of the excitement of the trip, the new boat, and the hectic times. To do it all, we went full tilt. Three months later was the first time I really had a downtime. I missed the children. I missed the house. I was homesick and ready to give [cruising] up."

It took Gail about four weeks to get over the sadness of leaving. "I persevered," she says, with a satisfied grin. When Gail looks back, she remembers that the depression over leaving happened the first chance she had to stop and be still. When you are busy preparing and moving on to new countries, cruising is "new and exciting. Then it hits you—the enormous step you've taken," she says. "In port, talking to other cruising women always lifts my spirits, even when we share our woes."

For Barbara Marrett, a connection to friends and family is a source of strength and joy. "In the sea of impermanence, it's nice to have the connection to long-term friends and family," she says. "One of the best things that I did was surprise my family by flying back from Fiji. The whole family had not been together at the same time for ten years. They were so excited. It was wonderful to be around the family."

Family Issues and Events

Being the caregiver for an aging parent is a heavy burden. You may be blessed with several siblings who share this responsibility, or you may be your parents' only source of help. On the other hand, your parents may not require care or may not want you to plan your life around their well-being. Whatever our situation, most of us don't leave home without serious consideration of our family's needs.

I told my sister when we left in 1995 that I would stay in touch as often as possible. Our father was 92 years old, living alone, and extremely independent. He had, however, suffered a minor stroke, which his doctor said was a precursor of things to come.

Six months into our cruise, my dad was hospitalized. His future was in doubt, and his days of independence were clearly over. I needed to help take responsibility for the decisions to be made, and I flew home. My dad did not want to accept being limited, and my sister and I needed to work together to get his cooperation. We moved him to a nursing home, put his personal affairs in order, and tried to keep him happy. I returned to the boat a week later. My dad survived for two weeks before he slipped into unconsciousness and died quietly. I was fortunate to be able to go home and assist.

My father-in-law died of cancer while we were at sea. We did not make it home to his bedside during his final days. Fortunately, we had seen him when our entire family gathered for our youngest daughter's wedding. My husband and I sailed with his fullest blessings. "We didn't raise you to stay at home," he told us, and we took joy in his enthusiasm for our plans. Remembering our last times together as a family is poignant, not regretful. Our last memories of him are associated with a beautiful event and a happy time.

If you have siblings at home, it is important to you and to them to have some understanding of how they and you will handle these situations. You might decide to postpone a departure if you really need to be present. Your plans might not be flexible if you have a narrow weather window; hurricane season or winter storms in some latitudes limit you to a few weeks of opportunity.

Cruising near home or staying within your country's borders might be an option. You can fly home or rent a car if time and distance permit. You need to think about what you can do. When my father-in-law died, we were on the east coast of Mexico. This was during a time when being the captain of any vessel meant that you could not leave the vessel to travel to another country without a legal passing of title. In our case, it would have required finding a lawyer, my husband and the lawyer appearing in court, and filing papers making me the captain while he was gone. The cost and time involved in doing this and a flight back to California were beyond us. It was hard for my sister-in-law to accept our failure to appear. It was some time before she understood the red tape of our situation.

I have been fortunate to have been able to field family situations during my years of cruising. You need to be realistic about your family's future and discuss potential issues with family members before you set off. Having a contingency plan for the issues you and your family might face is essential for your peace of mind.

Becoming a Grandparent

Special events, such as the birth of a grandchild, may warrant special plans. One woman I know circumnavigated, yet she was also able to fly home several times for the births of grandchildren. "I flew home from Fiji for a baby, and then I flew home from Darwin," she says. "We flew home from Cyprus, and then again from London. We had two homes—the apartment and the boat. I think we were very fortunate."

This cruiser was indeed fortunate, in several respects. Trips halfway around the world may not be in your budget. If you expect to go home frequently, set money aside for this expense.

Leaving your boat in a foreign country at an unfamiliar marina is not always a positive experience. If you don't know an area or feel confident about how your property will be managed, leaving your boat in someone else's care can be unnerving. Researching your options, as well as getting references from other cruisers, will make it easier to leave your boat for a trip home.

Disasters at Home

Being separated from family when disaster occurs is a frightening experience. We were at sea when northern California sustained a major earthquake in 1989. When we arrived in port on the coast of Morocco, a fisherman pointed at our transom and shook his head. Our home port of San Francisco, written under our boat name, was familiar to him. When he told us about the earthquake and its magnitude, we were stunned: our oldest daughter lived in the area.

Being halfway around the world, we could only watch television reports that filtered through and wait until the telephone office opened the next day. When the phone rang in our daughter's apartment at three o'clock in the morning, her first words to us were "I'm all right. Everything is okay." She knew a phone call in the middle of the night would be from us.

Our phone call to California got through via satellite transmission while the phone lines in California were down, so perhaps we were luckier than those closer to home. In retrospect, we would have been frightened by the news of this disaster whether we were at home or at sea. The possibility of disaster is part of life, regardless of where you are or what you are doing.

Emergency Contact

I don't have a plan for emergency contact, so I haven't had to deal with someone wanting to reach us in an emergency. It may sound like we don't care. The truth is, we made a conscious decision not to have an emergency contact plan.

My husband and I recognize that any number of terrible things could befall our family. But we would not be able to respond immediately unless we were in a major city with an international airport. For me, knowing about an emergency and not being able to physically respond is worse than learning after the fact.

Your attitude toward this situation may be entirely different, and you can create a plan for emergency contact via ham radio networks and SSB radio, as well as through satellite communication systems using faxes, telephones, and e-mail. (These modes of communication are discussed in the next chapter.)

We did make a different kind of plan—we each wrote a will. We recognized that if we died while in a foreign country, there would be a set of problems to solve. We outlined what would constitute our estate. We told the children that we did not want our bodies brought back to the United States. If we were close to a medical school, our bodies were to be donated. If we were in a more remote locale, body disposal was to be quick, inexpensive, and according to local custom. We made it clear that they were not to invest in ceremonies or cemeteries. The one thing that was required was that they throw a big party to celebrate how we lived.

We had a farewell dinner and told them all of this. They were uncomfortable at first discussing the topic. Next, they began to ask questions we could not answer: where exactly were we going, how long would we be there, etc. Finally, they acknowledged what we said and thanked us.

It is not easy for people to realize writing a will is important at any stage of life. Likewise, it is difficult to discuss with loved ones what you want them to do. The response is often "this can wait." I think that putting off this task creates enormous problems for those you leave behind. Writing wills was good for us because it permitted us to tell our children once again that we love them.

We try every chance we get to tell our family that we love them. If we lose one of them, or they lose one of us, we know that we have said the most important thing they need to hear.

They Don't Want Me to Go

We spent time with a couple preparing to leave on their first cruise. Their family and friends felt they were abandoning their responsibilities and doing something frivolous. It was unthinkable, this couple was told, that they were not working or shouldering their social obligations. After some consideration, the couple realized their family and friends were not truly worried about irresponsibility; they simply were jealous.

Outrageous as this may sound, the reality of doing something that many people only dream about provokes amazing responses. Fortunately, this couple's commitment to cruising kept them on track, but it was not easy. In their letters, they told us they felt harassed and alone rather than excited about their adventure. They finally agreed that the message to friends and relatives needed to be straightforward: Please don't make us defend our life, because we are not asking for your approval.

Some people might call this couple selfish. Yet you alone make the choice about how to live your life. Making life choices in order to please others means your life is not your own.

Controlling relationships are established over a long period of time, and they usually don't start just because you decide to go cruising. It is important to examine what kinds of relationships you have before you make important decisions about cruising.

I know a woman whose mother had been an intimate part of her daily life for more than forty years. She expected to be constantly informed about her daughter's life, and when she was left out, she became ill. The daughter shared her cruising plans with her mother during the construction of her boat. But as soon as she and her husband left the country, the daughter was summoned back by her mother.

She had a difficult time deciding whether to return to the boat or stay at home with her mother. This was a sad situation for her husband, who admitted that perhaps his wife didn't really want to return to cruise with him. Maybe his mother-in-law was just an excuse. In the end, she did not return, and the couple split up.

Families can also play a different role. Nancy Bischoff, who cruised with her husband and their sons, says that her family "worried about our safety. But they didn't say it to us. Just to each other. The whole family was very supportive." Nancy explains that no one family member wanted to worry her with their fears, so they each told her: "They're worried about you. But I'm not."

None of us would be happy thinking our loved ones didn't care about us. But I believe the attitude in Nancy's family is the important one to remember: Her family cared enough to worry, but they cared even more that she enjoy the dream of going cruising.

Guilt

The most grievous thing that happens to cruisers is guilt. In some situations, it's very subtle. But in the end, guilt has the power to push you to give up cruising and go home.

The feeling of guilt is common after reading mail from home or having a telephone conversation with a loved one. When someone you care about tells you how much they feel your absence, they put you in the position of justifying your being away. Friends and family don't mean to put this onus on you. They are expressing a sentiment they genuinely feel. But you are missing from a chain of contact that is well established, and your absence leaves a void.

Analyzing my own feelings, I realized that I was absent by choice. It was more important to me to be where I was than to be with my family. I still missed them, so my solution was to encourage them to come visit us.

Whether your boat is big or small, bringing family to visit can be a wonderful experience. "My mother had never been to Europe, and my brother sent her. It was a great kick," says Patience Wales of her mother's visit during a circumnavigation. Even if you have a tight budget, with a little planning you can afford tickets for the occasional visitor. In some families, it isn't a matter of having the time or money for a trip—it's a matter of waiting for an invitation.

Every member of my immediate family has visited us in at least one foreign port. We can accommodate extra people on our boat. Even so, we have had visitors who stay part-time on the boat and part-time on shore. Older family members like the convenience of real plumbing and beds that don't rock.

Having friends and family visit is one of the best ways to establish your love of cruising with them and alleviate their fears.

And when they communicate how they feel about your absence after they leave, they often say, "I had such a good time seeing you. When can we do it again?"

The bottom line with guilt is your own attitude about what you are doing. If you love cruising, it is easy to share the joy of your experiences and turn your absence into something positive. If you are unhappy cruising, then guilt can drive you home.

10

STAYING
IN TOUCH

COMMUNICATING WITH FRIENDS AND FAMILY once you start cruising is very important. Few if any of them will have a clear concept of how you live, what you do, and why you left in the first place. Cruising close to home makes communication simpler, but even the ubiquitous cell phone won't solve all of your problems. No matter where you go, there are still bills to pay, gifts to send, and parts to replace.

Who Forwards the Mail and Pays the Bills?

For years, we had a business manager who took care of money matters, taxes, and sorting out problems. Those services are not as critical nowadays because with e-mail, computers, electronic bill paying, and automatic deposits you can usually manage no matter how far you are from home. If you don't want to do any money management, you can ask a relative or hire a professional.

Some cruisers are more comfortable with the idea of money matters staying within the family rather than hiring a stranger to look after finances. Others prefer using a professional manager so they don't jeopardize family relationships. Whomever you select, you need to work out exactly what you expect them to do. Specify what tasks they are responsible for and what deadlines they need to meet. Should you decide to do it all yourself, it's a good idea to have a backup plan in place in the event of an emergency.

Accessing Money

When we first started long-distance cruising, we encountered a man who had an unusual approach to cash. Before leaving the United States, he converted everything he had into U.S. dollars. Moreover, he carried all the cash with him in a trunk. Although U.S. citizens who carry more than $10,000 into or out of the United States are required to complete a Treasury Department form and file it with a U.S. Customs officer at their port of entry or departure, he was willing to risk the large fine and possible imprisonment. Certainly, a trunk full of cash means you have easy access to your money; on the other hand, it seems like a huge chance to take.

When we travel in North America, we can use credit cards and ATM cards. Twenty years ago, we were dependent on travelers' checks because they were the safest way to carry money. Since you had to go to a bank and wait in line to cash a check, there were mornings when it took more than an hour for one simple transaction. Now you can walk up to an ATM and withdraw what you need. In Mexico or Canada, we can withdraw the local currency. The same precautions prevail anywhere that you use an ATM, however: be observant, don't withdraw huge sums, and try to have a friend or crew with you. Don't expect an ATM on every corner. Every year the numbers increase, but small beach resorts and fishing villages are generally the last to benefit from electronic conveniences.

We use our credit cards to make major purchases. Purchasing fuel or restocking the galley at the local supermarket is just like home. If your plans change or you have a sudden emergency, your credit cards can be a lifesaver at the airport, the boatyard, or a hospital. If your voyage is long term, be sure that your credit cards and ATM cards have different expiration dates. If everything expires at the same time, you could be stuck until the snail mail catches up with your new ones. One caution when you use credit cards: if the local exchange rate is in flux, some businesses might try to hold your charges a day or two to get a better exchange rate. The surprise comes when your credit card bill arrives and your billed amount is more than you calculated.

I have always kept track of our expenditures. In the old days, I had ledger books with multiple columns so I had the year at a glance. In foreign countries when I used local currency, I converted everything into dollars to have a basis for comparison. All these years later, I sit down at the computer and enter income and expenses. The computer converts to dollars, summarizes expense by category, and saves it all for my year-end tax report. I need to know how much I am spending and in what categories. Do you have to do this to cruise? Of course not. However, when I want to know if I withdrew more than $200 at an ATM on a certain date, all that information is in one file on the computer. Fraud can occur while you're in your own living room; it certainly can happen when you're 1,000 miles away.

Electronic Bill Paying

As long as we have access to the Internet, we use electronic bill paying. For bills that come at a regular time for a fixed amount, we schedule in advance for the bank to make direct payments. Those bills that fluctuate are the ones you need to monitor. Many of the bills you have now are likely to disappear while you cruise: car payments, landline telephone bills, health clubs, etc. If cruising is in your future, try electronic banking. Have paychecks and other income deposited automatically. Put all regular payments on a monthly cycle. You can also designate flexible payments by simply putting a cap on the payee. Electronic banking is not practical at sea because of current Internet connectivity issues.

A Deliverable Address

So much of our communication is electronic that we forget about the need for a snail mail address. Our old system was to pick up mail every couple of months from an American Express Office. All of our mail went to our business manager's address. She would forward personal mail to the next Amex office on our list. Getting mail was like Christmas. We would read it repeatedly, and then spend hours responding. We really looked forward to these occasions.

We felt sorry for people who depended upon the local harbormaster or port captain. The mail collection area was usually a shoebox of letters that were grimy from handling and some had postmarks that were several years old. It wasn't monitored, so anyone could go through the mail; once something landed in the box, it often died there—or disappeared. By comparison, Amex recorded each piece of mail that came in and kept it in a safe or locked container. If your name corresponded with a name on their registry, they would find it and give it to you. If mail was more than thirty days old, Amex returned it to the sender. The drawback was riding a train or bus to another town where an Amex office was located.

This system was excellent except that we couldn't receive packages. With the continuing fear of dangerous packages, sending and receiving them is difficult. Typically, repairs and parts sent to a "yacht in transit" are not subject to duty. Unfortunately, that isn't universally true. We made the mistake of having a package sent to a U.S. Consulate through ordinary mail. We paid nearly twice as much in duty as the part was worth. The rationale was that delivering the package to a building had nothing to do with yachts. If you have the choice, arrange with a harbormaster or port office to use their address. There's a better chance of not paying duty in that situation.

In some countries, the international delivery companies will act as your address, but you will have to go to their office to collect your package. Government postal services can be problematic. Mail can be opened without permission or lost or stolen. For both sending and receiving packages, we tried to avoid them. Early on in our cruising career, we learned to watch our package until the postage had been canceled. In some countries, it is common to sell the same postage repeatedly by peeling off postage you have just bought and selling it to someone else.

If you have contact with cruisers who are going home for a visit, they may be willing to carry your mail. Of course, they will have to be ready to wrap your item for shipping when they get to the United States. In the United States and Canada there are fewer problems with shipping, but when you are receiving mail while cruising, you need a deliverable address or a personal courier. Sometimes the local shipping agent will receive your mail for a fee. If other cruisers have successfully used the harbormaster's or port captain's address, investigate the possibility of using it for a package delivery.

We took one other precaution when we were concerned about a package going astray. The wrapping on packages our friends sent to us was unique; garish colors or strange designs made them stand out and hard to miss. Yes, they were obvious, but that made it harder to lose them.

I think there are still times, despite electronic advances, that I would still use snail mail. Our friends who collect stamps are in ecstasy when they receive foreign stamps with foreign postmarks. Our children and grandchild love the postcards from exotic places. You may ask why we don't e-mail photos or photo cards; we do, but there is nothing like the excuse of postcards for initiating yet another shopping trip!

Telephone Communication

The giant steps made in electronic communication have made the elaborate arrangements for communication that we struggled through twenty years ago virtually obsolete. At the time of our departure, facsimile transmission was new. It was the fastest way for direct communication if you could find a fax machine. Making long-distance calls required calling a local operator who would connect you with an international operator who would connect you with the in-country operator to connect you with your intended party. We participated in the first international direct-dial program between Telecom Australia (now Telstra) and AT&T while in Australia in 1987.

Direct dialing was so successful it actually constituted news in the foreign editions of U.S. newspapers. The program was popular and grew rapidly; we regularly purchased the Tuesday issue of *USA Today* to get new country codes. The hard part was remembering the sequence of the numbers that we needed to dial. The process was to dial the number of the country, in our case the United States. That number would be answered with "AT&T, what number are you calling?" Within a year or so, we completed calls without any operator assistance.

Cell phones made a difference in our communication, but it doesn't compare to the effect it has had in the rest of the world. In many countries, it used to take a year to have a telephone installed, but cell phones have opened up communication for everyone. Most of the world uses GSM (Global System for Mobile Communications) technology. We purchased GSM phones and used them all over Asia. GSM technology has only recently been introduced into the United States, and GSM phones are locked, which means that U.S. GSM phones do not work outside the United States, and GSM phones from elsewhere do not work in the United States. We use our "regular" cell phone in North America, and no doubt the technological differences with the rest of the world will be resolved at some point.

Below we'll discuss some cruising communications options that go beyond the telephone and snail mail, arranged from less expensive to more expensive. All of them are faster than snail mail. But none of them can replace a postal or express carrier when you need to send packages.

Radio Communication
VHF Radio

VHF radio is ubiquitous. You can use it to call for help, to contact a harbormaster, to call home, or to talk with other boaters. Fixed-mount versions are available as well as handheld, portable models. Fixed-mount radios have a transmitting range of about 10 to 15 miles, whereas handhelds have a range of about 3 to 5 miles.

All fixed-mount radios manufactured since 1999 are equipped with digital selective calling (DSC; an automated distress signal), but most handhelds are not. A DSC-equipped VHF costs about $350; a handheld costs about $150.

Ham Radio

At one time shortwave amateur ham radio was the standard for boat-to-boat communication and boat-to-land communication. It is still available but has a dwindling audience among younger cruisers. To operate a ham radio, you are required to have a license issued by the Federal Communications Commission (FCC) for which you must pass an exam. I struggled through Morse code and acquired a license. In the past two decades, the exam requirements have become fewer and fewer.

Many ham operators love the camaraderie that comes with worldwide conversation, and the American Radio Relay League (see the Resources appendix) sponsors events that make this a great hobby. Ham radio operators may not conduct business of any kind. We have heard ham vigilantes break in on a transmission and threaten others for violating FCC regulations.

Ham radio is the least expensive of the long-range electronic communication options. It does require some hands-on skill in tuning, but if the licensing and the hands-on skills don't present a block to you, this may be your best option. Once you buy the radio, tuner, and antenna, and get your license, there is no cost. You can connect your radio to your laptop computer and send e-mail. Since just about everyone cruises with a computer, we didn't factor in the cost of a computer. After surveying dealers and ham operators, we found a range of costs. It's possible to purchase a good "rig" for less than $1,000.

You'll also need a specialized modem, which will run about $1,200 to $1,400. However, the total of $2,400 is the lowest cost in radio options for long-range electronic communication. One suggestion from an experienced ham operator is to stay away from small transceivers as they are harder to tune. A slightly larger radio makes life easier on a moving boat.

SSB Radio

SSB radios are more common on cruising boats than ham radios. You also must obtain a license, but that only involves filling out a few FCC forms. The license also covers your VHF radio, your radar, and your EPIRB. Many cruisers find SSB radios easier to use than ham radios. An automatic tuner quickly selects the frequency you want; you don't fiddle with any knobs. SSB radios are set for the specific frequencies the FCC designates for marine communication. In contrast to ham radios, you are allowed to conduct business on an SSB, so you may order parts, make a plane reservation, or manage your business.

The SSB also uses a modem to send e-mail. SailMail, a common SSB e-mail service, has an annual service fee of $250, which helps cover the expense of maintaining and developing the land-based stations. (Winlink, a ham radio e-mail service, managed by land-based volunteers, is free.)

The SSB communication package including the modem costs between $4,000 and $5,000.

Radio networks, commonly called nets, are used by cruisers on all three types of radios. VHF nets exist in local areas to spread news. In Mexico, most of the marinas have some portion of the population that is year-round. The nets in those marinas are your best source of current information. Each morning, usually around 0800, the net begins with everyone checking in. It's like taking attendance. New arrivals are contacted so that they know to participate. Arrivals are welcomed, departures are bade farewell, services needed or available are mentioned, group potlucks are announced, weather is given, and so on. The network is very much like the old party-line telephone; everyone listens in and knows what everyone else is doing.

On long-range radios, networks serve essentially the same purpose with people who are more far-flung. The radios have a longer range, and using them at night is more successful. They begin with check-in, and each boat gives its location. Reporting the weather and exchanging the news about who is traveling in what venue updates everyone in the fleet. Questions on nonurgent health issues, good and bad services in different ports, and the latest gossip from the fleet are shared.

Satellite Communication

Satellite-based communications systems offer global coverage. Satellite communication is easier and more popular on powerboats and multihulls. This does not imply anything about the owner's income, just that it is easier to use satellite communication on a boat that doesn't heel. You should shop around, because various systems offer varying rates of transmission, and varying costs (see the table on page 147).

SkyMate

SkyMate offers e-mail, weather reports, and a vessel-monitoring system that will alert you when you are away from your boat. SkyMate uses the Orbcomm satellite system. The basic gear is a small box referred to as the communicator, an antenna similar to a VHF antenna, and a computer. There is no radio involved.

You can write an e-mail on your computer with the SkyMate software and then send it out via the communicator and antenna. The limitations are that a satellite must be in the vicinity to pick up your transmission. The software tells you when the satellites are passing over and dispatches your e-mail. Your computer does not need to be powered up when e-mail is coming in. Your communicator will flash a signal when e-mail is waiting.

The messages are text only, which you can limit in length, and you cannot use attachments. Most of our friends found it easy to communicate with us, except for the length requirement. Frequently we would receive a truncated message that carried over to more than one e-mail. The number of characters sent and received in messages determines the amount you are charged. This includes any preliminary or subsequent characters that are part of e-mail transmissions. For regular contact with business and family, the charges can add up. Another difference to consider is that it does not offer the possibility for general conversation that nets do for radio users.

The one blessing was that we did not receive spam. SkyMate has a very good filtering system for spam. In addition, you can request that certain subjects be filtered out. You do pay for the characters received, so you should carefully select who you give your e-mail address to. A new feature is blogging. You can blog and send it to the SkyMate weblog. Your friends and family can go to the website without using up your character limit.

SkyMate equipment costs about $1,200. The most expensive service program is about $70 per month and allows you to send and receive 50,000 characters. There is an additional charge of $1.40 per additional 1,000 characters received and sent. An annual budget figure would be about $2,500. You can change plans if your usage drops. SkyMate also offers a DryDock Plan that we use during the months that we are not underway. We use the computer in a cyber-café or look for a wi-fi connection while SkyMate is "dry-docked."

Iridium

Iridium provides handsets that look and feel like a telephone, although they are bulkier than cell phones. You can make voice contact and can send and receive e-mail.

Handsets cost about $1,500. You'll also need a data kit to use the phone for e-mail or an external antenna and docking station to mount the phone in your navigation station. The top-of-the-line gear is about $3,400. Regardless of where you are, the cost is $1.50 per minute plus a monthly service fee of $20 to $30. You can also buy prepaid cards in 500-minute blocks, which must be refilled annually, in which case you don't have to worry about a monthly bill. Voice mail is $10 per month; if you use a prepaid card there is no service charge or voice mail charge.

Under some conditions, e-mail transfer rates can be as high as 10 kilobits per second (kbps). (In contrast, the marine SSB or ham radio maximum is 4 kbps.) Remember this is much slower than the 56 kbps that is common for Internet usage, so your minute charges can add up rapidly.

Inmarsat-C

Inmarsat-C has no voice capability but can transmit and receive data, so you can use it for sending and receiving faxes and e-mail. You are charged per character, and the cost per character varies based on the location of the sender and receiver. The hardware has a built-in GPS, and weather information and safety alerts are free. A distress button on the face of the unit automatically transmits your vessel's location and identity. The hardware costs about $3,000. The use charges vary depending upon location and range from 25 to 33 cents per 32 characters.

Inmarsat's Mini-M offers voice, fax, and dial-up Internet access. Before you get too excited, the maximum speed is 2.4 kbps, and it is very expensive. The hardware costs about $5,700 and the use fee is about $2.50 per minute at peak and $1.50 at off peak. Once you have purchased the hardware, you pay the time charges monthly, or you can buy a prepaid phone card. If you need to conduct business underway, Inmarsat may be your choice.

Globalstar

Globalstar offers portable phones that provide voice and data coverage up to 200 miles off the coasts of North, Central, and South America, much of the Caribbean, Europe, Australia, and New Zealand. The handset is similar to the Iridium handset but costs only about $600. Airtime costs about $1 per minute plus a $20 monthly fee.

At present, cruisers who don't want the traditional radio systems find the combination of Iridium and SkyMate efficient and reasonably simple to use. We know a number of cruisers who need to maintain voice contact with ailing parents or make quick business decisions, and they use this option.

If you are investing in the long-term cruising lifestyle, selecting the method(s) of communication will be one of your most important decisions. Communication with other cruisers via a net will require radio. Voice communication with your family or business will probably require a satellite solution. Cost, dependability, and simplicity of operation are important issues. How much contact you want is your choice.

COMMUNICATION COST COMPARISON

	System				
	Iridium	**Iridium Prepaid**	**Inmarsat-C**	**SkyMate**	**Marine SSB/Ham**
Services	Voice Data[7]	Voice Data[7]	Data Weather Safety	Data[3] Weather Safety	Voice Data[7] Weather Safety
Cost of Use	$1.50 per minute	$1.50 per minute[2]	$0.25–$0.33 per 256 bits[6]	$0.003 per character	No charge
Monthly Fees	$30	$0	$0	$15.99[4]	$16.67[5]
Equipment Cost	$1,495–$3,395	$1,495–$3,395	$3,469	$1,199	$3,400–$4,500
Data Speed	2.4 kbps–10 kbps[1]	2.4 kbps–10 kbps[1]	Not applicable	Not applicable	2.4 kbps–4 kbps
Voice Mail	$10 per month	Included; no charge	Not applicable	Not applicable	Not applicable

[1] 10 kbps data rate achieved through software compression; your results may vary.
[2] Prepaid cards must be purchased in 500-minute blocks. Cards must be refilled annually.
[3] Limited one-way voice and fax services are available.
[4] Silver Plan.
[5] Fee for SailMail service is $250 paid annually; the Winlink system for ham radio licensees is free.
[6] Cost varies with location e-mailed/e-mail termination point.
[7] Supports e-mail attachments such as weather GRIB (gridded binary) files. [GRIBs are detailed weather files that can be downloaded from several Internet sources with the appropriate hardware and software.]

Source: H.F. Radio On Board, November 2006

11

CAREER PLANNING
AND
EMPLOYMENT

W HEN MY HUSBAND, Jim, and I had our first serious discussion about long-term cruising, it came to a grinding halt when I posed the question, "But what about my career?"

His offhand answer, "You can always start over," offended me at first. But after my anger subsided, I realized that I could start over. I had many contacts in the large shopping center corporation I worked for, and I could maintain work contacts during our planned five-year absence.

I planted the seeds for my return to the work force before leaving. I informed cohorts that I would be looking for work when I came back, and I completed a professional certification in marketing and management before departure to ease my reentry into the professional world.

If you weigh what I gave up as a career woman against what I gained as a cruiser, you might not be convinced that I made the right choice. I gave up a substantial salary and the status and satisfaction I gained from hard work and proven results. But for me, going cruising was the right decision. I gained the freedom to run my own life, and I proved to myself that I could live without the safety net of a corporate career.

Facing the prospect of giving up a career is difficult. Women who have spent long hours improving their salary status, accomplishing important results, and gaining respect from their peers need to consider the choices carefully.

Some cruisers give up their occupations when they leave. Some view cruising as a sabbatical from work. Some find ways to blend their careers with the cruising life. And for some, the experience of cruising helps them make a career switch to an on-the-water vocation.

The Option of Timing

A career may be important in your life plan, just as having a family may be important. Remember, you have control over when you cruise and when you pursue your career. One option is to cruise first and work later. "We're 'retired' now. We'll go to work when we're 65," says Lin Pardey, who has turned her cruising into a career.

Lael Morgan cruised as a young woman. People kept asking her, "Why are you doing this now? Wait, in ten years it will be easier." As Lael points out, she and her husband may not have had much money then, but they weren't encumbered with a house and family either. Forty years later, her attitude toward waiting has not changed. "So many people wait until they're too damn old," she says. "I saw so many people who retired with more boat than they could handle."

For Lael the decision was easy. "It was his dream, and I went along because I didn't have a dream of my own. I never conceived of being away or taking that kind of time off. I haven't kept a straight job since." Now Lael is land based and works full-time. Since cruising, she has written numerous books and won awards in journalism and photography. Twenty years ago, she completed an advanced degree in communications, and currently is a visiting professor in the Department of Communications at the University of Texas.

Expectations

If you are planning to blend a career with cruising, think first about what purpose work will have in your cruising life.

Do you plan to work because you will need money along the way? How much money will you need to make? Do you want to work for your own personal enrichment or to stay current in your field? Is working in a cruising destination a way for you to stay in one place for a while and get to know the community? Are you looking for short-term work for extra cash or positions that will help you build your career?

If you want to mix working and cruising, advance planning will help you lay the groundwork. Think about what you want to do and how you will do it. Talk to other cruisers to find out how they mixed working and cruising.

Also consider the red tape. You should know what official statutes pertain to you as a foreign national seeking work.

Combining Work and Play

Some cruisers alternate working at their chosen career with cruising as a way of "having their cake and eating it too." They typically cruise to a destination and stay there to take on a work assignment. The key is knowing where you can get work and arranging the employment in advance.

In the South Pacific, a number of Americans find that American Samoa offers possibilities because there are no employment restrictions for American citizens. American Samoa's location allows you to cruise for a couple years, stay in the islands to work, and then continue sailing at the completion of a work contract. The U.S. government employs people there in several areas, including health care, construction, and teaching. Cruisers negotiate these contracts in advance.

We met a couple in Pago Pago (American Samoa) who had sailed there so the husband could supervise a construction project for two years. The wife quickly found a job in retail. Her background made it possible for her to move up into management almost immediately. After a two-year stint, they decided to move on and see new places.

Other good cruising destinations for U.S. citizens who want to work and play are Hawaii, Puerto Rico, the U.S. Virgin Islands, Guam, Wake Island, and Midway Island.

Working in foreign territories is more complicated, but you may be able to achieve results with some planning and forethought.

Before setting out, check library reference sections for employment information. Look online for sites that describe job opportunities in different areas of the world. Information is also indexed by profession, and you may find areas where your skills are needed.

Teaching English is a job that allows you to work in a variety of countries. Requirements vary from being a credentialed teacher to being a native English speaker willing to fit into a school system. Such opportunities can be satisfying and typically pay well.

I have great admiration for a nurse I met in the South Pacific who was using her expertise to her advantage as a cruiser. Her training, including an advanced degree in public health, was in great demand. When we met, she had a contract that would begin in eighteen months' time in Saudi Arabia, and she and her partner were working their way to the Red Sea. Working in a strictly controlled Muslim society that limits personal freedom is unappealing to me, but her outlook was pragmatic: "I can be a nurse anywhere, particularly if they pay me $90,000 a year."

If a career is important to you, there are ways to combine your interests with cruising. Lura Francis had an established career as a painter, but it was very important to her to cruise with her husband. She sketched everything she saw while cruising and filled books with images that she planned to use one day in her painting. When she and her husband returned to California, they moved ashore. Lura used the sketches to re-create her cruising experiences in her paintings, and her one-woman shows were very successful. As a widow, she continues to paint. She has expanded her career to include teaching painting, directing local art festivals, and running her own painting website.

In Phuket, Thailand, we met an American woman who entertained every night in a large hotel. She played the piano and occasionally sang. Having music in common, we spent time together in the afternoons talking about her work. She was one of several Americans we have met who entertain in restaurants and hotels around the world. In addition to a salary, many of these entertainers receive meals and guest privileges from the establishment, as well as tips from patrons. The biggest problem she had was getting regular practice time when she wasn't employed, so she carried a battery-powered keyboard to keep up her skills. Musicians can find work with varying time commitments.

Technological advancements in electronic communications are paving the way for other work opportunities. Many land-based people work at home and never go into an office. Online connection for computers is expensive, but the capability exists. Satellite communication systems are being developed in more compact units with smaller price tags.

If you have an established career that does not require you to be in a specific location, consider taking the career with you. It would be hard to run a day-to-day business requiring daily contact with clients while you are cruising, but you could consider being in port during certain time periods to handle large projects. Or you might arrange work that you could accomplish on your own time while you are cruising and then deliver to clients as you complete it.

When Is Recess?

There is a downside to cruising and taking a career with you: When your mate is snorkeling, sightseeing, and visiting with other cruisers, you may have to keep working.

I take my career as a writer with me as we cruise. More and more, I am asked about writing as a career and a source of income. It is fair to assume there is potential in writing about cruising. The sailing magazines are full of cruising articles, and the shelves at the local marine bookstore are filled with cruising books. Unfortunately, the market for articles and books is small. What if you wanted to write about topics other than cruising? Take travel, for example. There are many magazines and guidebooks. There are also thousands of travel writers who are already established in the profession.

If you are an established writer before you set out cruising, it is easier to get published. As a contributing editor for a cruising magazine, Barbara Marrett uses her cruising experiences in her writing. "The key is to find what excites you about the trip, to have something that you can focus your energy on if just cruising isn't enough for you. I really like writing articles and taking pictures."

Becoming established as a writer is extremely hard unless you have regular access to a phone, fax, and e-mail—and don't mind rejection. You need to find your niche, establish regular contacts with editors, and stay in constant touch. Even established writers must continually communicate with editors to get assignments and keep the flow of work going. I love to write, but I know I have to skip recess—the snorkeling, sightseeing, napping, or partying—when there's a deadline to meet. And as a writer, I have learned that after every deadline, there is always another one.

Migael Scherer is a writer, and she points out what the difficulties are for her. "As a writer, I need time by myself. I can take notes, keep a journal, and write letters, but revising, perfecting, and shaping take solitude and time. I can't write while I'm running a boat and cruising. The boat is a whole entity that needs care. I respond to the boat, the wind and currents, and what the engine is saying to me. I need to be aware of the boat."

Sabbatical Cruising

Another possibility that allows you to cruise and maintain a career is making short excursions on a sabbatical basis. Teaching is a profession that offers sabbatical leaves after a specific period of employment. Others find ways to make a sabbatical cruise part of their business life.

A young Swiss doctor who sailed with us filled hospital contracts that lasted six months to a year and cruised between assignments. She worked in the hospital when others took extended leave. She found the work interesting, and it was helping her decide what area of medicine she would eventually specialize in. This kind of sabbatical leave is typical in Europe and Australia and is becoming more popular in the United States.

An old sailing buddy of Jim's is an optometrist in San Diego. He loved cruising. His very successful practice was important, but he and his wife wanted to cruise before age and health became an issue. They started by cruising in the Caribbean, but soon realized that going to and from San Diego could be difficult. Therefore, they bought a boat in San Diego that became their second home. They cruised the islands in the summer and spent the winter on the powerboat in California. When he finally decided to retire, they moved their powerboat to Canada. The sailboat is in the Caribbean and the powerboat is in Sidney, British Columbia. Their choice—Sidney in the summer and the Caribbean in the winter—is perfect, and the cruising variety is amazing.

Adapting a career to cruising, or tailoring cruising to fit your career, is possible. It requires thought and creativity on your part, as well as the cooperation of your cruising partner. Not all professions can be easily adapted to life on a boat. But if you want to cruise, you may find some interesting solutions.

Making a New Career

When we came back from our first long cruise, I discovered that I truly could start over again and return to my prior career in the shopping center business. The problem was, I didn't want to. After nearly seven years of being barefoot and carefree, the appeal of a job I once loved had waned dramatically. The idea of dressing up every day, driving on the freeway, and spending the entire day in an air-conditioned office with no view and no fresh air couldn't compete with the life I had been living.

With a glimmer of encouragement from my husband, I began a new career. I combined skills from my earlier career with new information and experiences. I started writing, training, and lecturing about different aspects of sailing.

My husband suggested I try my new career for a year to see what direction it took. Working on my own terms and setting my own goals became a whole new way of life. At the end of the first year, I had gained confidence and earned some money—despite lots of rejection letters. My husband said, "Keep going!" The financial rewards were not as great as they were in my former career. But

I no longer needed to drive a car or maintain a big wardrobe. The trade-off was worth it to me.

On-the-Water Professionals

Some women are fortunate enough to have an on-the-water occupation. Patricia Miller Rains earned her 100-ton captain's license, and she and her husband, John, work together delivering yachts and writing the definitive boating guide to Mexico.

Irene Hampshire and her partner, Jon Shampain, live aboard their own boat, but they are responsible for a racing yacht kept in the same marina. They sail as crew when the boat is racing to a far-off destination such as Mexico or Hawaii. After the race, the two of them—often along with their sons—spend months bringing the boat home through interesting cruising venues.

Dawn Riley is a full-time professional sailor and is in demand worldwide as a racing skipper. When she started out, she described working as a professional sailor as being "between jobs." The races and the boat deliveries became her job, and she eventually was invited to crew in major events as a paid professional. Dawn is preparing for her fourth America's Cup campaign as the general manager of the French team. Her career is sailing, and it has led into many types of jobs—motivational speaker, author, clothing designer—and she's still in her thirties. Not everyone aspires to this level of skill. But being an internationally known racer offers a career on the water and travel around the world that is extremely satisfying.

I met three women working with their husbands as full-time, professional charter crew. After years of cruising, they needed to earn money so they could continue sailing—and staying on the water was a priority. All three couples are full-time crew aboard privately owned yachts. One couple was on a large sailboat on the West Coast going to Florida, and the others are on powerboats that cruise the Caribbean, Mexico, and the Intracoastal Waterway. My first impression of their life was that it was glamorous. But that is not how they describe their work.

When the owner is on board, work begins at 5 A.M. There is fresh food to prepare, systems to check, and watermakers to turn on.

Their workday ends at midnight, after the owner retires. The crew then does the cleaning and the laundry. In some cases, they need to get underway because they must be in another location by sunrise. During their workday, they are deckhands, engineers, tender drivers, babysitters, cooks, dishwashers, stewards, navigators, bartenders, and medics. This pace usually is maintained for a period of weeks, until the owner goes home. The crew can then be on their own for months until the owner's next visit. But in the intervening time, they must handle maintenance and repairs and perhaps move the boat to a new destination.

Working those long hours is hard to imagine. However, the rewards for what appears to be slave labor are very good, if you're good. A "team" crew—husband and wife or boyfriend and girlfriend—can expect to earn about $60,000 to start. Our friends Marja and Stephen Vance have been a "team" since 1991, and now draw a six-figure income. As a qualified team, he's captain and she's chef. They can do other jobs or work with additional crew, but with fifteen years of experience as a combination, they receive higher pay.

Looking at these numbers may not impress you. However, consider the fact that they have no living expenses, and they have a month off each year; they do very well. A novice crew serving as steward or deckhand can expect about $1,200 per month. The only downside they mentioned was moving from the luxury of a megayacht to a (inevitably smaller) boat of their own. This kind of career is not for everyone. If you can persevere, the rewards are great.

Many cruisers carry diving equipment. They can enjoy their hobby as they go, and they may find the opportunity to do salvage work, boat-bottom maintenance, underwater photography, and diving instruction (the latter requires certification, but instruction is in demand in popular cruising areas).

Peddling Your Skills

Learning basic skills—such as haircutting, massage, or sewing for sail repair—can help you create an interesting, portable career.

Your skills may be in demand in places where cruisers congregate because such services are not always available. Your skills give you the chance to meet lots of people and establish a flexible business that goes with you. The equipment and space requirements are minimal, making this an attractive option for some women.

Many cruisers carry sewing machines to do sail repairs, canvas work, and make clothes. If you are not experienced with a sewing machine, doing it yourself can be frustrating. For those with experience, the sewing machine offers a variety of opportunities for work. Expecting to turn your boat into a floating sail loft may not be practical, but the ability to repair sails in your forepeak or in the cockpit is very valuable. You will need to carry repair materials with you and keep your machine in good working order, which is not always easy to do. Working with canvas requires a similar effort.

If you are a good seamstress or tailor, you can find opportunities to be creative, even if you are only making pieces for yourself or your own boat. The batiks of Asia, the hand-painted fabrics of the South Pacific, and the lovely textiles of Central America all make exquisite garments and accessories. Creating a unique product requires talent, but the items can create their own demand.

A friend with past cruising experience has remarried and is planning to go cruising with her new husband. She has spent the last three years learning how to create elegant jewelry with simple wire and exotic beads. The designs she turns out become her inventory, and she can create jewelry to specific requirements, such as color and length. The materials and tools take very little space on the boat.

Beautiful clothing, artwork, and handicrafts produced by talented people who want to express their creativity are found in anchorages around the world. We met a woman in the South Pacific who had been collecting shells for a number of years. But her boat was small, and her collection was growing rapidly. Her solution was to keep the most perfect example of each type of shell and attach a small, gold jump ring. She sold or gave away that perfect shell whenever an unadorned gold chain came into view. With each piece, she provided encyclopedic knowledge about the shell and its habitat.

Constraints and Regulations

There can be problems connected with careers and cruising. Just as the government in the United States has rules about noncitizens working, other countries have similar regulations.

Working in a U.S. territory or a possession of the United States typically is unrestricted. However, you can run into local biases. If you have skills that are in demand, a job is not too hard to find in these places. Indeed, some places are anxious to have skilled workers, even for short periods of time.

In foreign ports, working can be more problematic. Working without permission, and being paid "under the table," is not uncommon in Europe, Australia, and Asia. Jobs waiting tables, tending bar, and doing repair work are readily available. These jobs may be short-term posts, but they are perfect for cruisers willing to take the risk and looking for quick money, not careers.

There often is work in favorite wintering spots, but those jobs, too, can be risky. Once, we were hauled out in Cyprus and working on our boat. Our neighbor in the boatyard was doing the same, but he was also doing small repairs for other cruisers. We were regularly visited by the local immigration and customs officials, who wanted to make sure we were not doing work for other people. Our neighbor was eventually caught and was expelled from the country.

If you want to find a job in a certain port, ask other cruisers what their experiences have been with local officials and local workers. Ascertain whether you are breaking laws or threatening local employment before taking a job. Most cruisers are given a tourist visa upon entering a foreign country. If you intend to work, make your intentions known. Failing to have the proper visa when you take a job can carry the same consequences as it does in the United States: You can be sent home.

Some cruisers don't want to work. As Nancy Payson says of her decision to go cruising, "I was presented the opportunity of quitting my job and going sailing. That lasted for two years, until we ran out of money!"

12

HOME IS
WHERE THE
HEART IS

GOING CRUISING DOESN'T MEAN giving up a home. It means changing where your home is.

Each of us needs a home of some kind. The definition of "home" differs from person to person, but the old adage rings true: Home is where the heart is. As a cruiser, even if you keep a house on land, your boat is your home.

Your Boat Is Your Home

You and your sailing partner need to agree on the concept of your boat as home, and you need to give it the same consideration as you would give a shoreside home. A boat is not just your means of transportation from port to port. You sleep, eat, and entertain on your boat—just as you do in a home on land.

I am a firm believer in making my boat as homelike as I can. Take time selecting your boat. Take into consideration all the things you will expect from this new home.

Regardless of how big your boat is, it will never seem as if there is enough space. That is the nature of boats. You will be forced to make choices about what to have on board. The things that are most important to you may be books, a favorite chair, or a special set of dishes. If they are important, take them along.

There are, of course, limits to that line of thinking. It was clear my baby grand piano would not be included in my move to the boat, but an electric keyboard kept inside a special case that fits into a safe niche on our sailboat was a first-class substitute; it will have a similar safe location on our trawler when the rebuild is finished.

Some women may liken life on a boat to life on a wagon train. It doesn't have to be that way. If you look at the boats of long-term cruisers, you may be surprised at the unique, personal atmosphere each cruiser has created. This is not accidental; it is a deliberate act done with pride and care.

The basic design of a good boat should not be sacrificed for space as in some condominiums we've seen. The boat takes care of you and should be constructed so that it will take more punishment than you can imagine. Your boat space is fixed, and the challenge for you is to make it yours.

Boat Units

You need to set aside enough money to create the kind of home that will make you happy. When I talk with would-be cruisers, I use the term "boat unit," which I define as $1,000. It represents the investment to start the installation of each new system in your boat (please note I said "start").

The expenditure of those units is usually focused on electronics, radio gear, dinghies, and outboard engines. But I encourage women to think in terms of designating boat units for the things that are important in making a home.

On our sailboat, *Nalu IV*, we cruised with crew or guests a great deal. The galley had to be efficient and easy to use. Refrigeration was important, because we ate fresh meat and poultry regularly. The propane stove had three burners and an oven. There were salt- and freshwater foot pumps at the sink, and we had pressurized water with an electric water heater we could use when we were connected to shore power. We had stainless flatware and Corelle dishes for eight. We used placemats and cloth napkins, and most of our serving dishes were souvenirs from cruising. When we discussed the relative merits of purchasing electronics or galley equipment, my argument to my husband was straightforward: "Until you can show me a GPS or radar that will cook three meals a day, I want the best stove money can buy."

It should not be a question of a stove or a GPS. Plan your budget so you can afford both. Your partner doesn't want to do without creature comforts any more than you do. But the wonderful world of boat gear can overshadow the simple amenities on board that we can easily take for granted.

When we moved aboard our trawler, the cubic interior space seemed huge to me. Unfortunately, the actual space for storage and the space for work areas wasn't as usable as it had been on the sailboat. A huge, open saloon was an unsafe place to be. Rough water quickly put the area into chaos. Nothing—the sofa, dining table, side tables, or chairs—was fastened down. Only the electric power cord held the refrigerator in place. The lockers lacked positive fittings so doors flew open on their own. The glass-topped coffee table was a tragedy waiting to happen. Although the trawler was capable of offshore cruising when she was built, previous owners had removed those items that made her safe at sea and added dangerous furniture and appliances.

To make the boat safe again, we returned the saloon and galley to their original design. The galley was an L-shape, and Jim rebuilt it in the original U-shape. The new galley is much safer, and I don't need to worry about being thrown across the cabin. Jim secured the refrigerator—a household type—to the bulwarks at the top and bottom. We latched the dining table to the starboard side with bolts and hooks. The sofa was replaced with a smaller unit that fits into a corner, and wells hold the feet of the sofa in place. Closed cabinets stay closed. The glass-topped coffee table that I put next to the Dumpster one morning disappeared that afternoon.

Great Things Come in Small Packages

The practical considerations of planning your boat interior may not fit your idea of a perfect home.

Boats should not have movable furniture. The interior layout of a boat is structural, which limits your ability to change it. Just as a house has bearing walls that carry the structural loads of the roof and floors, a boat has structural bulkheads that give the boat its shape and strength.

Complete privacy on a boat is nearly impossible. You can have a boat with a separate cabin, but footsteps on deck and noises from the head and other staterooms are part of life. Areas of a boat interior can be separated with doors, but doors on hinges take up more space than sliding doors, canvas doors, or no doors at all. Complete privacy on a boat becomes a state of mind.

Moving Aboard

I think it is essential to live aboard before you set off cruising. It isn't always possible to move out of a house or an apartment six months, or even six weeks, before you depart. But if you do, it will make your adjustment to cruising and living on a boat much easier.

When you commute, you are still using your boat with a temporary frame of mind. Commuting to your boat on weekends allows you to bring extra things and take them home again. You need to live on board full-time before you know what you can live with, in terms of the space on board, and what you will change.

Remember what it's like to move into a new house or apartment. If you unpack all your belongings immediately, put up the paper-towel rack, and put all your kitchen appliances in place, you often find yourself rearranging everything a week later. Getting the feel of a new space is crucial before making decisions about how you can best use it. And that takes time. If you know you need to change space, plan, plan, and replan.

We moved on board several years before we went long-term cruising. In the first two months I filled, emptied, and refilled the drawers and lockers at least three times. My husband could never be sure where his sweatshirts and socks would be. Moving onto a new boat after twenty-two years meant starting all over again.

Selecting the Systems

Most cruisers find that less is better. Louise Burke, who has many years of experience at sea, believes that "the longer you spend at sea, the less you find you need or even want. Life becomes wonderfully simple."

The KISS Principle

There is a reason why some people follow the KISS principle—"keep it simple, stupid"—and keep their boats simple. The farther you venture from home, the more dependent you become on your own skills to repair and maintain everything on board. In our home port, there are mechanics, electricians, refrigeration repair services, and spare parts. In foreign ports, you may face long waits and huge expenses to repair even ordinary things.

Diagnosing the problems with onboard systems is essential. You can do it yourself or—if the system is complex—you may have to fly in a mechanic. The challenge of understanding mechanical, electrical, and plumbing systems is not for everyone. Weigh the importance of having refrigeration, a watermaker, or hot pressurized water against the time and skill it will require to keep those systems running.

What Are the Choices?

Some cruisers don't have engines on their boats; they generate electricity from the wind or the sun. Some don't have electric lights; they use kerosene lamps. Some don't have refrigeration; they use block ice when it's available. Some don't have holding tanks; they use a bucket.

The cruisers who live on those boats seem just as happy as the cruisers who have electric appliances, freezers, refrigeration, watermakers, and even washing machines. You and your partner choose how you want to live.

After many miles and many years, we added two luxuries to our sailboat: an engine-driven watermaker and an autopilot. These were not essential, but they were bargains we found hard to refuse. After we installed and played with the new toys, we got to know the peculiarities of the systems.

The watermaker could be run only in relatively clean water and had to be used regularly. If we used it in dirty water, the filters clogged. If we didn't use it, it had to be cleaned and "pickled" to prevent damage to the membrane.

The autopilot could be fine-tuned so it responded to changing conditions. But the more finely it was adjusted, the more electricity it used. Occasionally, the autopilot's tiny brain malfunctioned for no apparent reason, and it chose to operate sporadically—or not at all.

Until we completely understood these systems, we spent hours learning to operate and repair them properly. It was reassuring to know we could go back to our old, simpler ways without feeling a great loss. Many of the systems on our trawler are familiar from our sailboat years. We also have a generator and air-conditioning, and because of our twin diesels, we have lots of redundancy.

I have made electrical and mechanical systems sound nearly impossible. But there are lots of boats with multiple useful gadgets and conveniences that are kept running. If you have electric power, then lights, a stereo, and video or DVD players become part of your life. With a watermaker, longer showers, pressurized water, and a washing machine are possible. There are appliances that run on your battery's direct current (12-volt DC), such as blenders and vacuum cleaners. If you install an inverter that changes DC battery power to AC power (which is what you have in your house), you will be able to use drills, sewing machines, coffee grinders, and food processors.

You and your partner need to decide what conveniences to install and how many boat units you are willing to spend.

Comfort Comes in All Shapes

On the Whitbread Round the World Race, "a dry sleeping bag was luxury," says Whitbread skipper Dawn Riley. For racing sailors, a dry place to sleep and dry clothes are often the most important things. Most cruisers don't put themselves in those situations. They are living on board full-time—not just camping out. In fact, most cruisers don't sleep in sleeping bags. "A boat becomes your home when you make sure it's clean and pleasant," says Barbara Marrett. "Replace worn cushions. Put down carpeting. Put up a few pictures.

Sleep in sheets instead of a sleeping bag. Have real dishes instead of plastic or paper. And have it be your space."

What Barbara advises is possible on small and large boats. When she sailed on a 31-foot boat with John Neal, "there was a rug. The boat was very clean, and it felt like a home. It didn't smell bad. It was cozy and had beautiful wood."

Aesthetics are important, particularly to women who are cruising on small boats. Lin Pardey's *Taleisin* is less than 30 feet long. Still, she believes in having luxuries in her home. "I have a few special things from other countries: fine Victorian china, wine glasses, and velvet upholstery." Many women would consider those luxuries, whether aboard a boat or on land.

Some creature comforts are very practical, such as Nancy Jewhurst's desire for a comfortable chair. "I missed having a comfortable place to read, because on our boat we didn't have one." On a subsequent visit aboard their 32-foot boat, I saw she had purchased a long plastic lounge chair to use on deck. It can be folded up and put away when it's not in use.

Many cruising women find doing laundry a problem. Paula Dinius invented a solution for taking care of laundry when they were not in a port with washing machines. "I got an ice chest and strapped it on the bow of the boat. I'd leave it for a few days. It would agitate the clothes [inside] and then I would change it and put in fresh water." Her only problem was washing heavy items such as towels and sheets.

"I found a little washing machine in Gibraltar and installed it in the shower," says Gail Amesbury. "It only worked in port, when we had water and electricity." Before she had the machine, "laundry could be fun. We'd go to a laundromat and meet people. . . . For the easy lifestyle, it is a small price [to pay]."

For Nancy Jewhurst, when you are cruising, "You have the time [to do laundry], so the things you don't have are not a major issue."

Lael Morgan cruised during the 1960s when creature comforts were few on boats. "I didn't miss anything, but I could have used a new library halfway across [on a passage]. Our boat was slow."

Nancy Payson enjoyed the improvements in her home as she and her husband changed from a wooden boat to a fiberglass one that required less maintenance and provided more amenities. "Initially, we did not have refrigeration or ice. And we had an alcohol stove, which by today's standards is primitive. As we gradually got things, I really appreciated them. Now we have refrigeration and a propane stove. You never have enough water. But I've lived with that so much you just appreciate being ashore when you can get it."

Giving up comforts doesn't seem to be a problem for many women. Patricia Miller Rains said, "I just substituted 'boat friendly' material comforts for the ones I was familiar with on shore. I substituted functional galley gear instead of the mountains of marginally functional junk tossed into cupboards. I substituted sleeping pockets for sheets and blankets. Giving up the car and learning to get by with bicycles and public transportation was the hardest."

There is one other item that sometimes is missed. As Irene Hampshire, who lived on a 33-foot boat with her partner and two sons, said, "We could have used a bigger boat, and a door to slam once in a while."

I Don't Need It

I expected the women I interviewed to want more creature comforts. Women who are planning to go cruising often identify things they believe they must have, but many full-time cruisers don't mention these items. These are some of the things that cruising women did not miss:

☐ *A double bunk that you can walk around.* A big double berth that you can walk around and make up easily at the dock is a monster in rough weather, because you can't wedge into a corner for a nap or a good read.

☐ *A galley with a microwave oven and a bread machine.* A galley with a microwave, bread machine, and pressurized hot water is still a challenge when it's tilted and everything is slipping and sliding.

☐ *Air-conditioning and heating.* Accommodating the unit
and its ducting can present a space problem. Cruisers
typically want to preserve space for other uses. Most seem
to feel they can acclimatize to local temperatures. In
severe climates, such as Alaska, a diesel stove can be used
for cooking, heating, and making hot water. Small, 12-volt
circulating fans move the warmth through the boat.

☐ *A bathtub.* In warm climates, cruisers jump over the side,
take a bath, and rinse off with fresh water from a sun
shower. On cool days, a warm shower from solar-heated
water takes the nip out of the air temperature. My favorite bathtub was a tiny freshwater stream in Malaysia.
My husband and I built a dam, inflated empty boxed-
wine bladders for pillows, and soaked in our private
paradise until we looked like matching prunes.

Your Home Is Your Nest

You are the only one who can decide what will make your home acceptable for you. For some women, the galley is critical, since cooking is their passion. Other women want unique decor and colors
that are pleasing to the eye and the spirit. Some women need plants
and pets to satisfy their desire to nurture living things. Perhaps you
need many different things to create a satisfying home.

Before we put anything on our boat we ask ourselves if it has
two uses. This test does not apply to the life raft or the EPIRB, but
it does apply to souvenirs and creature comforts.

My husband thought a hand-crank clothes wringer did not
make sense. He argued it was heavy and hard to store, and I pointed
out that it would make laundry easier, particularly with my advanc-
ing arthritis. He raised the two-use test, and I had to think quickly. I
told him we could also use it for making pasta and rolling out pizza
dough. (Fortunately, he never asked for a demonstration!)

For Migael Scherer, "When you live in a small space, everything
can be beautiful. Everyday things should be beautiful and everything

should be nice. Frivolous things are good for the soul." She collects fabrics as souvenirs and makes cushions.

Cruisers' homes carry stuffed animals, sterling silver, native handicrafts, earring collections, and herb gardens. Those items can be useful, frivolous, or aesthetically pleasing. The spaces they occupy are big, small, old, new, wood, fiberglass, and steel. Different as these spaces are, they are home to each owner.

One of the women I interviewed grieved about the sale of her boat. She felt she had lost her home when they sold their boat and got a bigger boat for a different type of cruising. "I only had a few drawers in the aft cabin [of the new boat]. . . . It was a bigger boat, but I had less of me aboard. You don't sell something you love. It's like selling your soul."

Your boat is your refuge and your nest, and it can give you peace and security. Cruising is best when you do it in your own home.

13

MEMORIES
AND
MEMENTOS

Y OUR BOAT IS YOUR HOME, but it doesn't have an attic, a garage, extra closets, or a tow-along storage locker. You are faced with hard decisions about what material possessions to keep and what things to discard when you move on board. Sorting and separating is never an easy task. But when you move on board, space reduction is drastic, and managing your possessions becomes a tougher job.

Inventory Reduction

Our solution, although not planned, was a gradual reduction of items. Our first step was our move aboard the boat. This eliminated nearly all our furniture and carpets, major appliances, extra linens, and decorative items. With three children about to leave the nest, we decided there were some items they would want. We rented a storage locker and saved those items for them.

We changed to a larger storage locker twice before we even departed for our first long cruise. We found that household items were not the only things we had to store. We had every imaginable tool for building houses and boats, plus plumbing, wiring, and painting materials. Our boat had been used for offshore racing, and it came with an inventory of twenty sails that had to be stored. Over a period of three years, we managed to accumulate more things rather than reduce our possessions.

As D-day (departure day for our first long cruise) approached, we went through another inventory reduction. We turned over to the children the things we had saved for them. We gave extra tools to friends who could use them. We recut two racing sails for cruising, stored five spinnakers in a friend's attic, and sold or gave away the rest of the sails. We saved some materials that could be used as spares for the boat, and gave clothes to charity along with extra blankets, towels, and kitchen goods.

But we weren't finished.

We still had to deal with years of trophies, pictures, photo albums, yearbooks, and the like. A collection of souvenir clothing from a variety of regattas filled two large plastic bags. Sterling silver and pieces of jewelry loomed as a major problem. This was the hardest part. Some of the items we had to dispose of had monetary value, and some were valuable because they were linked to significant memories. Our solution was to keep most of these items, store them in boxes, and leave them with friends.

Seven years later, when we returned from our first cruise, we retrieved most of our boxes and stored them in an office. When it came time to go cruising again, we gave away or dumped the items—we had accumulated so many memories in the intervening years that new memories displaced those attached to our old things.

We gave our oldest child the silver. The trophies went to former crewmembers and yacht clubs. We gave away yearbooks and unused clothing. We sold three spinnakers. The pictures, both slides and prints, had increased twenty-fold; they were given to the children to sort, keep, or toss. We asked our oldest daughter to put together one album of family photos, including important events and places we had visited. We now carry that album on the boat.

We learned an interesting lesson. Memories and mementos keep accumulating with time. Unless we wanted to establish a collection akin to a presidential library, there was no place where all our possessions could be housed. And, it occurred to us, who besides ourselves would want the accumulation of our life?

When it became apparent that we would live and cruise differently on the trawler, I approached mementos with a new attitude—why not make use of them? The linen tea towels from Ireland, England, and Australia that were turning yellow in a drawer are now in frequent use—there's always something to wipe! The sterling silver we had given to our eldest child was stuck in a box in a storage unit; we retrieved it, and now it sees three meals a day on the boat. I'd acquired a pile of *molas*—colorful textiles from the Kuna Indians of the San Blas Islands—in Panama; I turned small ones into potholders and, since we had a new couch, larger ones became decorative pillows. Talavera pottery from Mexico—which had been too heavy for our performance sailboat—now holds soap in the guest head, keeps potted plants from leaving rings, and appears at dinnertime. Baskets from Mindoro, Tonga, and Morocco work the gamut from holding sewing materials, fruit, and extra hand towels to bread and cookies. I still have a stash of unusual containers, but it is dwindling because I give them as gifts.

You will acquire practical things as you cruise, and they rapidly become part of everyday life. When they break, rust, or get lost, you will find a new item in a new town, country, or hemisphere. Experiencing these new things is a part of cruising, and there will be new stories to remember.

I Might Need That

We all are inclined to think we need something and later discover that we were wrong. Your closet may be filled with clothes, but you wear only two or three items because they're your favorites. Still, if someone suggested you didn't need the rest of your clothes, chances are you might answer, "But I might need them."

When Gail Amesbury bought a home in Fort Lauderdale after the sale of her boat, she unpacked boxes of valuable things that had been stored in England for ten years. As she went through the boxes, Gail's reaction was, "I wonder why I saved all this stuff." Her attitude now is that "you should cut the ties with the possessions you've got, because in ten years [they] won't mean the same [thing]."

There is a lesson in going through items that were put in storage years ago. At the time, those things seemed important. But as Patricia Miller Rains says, "You don't know that you didn't need it until you do without it."

Keeping Valuables

The world of ocean cruising may not be the most practical place for some items, but that never stopped Nancy Payson from keeping a treasure. "I have my mother's sterling silver. I love it, and I want to live with it. Not that we're fancy, but it's part of us." A choice to have silver on board may mean extra work. But for Nancy, it's more important to keep that memento with her.

You cannot cut yourself off from your past any more than you can disassociate yourself from your future. The trick is determining what parts of your past are important. "It's important to keep things that have meaning," says Barbara Marrett. "I kept little things that belonged to my family or friends."

What's Worth Keeping?

Measuring the value of things is difficult. As Americans, we are raised in an acquisitive society. I grew up learning it was acceptable to go out and buy a gift or something for myself as a way to apologize, recover from a trauma, or perk myself up. Buying, keeping, and storing things is easy. That way, we never have to decide what things are really important and what things aren't. Reducing our possessions goes against the practice of accumulating. It requires us to measure the value of possessions in a way that may be completely unfamiliar to most of us.

Pick Something Small

"Your treasures [on board] tend to be smaller," says Migael Scherer, who has lived on her boat for over thirty years. "I have friends who have watercolors, pen-and-ink drawings, prints, and sculpture. I trade art with other liveaboards who have limited pieces." The size of those valuables has to be directly proportional to the size of your boat.

Some mementos are justified because they are functional. Our wooden pepper mill, wooden salad bowls, and fruit bowls are trophies we won. They are useful items, yet they kindle great memories and conversation.

Make a Choice

Think about how you would choose at a grand buffet table covered with everything you love to eat. If you fill your plate with servings of every dish, the result will likely be devastating to your digestive system—and your waistline. A more sensible approach would be to take a tiny serving of each dish or to sample a few favorite dishes. Consider applying this "buffet" approach to your mementos. Keep a tiny sample of each important item, or prioritize and select a few favorite items from the top of the list.

Saving Important Items

Even after the most discerning sorting process, cruisers often find themselves with things they can't bear to discard or sell. At the same time, they know there is no way they can take everything with them. At this point, they have to create a way to keep those precious items.

Home-Base Storage

Long-term cruisers are reluctant to use the word "home" because their boat, wherever it is, is home. Cruisers therefore use the term "home base," which can mean a variety of things. A home base could be a storage locker in a home port, a plot of land in the mountains that will someday become a residence, or a small home left intact. We don't have a home base, but at least half the long-term cruisers we know do.

Some cruisers are fortunate enough to maintain homes while cruising. Réanne Hemingway-Douglass finds a personal place essential to her well-being. "I like to have a home base. If I didn't, I'd go nuts. I want to putter, to read, to have my own books. I like a piano. I love to cook. I still have the best of two possible worlds—a land home on an island in the Pacific Northwest *and* a boat. Can't ask for anything more." Another woman had to downsize substantially when she went cruising, but she still kept a home base. "The thing I liked was being able to come home rather than moving in with the kids," she says. "I felt very fortunate to have this, a place to have our belongings."

For these women, the ideal situation was to keep a home base where they could keep everything intact and return after cruising. Cruising women who do not find keeping a home base an ideal solution have to search for other ways to handle possessions.

Borrowed Storage

Finding a place to keep things of value is not always simple. If you don't keep a base on land where items can be stored, you have to rent a storage locker or rely on family and friends for storage space.

Nancy Payson's situation is not unusual. "I couldn't bear to give up some things," she says, "so we stored them with my father, my aunt and uncle, and a friend. All of them had children. My relatives divorced. My father forgot, and everything got scattered and divided up [among] friends. So much for things I couldn't bear to part with. They parted from me."

What happened to Nancy is common, because our mementos don't hold the same value for others as they do for us. A better solution is to ask friends or family to take the things that they really like. Migael Scherer used that approach: "I retained 'visiting rights' to things we had to give up. An antique clock went to a friend. I still see that clock."

It may be a wise move to pass certain family heirlooms to the next generation when you leave. Barbara Colborn kept her heirlooms in the family: "David's daughter does have some family heirlooms . . . so we don't have to get rid of everything. Things are in good hands."

Safety Deposit Box Storage

There are some items you don't want to take on the boat when you go cruising, and they must be stored in a safe place. Items such as wills, copies of insurance policies, or valuable jewelry are best left ashore in a safety deposit box. Even though you're storing original documents, be sure to take copies with you for quick access. Migael Scherer houses her valuables on dry land: "We use the safety deposit box for valuable things. We leave photo negatives ashore and take the albums on the boat."

New Mementos

One of the great joys of cruising is collecting new mementos and memories. It sounds as if I am contradicting myself, but the truth is, you will find some wonderful items as you travel. If you have been selective in your original preparations, you will find the necessary nooks and crannies for new acquisitions.

As Barbara Colborn says, "When you go to a foreign country, there are just so many new things to experience: Why drag along everything from the past twenty years? You don't need it. You're experiencing new things."

Nancy Payson has a good attitude about new things. "I have accumulated such nice souvenirs from all the places we have been. The *molas* from Panama and carvings from the Marquesas and Tonga are associated with memories, and mean far more to me than the possessions we left behind."

You will find mementos and souvenirs that you want to collect but don't have space for. A gift of tapa cloth (cloth made from tree bark) a new friend in Tonga gave me, and a primitive, very heavy, handicraft in stone that Lin Pardey acquired would be fine on a cruise ship, but they aren't practical on cruising boats. Lin managed to keep her 118-pound stone sculpture by sending it to her home base in New Zealand. The two pieces of tapa cloth I was given were 6 feet wide and 15 feet long and too big even to store on the boat. I gave one away as a gift, and I used the second piece as a wall covering in the forward cabin of the sailboat. Some friends thought it was sacrilegious to cut the tapa, but I would never have been able to enjoy it unless I found a way to use it. Glued on the bulkhead and protected with several coats of varnish, the tapa was enjoyed for many years.

Another way to enjoy mementos is to use them to replace everyday items that wear out. Even if they aren't beautiful art, they may be unique because of the materials used, their design, or the memories attached to them. I use my mementos I got in what was then Yugoslavia in my galley nearly every day. I bought a small, red enamelware teapot in a government store in Bar, Montenegro, the night we arrived, and a heavy-duty stainless steel pan I purchased in Dubrovnik, Croatia, ended my search for a proper stovetop roasting pan. Blankets, rugs, and towels are practical mementos that can also serve as unique decor on your boat.

Most cruisers buy more *molas*, which use a reverse appliqué technique beautifully executed in layers of colored cloth, than they could ever use as gifts, pillow covers, or clothes. My small *molas* that became potholders made fine gifts for other cruisers (of course, I kept a few for myself).

CDs and cassette tapes of local music are souvenirs that take up little space and bring back great memories of places we have visited and people we have met.

Clothing is a great souvenir, as long as it is worn appropriately. In warm climates, it is tempting to buy clothes that are appropriate on the beach and in resort towns and to forget that those clothes are not suitable in the local marketplace or church.

Shoes bought in the South Pacific are more practical for the area than the ones you might buy before leaving home. The plastic "Mary Janes" found there are very recognizable, useful, and indestructible. (It's also fun to walk up to a complete stranger, ask them how they liked the islands, and then tell them that you knew they went there because you recognized their shoes.)

My favorite souvenir ten years ago was a gold charm bracelet. It was so small it fit into an old-fashioned matchbox that I could store anywhere. Birthdays, Christmas holidays, ocean crossings, and other important events were remembered with charms. A tiny heart my husband carved from teak when we were still at sea one Christmas and the tooth from a barracuda we caught in the Red Sea on my fiftieth birthday were two of the best charms. Other charms have been added over the years, and the bracelet is now full. Each charm brings back wonderful memories.

Disposal Systems

You can easily accumulate more things than you can make space for. Lin Pardey describes how her husband Larry solved the quantity question when they first started cruising. "I love to watch handicrafts being made. Larry gave me a shoebox and told me to buy every souvenir I wanted until it was full. When it was full, I gave something away. When we left the boat and took a trip in the Kalahari Desert, I traded lace underwear for some handmade beads." Lin's box is bigger today, but she lives on a larger boat. She also uses the items in the box as unique gifts and thank-you presents.

Shipping items to family and friends isn't always a simple task, but it is worth the effort if some of your souvenirs would make perfect gifts for folks at home. I can usually justify the purchase of an unusual item because I call it "early Christmas shopping." I enjoy the process of selecting and buying, and I gain great joy from passing on my treasures.

If you lived on land and tired of something, you might offer the item to a charity, a church group, or a local hospital. The same kinds of opportunities exist for your cruising possessions. I had a shell collection from Asia that outgrew the sailboat, and I found it a new home at an elementary school in rural California. I replaced a giant unabridged English dictionary with a smaller one, and the old dictionary became a welcome addition to the library of a Mexican high school.

Instead of using T-shirts or hats for trading, think about giving them away as a gesture of goodwill. Many places you visit as a cruiser are off the ordinary tourist track, and your visit will be well remembered by the items you leave when you depart.

The richest cruisers are the ones who have collected many, many memories. Precious things may be part of those memories, but things can disappear while the memories are yours forever.

14

TWENTY-FOUR HOURS A DAY

A REN'T YOU BORED?" Noncruisers ask me this question frequently. They ask because they cannot imagine what I do to occupy myself full-time, 24 hours a day.

Barbara Colborn described her initial reaction to the pace of cruising. "I worked in an office. I wore heels, nylons, and nice clothes every day, and I had a schedule. I was scheduled from five-thirty in the morning until six at night—and suddenly everything changed."

A Different Pace

The change is not a lack of activity. There are different activities when you go cruising, running at a different pace according to a new set of priorities. The first thing I do at the start of a cruise is remove my wristwatch. On land, we jam so many obligations into a day: keeping appointments; picking kids up after school; getting to the store before it closes. There is no hope of getting everything done without monitoring the progress of the day with a wristwatch.

On the boat, I want to control my time rather than have it control me. Cruising offers me the opportunity to set my own schedule and move at my own pace.

We still need to keep track of time on board. On the sailboat, we had two clocks on board: one set to local time and one set to universal time, which is the same as Greenwich time (or coordinated universal time). The latter clock was useful for keeping track of international broadcasts, weather fax schedules, or making sure our log keeping was consistent as we crossed time zones. The local time clock, which we still use, is handy for knowing when tides and currents change and when the local market opens. The clocks are also important for our system of watchkeeping.

I don't need a clock to tell me if it is time to eat or sleep; my body handles those tasks. Social invitations usually happen around sunset, or when you see the dinghy back at the boat. If you are more comfortable wearing a watch on board, do so. But let your body and your environment also have a say in your schedule.

I had a friend who wore a watch without hands. The face moved, and a little notch in the face revealed a rainbow of colors underneath. She couldn't tell if she was 5 minutes early or 5 minutes late, and she didn't care. She kept time based on whether something was blue, lavender, or pink. It was the perfect watch for cruising.

You may wear a watch because you want to keep a schedule. But when you are cruising, you will likely find people who don't value time in the same way you do.

At home, you expect to pick up your laundry on a specific day, at a specific time. Rarely does your laundry service fail you. If they do, they know you will take your business elsewhere. But in some countries, it is not really important if you have clean clothes today at two o'clock or tomorrow at ten o'clock. You will get your clean clothes, but you may not get them when you thought they were promised. And no matter what you say or do, you won't change deeply rooted local customs so that they conform to your schedule.

In some warm countries we have visited, activities cease during the hottest part of the day. I had to learn to live with the flow. We met a cruising couple in Mexico who worked as entertainers in a local restaurant. They worked from eleven o'clock at night until four o'clock in the morning. For some, the prospect of staying up all night to entertain—or to be entertained—is preposterous. Yet if you sleep through the heat of the day, dining late and dancing all night do make some kind of sense.

Americans have a reputation for being impatient. We don't expect to wait for service, meals, appointments, or people. When we think things need to happen more quickly, our solution is to offer money to grease the wheels of progress. I have had officials tell me they can't accomplish a given task on time, which may mean they expect me to pay for faster service. When I tell them I don't mind waiting, I usually get whatever I need in a timely manner.

Part of cruising is being willing to change your pace and your attitude. Learning to eat when you want to eat or sleep when you want to sleep may be hard to do if a clock has always dictated your habits. But even if you are on a short cruise, try to put your watch away and leave your time open rather than packed with commitments. I bet you'll be pleased with the results.

Schedules for Cruising

I said that your time is your own when you cruise. But I have to backtrack. When you are underway, your boat and Mother Nature determine the sequence of events. You order your day with a variety of activities, yet you know that at any time, plans may change: the weather changes, sea conditions change, boat gear breaks down. There are schedules to keep as you cruise, including your watch system and set hours for radio nets.

Standing Watch

Our watch system is ordinarily 2 hours on and 2 hours off at night. During the daylight hours, we switch to 4 hours on and 4 hours off. Sailing at night is very pleasant. But because it is hard work to pay attention at night, we do shorter watches. This way, over the course of the night, each of us gets a total of 4 hours sleep in two 2-hour blocks of time. We also take naps during the day.

I love the early morning, and I prefer the watches from midnight to 2 A.M. and 4 A.M. to 6 A.M. My husband is a night owl, so he is on watch until midnight and then takes the 2 A.M. to 4 A.M. shift. Our pattern usually works well.

When I go off watch at 6 A.M., I will not be on the helm again until 10 A.M. If I'm really tired, I sleep for an hour, get up to make breakfast, then read or write or go back to sleep. Or if I am very awake at 6 A.M., I make breakfast, then sit in the cockpit to chat. When my husband goes off watch at 10 A.M., he usually sleeps for an hour or two, washes the breakfast dishes, and makes lunch. When I go off watch at 2 P.M., I like to handle specific boat tasks. If we are busy doing sail changes, I stay on to help out. By late afternoon, I want to do two things: get cleaned up and organize our evening meal. When I go back on watch at 6 P.M., we have a glass of wine, and Jim gets cleaned up and serves dinner. He often reads or catches a quick nap and does the dishes before going on watch at 10 P.M.

At the 10 P.M. watch change we discuss things that are important for the upcoming night. We keep hot water in a thermos for chocolate or coffee, and there are cookies or candy for a sugar charge on watch. If it looks as if the wind will get stronger during the night, we might put a reef in the mainsail or change the jib. We don safety gear and discuss any navigation issues—particularly if we are sailing inland or close to a coastline.

We maintain the same pattern in heavy weather, except the person off watch sleeps on deck during the night. This allows either of us to respond quickly in case there is a problem. When there are only two people on board, safety harnesses are absolutely essential at night. In rough weather, harnesses are worn around the clock, in the cockpit and on deck. On the trawler, the person off watch sleeps on the bridge instead of the stateroom.

I am always surprised when cruisers tell me they sit and read a book or watch videos in the cabin during their watch and come on deck to look around every once in a while. Keeping a proper lookout requires being on deck. We don't use earphones on watch. They can block out the sound of the wind, buoys, or a running engine. In bad weather, with reduced visibility and the potential for problems, it is crucial that someone be on deck continuously, watching and listening to the boat.

We keep a log during passages, recording wind velocity, wind direction, barometric pressure, course steered, boat speed, and time of day. It helps us monitor our progress. It also helps us track regular patterns in the weather. We always include comments in the log, so the person who was off watch knows what happened while he or she was asleep.

Stick to a schedule that distributes work and rest equitably, whether you are cruising for the day or making longer trips. My husband has generous moments when he decides to stay on watch an extra hour to give me more sleep. But it doesn't work because my body clock knows when I have to be on watch. When it's your turn to sleep, rather than being a nice guy and letting the other person sleep, make the watch change on time. You need the rest, and the other person probably would not sleep soundly because his body clock says it's time to get up.

It generally takes three days to fully adjust to a watch system. If you have trouble sleeping during the day, try eyeshades. Even if you don't sleep, use the time to rest and relax. Your body will respond, and you will adjust more easily to the schedule.

Off Watch

What the person who is off watch needs most is sleep. Making sure you get sufficient sleep is as important as being able to stay awake on watch.

Still, there is time to do more than sleep when you are off watch. As Barbara Colborn said when she returned from her first ocean cruise, "On our passages, especially with the 4-hour watches, I'd have plenty of time by myself, and we would of course both be awake at certain times. We'd sit and talk and have wonderful times together."

On some boats, the off-watch person does the cooking. If only one person assumes responsibility for cooking, then a system needs to be developed so meals can be cooked without infringing on anyone's sleep.

The off-watch person can use waking time to take care of personal needs, monitor radio broadcasts, and handle minor repairs. He or she should take care of the cleanup when not cooking, so one person doesn't do all the domestic chores.

Off-watch hours on long passages offer great opportunities. I have taught crew how to knit on long passages. One morning one of our crew said he missed bagels terribly. We spent our off watch together making bagels. By the end of the passage he was the expert.

I put the sewing machine on deck during a pre-Christmas passage and made Christmas stockings for everyone.

Nets

As mentioned in Chapter 10, amateur radio operators and cruisers with VHF and/or SSB radios participate in nets. Communication at scheduled times on certain radio bands is organized by general geographic area. The cruisers congregate on the net to exchange information on weather, offer or ask for assistance with a problem, and gossip about which boats are sailing where. The first minute is always cleared for emergency transmissions. If you are in trouble, you can get on the radio and ask for help.

Informal, short-term nets often are formed when several boats plan to make a passage at the same time. The boats agree to communicate at a prearranged time on VHF, SSB, or ham radios.

The exercise is particularly good if you are sailing through unfamiliar waters. Faster boats can advise slower boats of changing weather and can let others know if there are any problems with port clearances.

In recent years, I have found more and more boats participating in these informal nets, particularly on VHF radio.

Weather Fax

Receiving weather information via a weather fax requires maintaining a schedule, although the weather fax can be preprogrammed just as you preprogram your VCR to tape a favorite television show. You can also receive weather faxes on your laptop computer via a connection to your SSB. Weather faxes provide satellite images and hand-drawn interpretations of images. Normally, they present current conditions and rough projections for the next 12, 24, 48, and 72 hours. This information can be especially useful during hurricane seasons or when planning a passage.

Time at Anchor

I have heard it estimated that most cruisers spend about 30% of their time underway and about 70% of their time in port. You can find boats that don't fit that ratio, but—even so—the estimate raises a key question: When you are not sailing, what do you do?

When cruising no longer is your vacation or a short-term experience and becomes your life, how you use the time at anchor becomes an important matter.

Everyday Life in Port

I asked Nancy Jewhurst, who cruised on her 32-foot boat with her husband and son, to describe what she did on a typical day at anchor. "The same thing everyone does in their homes everywhere," she answered.

Like many people the world over, her day was focused on taking care of everyday needs. "I got up in the morning, cooked breakfast, and spent half the day doing school[work] with Kyle. I did laundry, although there was less of it in a climate where you were not wearing too many clothes. Made lunch. Went shopping for food, which when you're cruising takes about four times as long as it does when you're living on land with a car."

As a cruiser, you don't just hop into your car and drive off to the store to pick up a few items. As Nancy explains, "You get into your dinghy, and row your dinghy to shore. You tie your dinghy up, making sure it's safe. You walk to the store—you might take a taxi—but you probably walk. You load up with groceries—if you have too many, you might take a taxi—and walk back. Load all that stuff in your dinghy, go back to your boat, unload it, and put it away. Now that's a long process."

Shopping can be an Olympic exercise. It can also be part of the fun and entertainment of cruising. We wanted fresh garden vegetables after an eighteen-day passage from Mexico to the Marquesas. A local said he would take us to a place where we could get everything we wanted for a small fee. We hiked up a steep mountain road for 45 minutes and finally arrived at his huge garden that was terraced on the mountainside. We picked our own lettuce, beans, onions, brussels sprouts, and spinach. It was much more than a shopping trip.

In many cruising venues, there are no supermarkets. Outdoor, farmer-style markets are common around the world. They are colorful, fun to use, but limited because they normally carry only fresh produce, meats, poultry, fish, and maybe bread. Staples in bags, bottles, and cans are more likely to be found in small stores. Coffee, tea, wine, beer, soda, and dairy products typically are in a third location. Cleaning materials and paper items might be purchased in yet another place.

I have spent an entire day doing the shopping in foreign countries. After making a list of what I needed, I had to translate the list into another language, study the currency, learn to count in the language, and learn how to ask questions. "How much?" and "Is it ripe?" are usually at the top of the list. Part of the enjoyment is knowing that the next trip ashore could be the story of the day. Stopping in the market to watch a local festival unfold or following a big turtle swimming across the cove can be part of that typical day in port. For more on provisioning, see Chapter 17.

Destinations

For many cruisers, reaching a destination is the reason for making a passage. A spectacular city, an ancient ruin, or a world-famous dive spot are the kinds of locales that draw people from around the world.

Most cruisers find there is not enough time to sample all a place has to offer and still handle necessary tasks such as boat maintenance, repairs, and housekeeping on board. I asked one woman if she was interested in joining a group of women who walked every morning for exercise. She looked stunned and responded, "I can't possibly squeeze in another thing. I just don't see how some women do it all." I neglected to tell her the destination was usually the market, so the exercise excursion was an outing that rolled fitness and chores into one.

When I discovered that a planned maintenance stop in Mexico would be prolonged due to lack of paint, I hired a tutor to help me improve my Spanish. Her hours were flexible, and she charged me $5.50 for a 2-hour session each afternoon. Not only did my Spanish improve, but I learned about new markets, local festivals and events, menus to test, and my tutor's family. It was an unexpected opportunity from which I gained numerous benefits.

One comment about cruisers' activities from Patricia Miller Rains is important to repeat here. "My first season cruising in Mexico, booze pervaded everyone's lifestyle, because we couldn't figure out why we weren't satisfied." She found that people had looked forward to cruising but they didn't know what to do with their nonsailing time except drink. There is always something to see or do, but you are your own motivator and inspiration. You can sit and do nothing—or you can fill your time with lots of activity. Look around to figure out what satisfies you.

Making Friends

At almost every anchorage, you will discover old friends and make new ones, and an important aspect of anchor time is socializing. "I didn't realize I would meet so many people and make so many friends from every walk of life," says Gail Amesbury. "It opens your eyes to the outside world."

We met Gail and her husband via radio contact during our Atlantic crossing. We traveled together for several months as nodding acquaintances, until they invited us to join them in "bowling on the green"—which turned out to be bowling on the beach. We spent several hours laughing and giggling together as we broke every rule of this "staid" English pastime. Although separated by many miles and years, we keep regular contact and share a special friendship.

Some cruisers exchange cards and collect them as mementos. We have a notebook that we ask other cruisers to write in. We ask for specific things—such as home addresses or comments on the locale and our shared experiences there. We paste a picture or their card on the page to help us remember them later.

Among cruisers, informal schedules develop around many activities. Afternoon snorkeling is best because the sun is just right or the air temperature is the hottest. Jogging, walking, or running is best early in the day or at sundown—because the weather is cooler.

Fishing is good just after sunrise or just before sunset, since the fish can see the bait better.

Radio nets also serve a purpose when you are in port. In some popular cruising ports, everyone in an anchorage turns on the VHF at sunrise to ask questions, welcome newcomers, and share jokes. The nets are a good way to hook into the cruising community in port, giving new cruisers an immediate sense of belonging.

At home, an enclosed yard, patio, or life indoors minimizes your contact with people next door. Business contacts—yours or his—may be part of your social life, but the friendship usually is limited because it is the focus of one person. Stopping to assist strangers is considered a dangerous practice.

When you are cruising, you easily establish common bonds with other people. You share meals, drinks, bad weather, dragging anchors, and lost dinghies. Even though you may only know cruisers' first names, you can have more in common with those fellow cruisers than most people have with longtime neighbors or business associates.

Among cruisers, friendships are strong because the basic rule is this: Take care of each other and always offer assistance. The problem of one boat becomes the problem of the entire fleet. If you have skills, you offer them. When you need help, your fellow cruisers offer assistance.

We were in the Caribbean when a catamaran lost her power and needed help to get into Rodney Bay on St. Lucia. Teaming up with another cruiser, we both put dinghies in the water, positioned the dinghies on each side of the catamaran, and maneuvered the boat through the channel and into the boatyard slip. Just as we were finishing the job, the transom of our dinghy collapsed. The other dinghy and the catamaran skipper got us to the beach before we lost our dinghy and our outboard engine.

Friendships lead to socializing that is fun and worthwhile. We come away from every occasion having learned something new or having heard a different point of view on a long-held notion. These friendly gatherings occur on the street, in dinghies, in restaurants, in cockpits, or along the beach. Unscheduled and informal, they fill hours and days with amusement and information.

Friends from Home

When we first started cruising, friends from home wanted to join us at various destinations along the way. We enjoyed one rendezvous after the next with several sets of friends. But it soon became clear that we were not in control of our cruise as long as we had to meet the schedules of others. So we set new parameters for guests.

We would give friends an arrival date and location with the proviso that we would be within 100 miles (about 24 hours' travel) of the location when they arrived, depending on the weather. We would leave word at a designated place about when and where to meet us. This hasn't really changed with our trawler, except that it's easier to get to guests.

We required one more change in planning: Guests had to allow a minimum of three weeks of cruising time. We hated sailing away from a lovely cove or interesting village to meet plane departures. We discovered that, with this change, we were happier because our guests had to be flexible with us. This change weeded out visitors who needed to adhere to strict schedules. And those who came to cruise easily shifted gears to our pace, rather than expecting us to keep to their schedules.

We found that those friends who joined us and felt comfortable with our casual lifestyle always wanted to come back. The repeaters acquired some habits that did make life easier for us. Before leaving home, they asked for a shopping list of things we needed. Even when there was no burning necessity, they would find something special to bring: pickle relish, peanut butter, cranberry sauce, and pipe tobacco. If there was a new bestseller or a notable video (now it would have to be a DVD), they added it to the boat library.

Will I Be Bored?

Only one of the cruising women I interviewed said she was bored some of the time. The rest of the women proclaimed their love for the cruising lifestyle. If you have the need to fill every moment of the day with planned activities, you may find that cruising is not for you.

In order to find out what cruising can be like, you need to let go of your old life, your old ways, your old schedule, and—maybe— your old wristwatch.

"I think the way to live is the way you live when you're cruising, which is to do everything at a slower pace," says Nancy Jewhurst. "You look around as you're doing it. You smell things. The number of things you have to do when you're cruising is much smaller, so you can afford to take the time to go at them more slowly. . . . There's usually no need to rush."

15

WOMAN
TO WOMAN

BAD HAIR DAYS MAY be a joke to some. But those days can make me feel miserable. Each of us has a particular trait that seems to be the stem from which confidence blossoms or shrivels. Hair is not of grave importance, but if the reflection in the mirror looks grim, it's hard not to have a rotten day.

Your focus in the mirror may be your clothes, your figure, or wrinkles in your skin. But, you may wonder, is appearance important while you are cruising?

That answer depends on the individual woman. To assume that all cruisers prefer to look shabby and unkempt is wrong. Yet cruisers are not constantly bathing, shampooing, and changing their clothes.

Deciding to stop wearing makeup, getting permanents, or bathing every day is your choice. But if your physical appearance directly affects your sense of self, then knowing how to take care of yourself while cruising is important.

Bathing

Patience Wales has cruised many miles, and her attitude toward bathing remains unchanged. "You learn to bathe in salt water and learn to conserve. You even conserve when you have a watermaker. We had a big 42-foot ketch, and we didn't go very fast. What you do is take a bath every day. . . . I couldn't imagine not taking one. You feel clean. You take 2 cups of water and a face cloth and go up on the foredeck and you get clean. I have sailed with people who simply don't bathe, and I think it's awful. You feel so much better." Two cups of water may not sound like a bath. But on a long passage with a limited water supply, it's a luxury.

The idea that you can bathe in salt water is hard for some people to accept, but it is how many of us stay clean, especially in tropical latitudes. Patricia Miller Rains says, "I loved bathing in the ocean with special soaps before rinsing with fresh water in the cockpit."

"I enjoyed bathing in the ocean. It was one of the things I missed: jumping over the side and taking a bath. A bathroom fogs up," says Paula Dinius.

Louise Burke points out another aspect of bathing that makes the whole prospect extremely romantic. "During passages . . . bathing and shampooing may be on deck with Prell and liquid Joy . . . topped off with a brisk toweling. It's refreshing, bohemian, and can be fun if you help each other in the waning twilight as your new home whisks you off to a new adventure."

Some people don't want to bathe in salt water or may be in an area where it is too cold. Others share Paula's enthusiasm for ocean bathing. Privacy when bathing is a problem for some cruisers. Modesty is a cultural trait. If there are only two of you on board or yours is the only boat in an anchorage, privacy isn't a problem. In other situations you may have to change habits or attitudes.

We discovered that bathing was the same as washing dishes or clothes in Papeete, Tahiti. All the boats were Med-moored, stern-to the quay, packed in like sardines. At about ten o'clock in the morning, our neighbors stripped down and proceeded to shower on deck, all the while carrying on conversations with us, people on shore, and anyone who happened to pass by. We quickly discovered this practice was the norm and followed suit. It was a liberating experience.

Bathing naked on deck or on shore in Annapolis or in a Muslim country might cause an entirely different reaction. We cruised on Lake Huron with a young couple from Switzerland. When they jumped naked into the water to bathe, a nearby boat with five young men startled us by whistling, shouting, and watching them with binoculars. Our friends were not embarrassed, but they wondered what caused the commotion.

On *Nalu IV*, we typically soaped up and rinsed with salt water, and then did a final freshwater rinse. With some soap products, you must use a large quantity to make a lather in salt water. If you try to rinse immediately in fresh water, the foaming properties seem to increase and it is nearly impossible to get all the soap off. We did not buy special saltwater soaps or Joy dish detergent. We used the same biodegradable liquid soap for bodies, hair, clothes, and dishes.

For freshwater rinsing, we used to use the black plastic showers that absorb the sunlight during the day to heat water. In the Mediterranean, we discovered that many cruisers use portable garden sprayers. The can holds about 3 gallons of water, a hand pump pressurizes it, and the sprayer is very efficient for rinsing. To make sure the water inside warmed up, we painted our yellow sprayer with black stripes. In cold weather on the trawler, we take hot showers inside. In hot weather, we shower in the cockpit.

Bathing is a nonissue on boats with watermakers. The luxury of essentially unlimited hot, fresh water is very common as compared to a decade ago. We caution you to take good care of your watermaker and always keep your tanks full.

Hair Care

When we left on our first long cruise, I had a neighbor come over to teach me how to give myself a permanent. Jim watched carefully, because I told him that I couldn't do the back by myself. Besides, I regularly cut his hair, and this would be his chance to return the favor. Six months later he had his first opportunity to give me a perm.

I carefully wound all the rods for the top and the sides, partitioning the hair, wrapping the ends with paper, and rolling the rods tightly. When it was complete, I gave him the comb, papers, and rods to finish the back. In a matter of minutes, he declared himself done. I was astonished at his speed until I saw the pile of unused papers and curlers. "I didn't need all of those because your hair is so thin," he explained when I questioned doing all of the back of my head on four curling rods.

Barbara Colborn had an adept and cooperative mate. Before they went cruising, her hairdresser showed her husband how to cut her hair. "The first few months it really wasn't very good," she says of her on-board coiffure. "But I told him, 'I want this and that differently,' and we worked on it. . . . He learned, and he got better and better at it."

Not having great success with my husband's hair-care services, ten years ago my solution was to get permanents in foreign countries as I needed them. I became expert on permanents around the world: Australia was no problem; in Djibouti, Africa, the salon was French, the permanent absolutely gorgeous, and it cost $100; in the Balearic Islands, I practiced my Spanish and had good success for about $30; the former Yugoslavia was undergoing incredible inflation, but I paid $6 in Dubrovnik and gave the woman who did my hair another $6 as a tip; Switzerland, Barbados, and St. Lucia were all hair successes. Later, I got smart, gave up perms, and grew my hair long. When we returned to the United States, I'd get it cut, then grow it out again at sea.

There are other solutions to hair care. Learn to cut your own hair. If you can cut only the front and sides, do that. Let the back grow and pull it into a ponytail or braid. Or locate another cruiser who cuts hair professionally. Without fail, we have found anchorages in the Caribbean and Mexico populated with professionals who do haircuts on their boats or on the beach as a regular business.

One caution for those who have not lived in the sun full-time: Sun damages hair just as it damages skin. The result is brittle, dry hair that is bleached and breaks off. Wear a hat and use protective shampoos and conditioners to ward off the ultraviolet rays.

For women who color their hair on a regular basis, this may be the time to try going natural. It is one less thing to worry about.

Skin Care and Makeup

I talked about sun protection for the skin in Chapter 7. I lost the battle before starting long-term cruising by sailing without wearing sunblock. In northern latitudes, the destructive power of the sun's rays are often discounted because the warm sunshine feels so good. As a result, the damage is done. And there is no wrinkle cream that can improve the situation. Plastic surgery is an option, but the expense and impermanence hardly make it seem worthwhile. I like to believe people when they say that wrinkles give me character.

Even though I can't erase my wrinkles and lines, I try to use a moisturizer with a sun protection factor in it every day. I never can remember to renew sunblocks or zinc oxide, but I do remember to put on moisturizer. Some moisturizers contain a color base or sunblock. Regardless of what you use, it is no good if you forget to apply it.

Protecting the skin is not limited to the face, although we do pay more attention to facial skin. The thin skin on the neck and the backs of hands shows sun damage quickly. Arms and legs have thicker skin, but wrinkles and discoloration eventually catch up. Unless you have no pigment in your skin, you have some tolerance for the ultraviolet rays. The extent to which you expose your skin will ultimately determine your skin condition as you get older.

Réanne Hemingway-Douglass said, "I want to stress the importance of protection against sun. Don was not careful and has had to undergo three surgeries for melanoma in the past decade. I paid more attention to wearing long sleeves and a hat and to applying sunscreen, and have had only superficial skin problems."

Makeup is an alternative for skin protection. Most women find makeup unsatisfactory in warm climates because of perspiration, and many forgo makeup when they cruise. Paula Dinius had no problem once they set out cruising. "It was harder living on the boat when I had a job, because I had to have more toiletries and face the world with hair done and clothes pressed. Once we left to go cruising, my lipstick never came out of the cupboard in five years."

Barbara Colborn, on the other hand, said, "I learned that lipstick and earrings go a long way to make you look good when you're wearing a T-shirt and pants."

Some women want the finished appearance of makeup and have found ways to make it possible while cruising. I encountered two young women in Australia who had just had their eyelashes and eyebrows dyed. A more extreme measure some women use is tattooing features such as eyebrows.

Each of us has a standard of appearance that we are comfortable with. When Barbara Colborn and her husband went cruising, they agreed on what their standard would be: "We wanted to be like those English adventurers who would go into the jungle in the old movies. You see them shaving, and the women would always have their hair looking clean and tidy. We wanted to make that effort to keep our personal looks together."

Clothing

Barbara Marrett recalls her first reaction to clothing as a cruising issue. "I'm not a real fashion plate so I really enjoyed simplifying my life. You can't take many clothes or much jewelry on a 31-foot boat. Most of the people you meet cruising are not judging you by your looks or what you're wearing, anyway. The more primitive people seem very astute at judging body language to learn who you are, rather than judging you by what you say or wear."

Clothing is still something many women worry about when they go cruising. Wearing only one color for months is unappealing (and unknown to most of us). On land, we have lots of clothing in closets, cabinets, and drawers. But when confronted with a single hanging locker and two or three drawers on a boat for everything you own, it is difficult to imagine how you will manage.

Most women don't limit themselves to items of all one color, although there may be some excellent reasons for that practice. There was a time when navy blue was the only yachting color. The best argument for navy blue is that it doesn't show the dirt; the argument against it is that it's too dark to be worn in hot climates. White was the hot-weather alternative, but cruisers have learned that white is rarely practical when you have to beach a dinghy, carry bags of groceries, or sit on thatched mats for a cold drink.

The space for clothing may be very limited, so you should wear the things you like that make you feel good. Patricia Miller Rains said her wardrobe in Mexico consisted of three swimsuits and two dresses. That may sound unrealistic, but she makes a good point: Clothing should be appropriate for what you do. Sailing and living on the water in a warm climate make swimsuits the preferred items of clothing. Dresses are more comfortable than pants in warm climates. And in Mexico, most women wear dresses rather than pants. If you have to scale down to a limited wardrobe, think about where you will be. Your clothing needs to be appropriate for other cultures. Through experience I learned that in order to gain acceptance as someone more than a tourist in Asia and the Arab world, I had to accept their dress standards.

There are times when you may need something special to wear. Most cruisers manage to pull themselves together for special occasions. Paula Dinius said, "We always had one special outfit to go out. You wear fancier shoes, do your hair, nails, and makeup. You don't have to be raggedy all the time. The guys would dress up, and we'd stand in the dinghy so we didn't get wet going ashore."

Lin Pardey describes herself as a nonmaterialistic person, and she managed very well with limited space. "I have two designer evening gowns, alligator shoes, and belt. When I go out, I dress as well as I wish."

After an absence of nearly seven years on our first voyage, we returned to our home port. We had worn-out swimsuits and underwear, because that was our standard attire on the boat. We still had T-shirts, shorts, pants, sweaters, and shoes that we carried around and didn't wear. We used our dress-up clothes and replaced them once, because they were very worn. Even though we thought we were traveling light, we brought home excess clothes.

The fabric your clothes are made of has much to do with your comfort level. Although many people advocate using synthetics because they are lightweight, warm when necessary, and wrinkle-free, we take the opposite stance. Most synthetic fabrics are too warm for the truly hot climates. Stores in Florida and California don't carry clothes that are warm enough to wear in Minnesota in the winter, and your stores at home are not likely to have fabrics designed for comfort in the tropics. Styles, customs, and fabrics vary with culture and climate. The clothes you own may suffice if you plan to cruise in U.S. waters. However, even the United States has great variations in weather on both coasts. Take favorite clothes with you and shop when you reach a new environment. The only caveat here is swimsuits. On the beach in Mexico, Tahiti, Indonesia, or Turkey, tourists wear the least clothing possible; in some cases none. But a couple of one-piece swimsuits that are flattering but not revealing work best for cruisers. Along with the swimsuits, have a one-piece caftan or cover-up to wear to and from the beach. If you look like a tourist, expect tourist treatment. Take along what you have that's appropriate, but leave room to buy something later on.

Sex at Sea

During a break in one of my seminars a woman asked me, "How do you have sex at sea if one person is on watch and the other one is asleep?" There are many times when both of you are awake and sharing your time. Sex is not something you put off until you get to port. Cruising couples make time for sex. But since you're not going to bed at the same time, you have to develop a different approach to sex.

"Sex is more natural because you are more in your body and less in your head," says Barbara Marrett. "If the sailing is really calm and nice, it flows." Migael Scherer shared Barbara's view of the surrounding environment: "Romance can be cultivated on a boat. On land, there are so many distractions. I think the boat helped us."

The freedom of sex outdoors in the daylight was appealing to some of the women interviewed. "Underway on passages you're out hundreds of miles from people. You have the cockpit, which is wonderful. It doesn't get much more private than that," says Barbara Colborn.

Louise Burke, who lost her seagoing husband but continued on as an offshore sailor, advised: "Become a team. Curl up at night in your new nest and feel confident and sublimely happy at sharing this new adventure with your lover or husband. Remember, a quiet anchorage, a strange harbor, and exotic night noises can bring out the best in the beast."

Cruisers are adventurers, and your sex life can be another area of exploration. Living on a boat, sailing across an ocean, or anchoring in a still cove offer opportunities: from lovemaking to swimming naked in the starlight, trying every bunk cushion on the boat, and slipping away from other people and boats in your dinghy. I find the dinghy is often the best answer because we can get away from the boat, especially when we have crew. At night, we drift under the stars to our hearts' content. We have had couples with us who simply retired early and asked us to turn up the stereo for an hour or so.

A trawler is more like a house, and a stateroom is more like a bedroom. Basically, if you can do it in your bedroom, you can do it in a stateroom.

16

MAKING
THE MOST
OF IT

WHETHER IT IS YOUR FIRST trip to the opera and you don't know the story, or you go to Wimbledon without knowing tennis, you may understand the significance of the event, but without the specific knowledge the magic is lost. Cruising is no different. It can be the event of a lifetime. But in order to make the most of it, you need to prepare and educate yourself in advance.

Cruising has many different aspects, and it is hard to know where to begin in your preparations. I learned the hard way when we sailed to Australia via the South Pacific. I had focused on all the necessary tasks before our departure, such as organizing provisions and boat gear. But I neglected to research the places where we would stop during our voyage. When we arrived in French Polynesia, I realized my mistake. I wrote to the States and requested that a guidebook and a French-English dictionary be sent out to us.

The books caught up with me in Fiji. Granted, I did see some wonderful sights in Polynesia, but I missed many others. The places I missed are not forgotten; I hope someday to return and have a second chance.

You won't have time to become an expert on everything you see and do, but you can prepare yourself enough to ensure you don't miss the once-in-a-lifetime opportunities.

Things to Learn for Independence

There are two areas you can focus on in advance of your departure that will help you be more independent and, I believe, improve your quality of life as a cruiser: operating the dinghy and speaking the local language.

Dinghy Operation

A friend once complained to me about being at anchor: "I prefer being in the marina. Then I don't have to wait on someone else to go places." When I asked her what she meant, she said, "I can't drive the dinghy, so I'm always stuck."

Learning to drive a dinghy may not seem important to you. But it is no different from not being able to drive a car or ride a bicycle. If you have to wait for someone to chauffeur you ashore and to other boats, then you are not independent.

If you are only cruising on holidays and vacations, going solo in the dinghy may not be important. But if you are going on long cruises and you want to make the early market or power walk on the beach at sunrise, being able to get yourself ashore is essential.

My friend chose not to learn how to use the dinghy. Her options were limited, and she remained dependent on her mate, or someone else, for transportation when they were not in a marina. The situation was even more limiting in areas without marinas.

If you are going ashore to do chores, sightsee, or handle business, you need to use the dinghy. You'll also need this skill if you want to visit friends, go snorkeling, or explore a lagoon. Using the dinghy should be second nature.

What do you need to know? For me the hardest part of dinghy operation is starting the outboard engine. After seventeen years, I was pushed to the point of insisting our outboard be replaced. Even when I got it started, which was rare, it would run briefly and die. Jim was having the same difficulties, and we agreed it was time for a new engine. The outboard we bought was easy to start and quieter to operate, and it had safety features our old engine didn't have.

Starting an outboard is a simple procedure. Read the instruction manual for the basics. Practice starting and driving. Learn to recognize if you have flooded the engine, which will prevent it from starting. Newer engines with pull starters are much easier to operate than older models.

Even though our newer model was better behaved, we still invoked the following plea as dinghy drivers: "Please God, look with kindness on this poor sinner and these two cylinders."

The first time I went off alone in our dinghy, I realized I could start it, stop it, and beach it. But I had never learned to pull alongside a dock or other boats. Fortunately, our dinghy was a rubber inflatable one, and it bounced off other dinghies, docks, and our boat. I got a few jolts—and some unpleasant commentary—but I didn't do any damage to others, myself, or the dinghy.

If you don't want to operate an outboard engine, learn to row the dinghy unassisted. Be sure that the oars, oarlocks, and seat accommodate you. It is easier to row a hard dinghy, which is designed to be rowed, than it is to row an inflatable one. Many boats have two dinghies, the same way families have two cars. It's a good idea if you have the space to stow them.

After moving to the trawler, I had to start over with my dinghy skills. The first issue was launching the dinghy. It is stowed on the boat deck (the roof of the saloon) and it's raised and lowered on davits. This 13-foot Boston Whaler has a 25-horsepower engine. It takes two of us about 10 minutes to uncover, launch, and start. It has electric start and a steering wheel. With the outboard and two of us aboard, it easily runs at 25 knots on flat water, but it is not a particularly "dry" boat when the seas kick up. We have learned that it is powerful enough to tow a water-skier. We are mindful that no one appreciates rocking from the wake and noise from an outboard, so we try to maintain low speeds and no wakes near anchorages.

Speaking the Language

A second way to increase your independence is with language skills. Being fluent in the language of your cruising venue isn't absolutely necessary, but having some facility with the language will enhance your enjoyment. English is spoken worldwide, and you can make yourself understood. But you cannot converse freely with the local inhabitants.

If you studied a language in school, brush up on it. Spanish and French are both valuable languages for cruising in the Western Hemisphere. Mexico, Central America, and South America (except Brazil) are Spanish-speaking areas. French is spoken in the South Pacific and on the Caribbean islands of Martinique, Guadeloupe, and St. Martin.

Acquire a basic understanding of grammar and pronunciation of a language before you go cruising. As you sail from place to place, you can acquire the vocabulary you need. Everyday tasks, such as shopping or going to the post office, are good times to practice a language. You need to learn how to count, ask for prices, and learn simple phrases of greeting and appreciation.

The rewards may be respect from the locals or freedom to travel off the beaten path, try out new places and new foods, and make new friends. There is some security in knowing you can ask questions and get answers. Language will expand your world. I recommend the two language books in the bibliography.

Grow as You Go

In the throes of planning for your departure, there is much to accomplish. You have to put some things on hold, but those things need not be forgotten altogether. You can work time into your cruising schedule for those endeavors once you are sailing.

"Dream up a list of five fun, rewarding, enriching, and absorbing activities, mental and physical, that you've always wanted to do in your spare time," recommends Patricia Miller Rains. "Adapt them to boat life . . . one at a time. Weave time for this activity into your daily routine and let it become a new habit. By the time you've completed this list, you'll have become a more interesting and organized person, and you'll already have dreamed up a new list." Those activities may include sewing, dancing, collecting shells, photography, and more.

Patricia discourages including things on that list involved with boat maintenance, such as varnishing. I agree to some extent, but I also know some women who love to varnish. They take pride in their work, which is better than anything a boatyard might do. The things you learn should be things you want to do for your own pleasure and satisfaction.

Cruising Skills

With the advancements in onboard electronic instruments, navigation today has been reduced to pushing buttons and reading dimly lit screens. Your cruising partner may be, like my husband, a nut about gadgets. Still, learning to navigate the old-fashioned way, by using a sextant, is essential.

Once you learn, however, your skills can get rusty unless you use them. We make a point of using our sextant periodically to keep our skills sharp. Plotting your course on a chart is another skill that gets ignored, and it's easy to get sloppy if you don't do it regularly.

I find plotting our positions on a chart and following our progress an absorbing activity during a passage. The geography-class explanation of latitude and longitude we all learned in school didn't have much meaning. But taking the latitude/longitude position from a sextant, or from GPS, and putting it on a chart gives me a picture of where we are. Some women have sailed with us for hundreds of miles and never bothered to look at a chart. My curiosity would drive me crazy if I didn't know our position and course. Plus it's safer if both of you know how to figure out where you are.

When we swap charts with friends, I like to match position plots to see if we sailed the same course and if we took the same amount of time. Notations written on their chart of what they saw—such as "Whales!" or "Caught fish!"—alert us to new activities.

The plotting activity has true value. Electronic devices can quit. But on your chart is a record of where you are. It is a safety net and valuable knowledge to have while you are working to get your electronic gear back online or dig out your sextant. If you are coastal cruising, plotting your course to avoid obstructions such as shoals and rocks is essential.

Learning to use a radio may not be something you have time to do before you go cruising. VHF and SSB radios only require you to have the FCC ship's station license in order to use them. After you make local contact with marinas and other boats on a VHF, you may be interested in reaching contacts farther away on the SSB.

If you enjoy learning radio procedures and regulations, you might consider getting your amateur radio operator's license so that you can participate in ham radio nets and have virtually unlimited communication. As you learn Morse code and regulations, you progress through different levels, acquiring more privileges and broadening your horizons on more frequencies. Contact the FCC for information on getting a ham license, or the American Radio Relay League for information on classes and local resources (see the Resources appendix).

Some women are attracted to learning the mechanical skills needed to keep various boat systems operational. Lin Pardey was the exception to the rule forty years ago when she started cruising. "I liked the mechanics of sailing. I'm quite a mechanical person and I like to know how the boat works," she says. "Just being around boats and understanding how they work, I found that men treated me special. It was a male-oriented world."

The basics of engine operation and maintenance may seem unfamiliar, but they are not complicated. Checking the oil, the coolant, the transmission fluid, and the zincs are often more easily done by a woman than a man because women's hands are often smaller and thus easier to get into tight engine spaces.

Barbara Colborn had thought of the engine as a black hole, but she learned it was more than that. "I'm gradually learning more about the engine through doing simple maintenance. Mechanics is like cooking. I wrote out the directions for changing the oil like a recipe: You gather up your tools, then you do step one, step two, step three. Women have smaller hands generally, and they can get in there very easily and do things quickly."

In the past, women had to fight stereotypes in order to do mechanical things. Today, women learn mechanical and electrical skills; many find those mechanical skills fun, enriching, and useful.

I rarely change the oil, but I still do regular checks of engine fluids and battery condition, and I keep maintenance records. On the trawler, twin engines means twice as many things to check and maintain!

Personal Skills

After you start cruising, you discover skills you never knew existed to add to your list of things to learn.

A talented young man crewed for us on a passage to Tahiti. He played the guitar, banjo, harmonica, and pennywhistle. During an evening's entertainment, he taught me to play the spoons. I would have never put that skill on a list, yet it proved to be fun and a good way to participate in impromptu musicales. I went so far as to have wooden spoons made by a Marquesan wood carver to create a new type of sound.

Musical instruments are always important for entertainment. Even when you can't speak a local language, the ability to play an instrument will break the ice and be your entrée to local activities. You can practice acoustical and portable electronic instruments on an ocean passage and play them on arrival.

Other forms of entertainment, particularly ones children enjoy, can be a great introduction to a new island or village.

We carry a variety of hand puppets on board that we have acquired over the years. On the quay in Manihi in the Tuamotu Archipelago, children gathered to watch the captain smoke his pipe. A raccoon puppet named Porky poked his head through a port to mimic the captain. The captain scolded, and we were suddenly in the midst of a Punch and Judy show. The children were delighted. The only downside was that about thirty children arrived on the quay at sunrise the next day chanting "Porky, Porky, Porky!"

Simple arts-and-crafts projects make great gifts and increase your enjoyment of cruising. Collecting seeds, nuts, and shells is popular. You can create something to wear, to give, or to display.

Acquiring things as you cruise is easy. Knowing what to do with them so they are useful and justify the space they occupy on board is difficult (see Chapter 13). Photography, sketching, and painting help you remember beautiful places and recapture memories. These activities also satisfy the need to do something creative and enriching.

Not all of us want to collect or create, and not all of us are inclined to perform. The one activity in which most cruisers indulge is reading. We've read hundreds of paperbacks and traded them for more. For a while, we read without any particular goal in mind. But we developed the need to have a library that would provide information about our destinations.

At first we read the standard travel guides for basic information about ground transportation, holidays, money exchange, and sightseeing. But then we wanted to get a better understanding of some places, and began reading more history. One of the most memorable books was David McCullough's *Path Between the Seas*, which is the story of the building of the Panama Canal. It gave the trip through the Canal more significance because we knew the human cost of the project. While in Japan we read *The House of Nomura* by Albert Alletzhauser, the history of one of the most influential financial groups in the world. We had the opportunity to meet Fumihide Nomura, the surviving member of this important family, and have dinner as his guests. It made all that we read very real and very personal.

Popular fiction with sound historical research, such as James Michener's *Mexico*, provides historical and cultural information with good entertainment. And don't forget to put a good atlas and encyclopedia aboard to use for reference.

If you enjoy writing but don't want to worry about deadlines and contracts, write for your own pleasure. Blogs are great fun and often useful. You might even develop a newsletter for friends and family eager to share in your adventures. Make and send copies, or send your original copy home and ask someone to copy and distribute it for you. When you make landfall, doing a newsletter electronically is easy. Since the available onboard e-mail systems are restricted, it's usually not practical to do this at sea (but see the SkyMate section in Chapter 10).

Most cruisers carry snorkeling gear. Snorkeling is a great activity for anyone. Jim refers to it as talking to the fishes. If we are at anchor in clear water, Jim is the first person over the side, saying "I have to check the anchor." That phrase means "I'll be back in a couple of hours." His enthusiasm for the water is contagious, and usually everyone else joins him.

The next step is diving with scuba gear. If you have the opportunity to learn before you start cruising, take it. Being a certified diver allows you to have tanks filled and to dive in many areas. There are some areas, such as Greece, where diving is tightly controlled. The unauthorized collecting of artifacts over the years has prompted the government to regulate scuba diving. On the other hand, there are locations specifically designated for divers with "walks" to follow underwater. We saw our first ones in the Caribbean.

Smell the Roses

"Herb likes to sail and I like to get someplace," says Nancy Payson. "I enjoy being there and walking, hiking, meeting the locals, getting to know the culture. Herb's an 'A to B-er,' but I make him slow down and smell the roses as we go along." Nancy and Barbara Marrett agree that for many women, the attraction to cruising is the travel.

Unless you are trying to set a record for speed or for the highest number of places visited on a cruise, spend time in your destinations. Travel the way the local people do—be it on foot, in trucks, on horses, or on camels. Attend the local church or festival to learn more about the people and their culture. Take along a camera and a tape recorder or a camcorder (if it doesn't offend people; always ask permission before taking pictures or recording near religious sites). A great way to learn about a country and its people is to get on a local bus and ride to the end of the line. If trains are the standard way to travel, pack a lunch, a water bottle, and tissues, and get on a train for the day.

We have found trains a fascinating way to travel. In New Zealand, the very old trains didn't have dining cars or toilets, so we stopped regularly at little country stations to sample terrific home cooking and use the facilities. In Sri Lanka, the train was so crowded that we sat in the vestibule on our sea bags. On the slow-moving train, we felt like characters in an old English movie. The Karanda train in Australia was like an amusement park ride; the track twisted into the mountains past waterfalls, brilliant plants, and wild animals.

We wintered over in the Mediterranean at Alcudia on Majorca. We had Eurail passes sent to us from the United States and spent three months riding trains, covering 14,000 miles and sixteen countries.

Don't wear a watch. Leave your schedule on the boat and sample something new. Let the days flow at their own pace.

A friend of mine often says, "You only go around once. But if you do it right, once should be enough."

17

A FEW
WORDS ABOUT
PROVISIONING

Twenty-five years ago, it was common for cruisers to set out for foreign waters carrying food and supplies for six months. In some of the less-traveled parts of the world today, such as the Red Sea, there still is trepidation about the availability of provisions. But when you set off on a passage, I think you will be surprised by your discoveries: You may not find your favorite granola in every port, but you will find good basic food.

What is very different from the "old days" is cooking. Many women have concentrated on careers and depended upon frozen food, ready-to-eat meals from the supermarket, or take-out meals rather than cooking. If you and your partner are not comfortable cooking, you need to find a solution to the situation. Start with a basic cookbook. Find an old edition of *Betty Crocker's Picture Cookbook* or the *Joy of Cooking*. First, these books explain basic techniques with basic ingredients. Second, they have diagram and picture references showing how to cut a chicken into parts or what part of the cow the tenderloin is. Cooking requires some basic skills and knowledge, just like any other discipline. If you are making a passage, you need to eat. Candy and energy bars, plus an occasional carton of yogurt, may be sufficient at home. Passagemaking for several days is another story. Learn to make at least one hot meal per day. Boiling water and stirring will get you started with ramen noodles. If you find that cooking is fun and easy, the variety of foods you encounter as you cruise will add a completely new dimension to your life.

Provisioning for Cruising

When I started daysailing, provisions were simple: soup, sandwiches, cookies, apples, coffee, and toilet paper. As I progressed to weekend cruising, so did the food on board. I would make turkey dinners and eggs Benedict (to name only two dishes), seal the meals in boilable bags, freeze them, then reheat them on board in boiling water. I didn't have a refrigerator, but for a weekend, food kept fine in a picnic cooler.

Provisioning for my first weeklong excursion was more complicated. But we anchored each night within reach of little country stores, and I had plenty of fresh food and staples.

The first offshore passage I provisioned for was the Transpacific Yacht Race from Los Angeles to Honolulu. The racing rules required that I submit a complete menu for twenty-one days, plus a listing of five days' emergency rations. Not only was I required to provision for three weeks, I was doing it for a crew of eight!

It took me nearly two days to write out a complete menu for the race. I considered the cooking skills of the crew: seven men, aged 18 to 50, and me. They all were expected to cook and do dishes, just as I was expected to steer and trim sails. I didn't have storage for leftovers, and refrigeration space was limited on board. I developed a grocery list from my menu, accounting for everything down to the last candy bar. By now I have had lots of practice, and I still write detailed menus for passages of more than 500 miles. If I plan off the top of my head as I shop, I am likely to forget a necessary ingredient. But with a written list, I can remind myself to get the ingredients for fun items, too: birthday cake, popcorn, and our special favorite—ice cream.

For me, planning menus down to the last jar of mushrooms is still the easiest way to manage provisioning. This planning may be the antithesis of the cruiser's credo of going where the wind takes you. But it is a way to learn.

Start by discussing the type of weather and sea conditions you are likely to have, and estimate the number of days you will be at sea. If you average 100 miles a day, and you are doing a 300-mile passage, plan on three days plus one more. If you make it in three days, you will have extra food on board for an unforeseen delay, such as a slow clearance into port. If you don't make your 100-mile days, you will have sufficient food.

Keep things simple for meals underway. Planning to do meals with many different side dishes when you are going to weather is an acrobatic feat. Food for a passage needs to be easy to prepare, attractive, fresh, and hot. Stick with familiar meals; experimenting with a new dish while underway is courting disaster.

The first day on a passage, I make mild food so no one starts out with indigestion, which might lead to seasickness. Chicken with rice, porcupine meatballs, or pasta are easily prepared in one pot. Served with bread and sliced fresh fruit, they make substantial meals that are easy to fix and eat.

I know one woman whose planning is excellent. She makes sure there are leftovers from the evening meal, then makes them the foundation for lunch the next day. Leftover chicken and rice can become soup; pasta can be used to make a salad; meatballs might be sandwich filling. The refrigerator doesn't fill up with leftovers, and lunch is something other than sandwiches.

Some believe that a planned-menu approach to provisioning does not leave any room for flexibility, but putting something in writing doesn't mean you can't change it. If the weather is too warm for hot soup, make cold soup. Or swap meals for something more appropriate. The reason for thorough menu planning is to guarantee you have all the provisions you need.

Even though I plan my menus, I like the flexibility of substituting a freshly caught mahimahi for, say, meatballs.

You can't plan on finding fresh fish along the way, so when you do, juggle a little. I store fresh food so the most perishable items will be used first, and I can see what I am supposed to use next. If fresh fish is plentiful, cook perishable menu ingredients so they won't spoil. Then find another way to use the meal, such as making meatball sandwiches instead of peanut butter sandwiches.

When gunkholing, I generally carry enough fresh food for three days. I trust our ability to locate a grocery store, friendly locals who have goods to sell, or fresh food from the environment. The plan has not failed me yet; I have never had to depend on fish, coconuts, or berries from the wild as a main source of food.

Shopping in Foreign Countries

Shopping is one of the most entertaining and educational experiences you have as a cruiser. Whether you are in a new town or a new country, food is a common denominator that helps you get acquainted with the local people and learn about the area.

Remember, in some ports you will have to translate your shopping list into a foreign language. Learning to count verbally is important—although you can always use your fingers. Knowing how to say thank-you is an essential part of your language lesson.

You will also have to do measurement translations. Metric measures are used in most of the world outside the United States. You will have to translate to kilos and grams in your recipes. My shortcuts for conversion are: a $1/2$ kilogram is slightly more than 1 pound; 1 liter is a touch more than 1 quart. Use a small pocket calculator to convert measurements, track spending, and convert currency.

For me, the first shopping excursion sets the tone for the rest of our stay. I learn about the people, their food, and their attitude toward me. I make every effort to put my best foot forward. I dress the same way as the local people: If the women wear skirts and cover their heads, I do too. I still may look different, but I try to avoid calling undue attention to myself.

The first shopping run also gives me the opportunity to judge prices and availability—in case we need to do major provisioning before we leave—and to learn the local market hours. In much of the world, shopping is done early in the day. It is not unusual for markets to open at 6 A.M. If you wait until too late in the day, the stalls will be closed or the shelves empty.

I also learn what kinds of extra containers I might need for my next trip. In some places, you need your own bottles and jars for oil, vinegar, honey, jam, and wine. For items such as beer and yogurt, there may be a deposit on the containers.

In most countries, the shopping bags are plastic. So wherever I shop—even in the United States—I bring my own bags and baskets to carry purchases. Disposing of plastic is a problem; it makes better sense not to accumulate it in the first place.

I have learned to bring specialized containers to market. I have plastic egg cartons, because eggs are often sold in open flats or loose in a basket. I have a long canvas bag lined with plastic to keep bread fresh and protect it from spray on the dinghy ride back. A string bag is great for fruits and vegetables.

On major provisioning trips, my own containers are not enough. I resort to paper boxes or wooden crates. Try to avoid bringing those local containers on board, since they may contain cockroaches. Dispose of paper wrappers, such as those on flour sacks or cereal containers. If they have been on the shelf for a long time, they might house insect eggs.

The other part of my shopping excursion is to check the availability and quality of water, as well as sources for propane.

After shopping, I have to get my goods back to the boat. Taxis, buses, bikes, and feet work fine if we're on a dock. Many cruisers use folding carts to manage heavy items, such as sodas and beer. I have both owned and rented motor scooters in various ports, and I find them ideal. A large plastic box wired on the back generally handles all that I want to carry.

If we are at anchor, the dinghy is the final mode of transportation to the boat. I like a big dinghy, since it carries people, provisions, water, and fuel—sometimes all at once. If you have any distance to go from shore to the boat, think in terms of a dinghy that will be capable of doing all the chores in one or two trips. Otherwise, you may be running back and forth when you could be snorkeling, sightseeing, or loafing.

What's Out There?

Whether you are passagemaking or gunkholing, your menu needs to reflect what you will be able to buy when you go ashore. The eating habits of the local population reflect what is readily available and appropriate for the climate.

Basic staples are available everywhere: sugar, flour, baking powder, salt, oil, beans, rice, and green coffee beans. I buy these items automatically every month, along with toilet paper, paper towels, soap, bleach, and matches. We can store these comfortably. Canned goods available around the world include fish, fruit, tomato sauce or puree, and beans.

Produce in the tropics is heavy on fruit—including mangoes, papayas, bananas, pineapples, guavas, and citrus. Peppers, tomatoes, onions, and squash are common. It is harder to find good potatoes, green vegetables, lettuce, carrots, and cabbage, because they grow in cooler temperatures. Tropical countries with high mountains offer a broader range of food.

Fresh dairy and meat products are harder to find in the tropics. Animals are not prevalent, and refrigeration is not common. Yogurt from sheep's, goat's, or cow's milk can be found in many small towns and villages. Fish, in one form or another, seems to be available anywhere you cruise.

We have found that bacon, salami, and ham are rarely available in Islamic countries. Beer, wine, and liquor are hard to find in Arab countries; in Sudan, for instance, religious laws are enforced by the government, and no liquor is available legally.

Countries at latitudes similar to our home port's have had the same foods. In Europe—including the former Yugoslavian countries, Turkey, and Greece—the problem was not availability, it was deciding what I wanted!

Many women are concerned about the quality of food, but I rarely find that to be a problem. Sometimes the inventory in a small store is depleted or the packaging is damaged. I have learned to ask for things, because there may be inventory in storage. If a store is out of bread or produce, ask when the next delivery is expected.

It's hard to find tender meat or chicken in countries where animals are eaten only after their productive years. A pressure cooker is great for making tender beef and chicken. Lack of refrigeration in some countries means you must select live animals. Usually, they are butchered and prepared according to your instructions. I usually select the animals first, do my shopping, and return for the meat last.

If you have never learned how to cut up chickens or what parts of animals yield roast, chops, or steaks, keep an old cookbook, such as those mentioned above, in your cruising library. I keep a cleaver for such tasks. I also use a food processor to make my own ground meats.

Lura Francis canned meat on board her Westsail 32 when she was in Cyprus. She follows a low-salt diet, and commercially canned meat is loaded with salt. Plus, she says her canned meat tasted great. She stowed the pint jars, separated by strips of bubble wrap, in lockers beneath the ship's bunks. During a six-year circumnavigation, Lura experienced heavy weather, including a hurricane, but never found a broken jar.

We regularly use certain spices and condiments in our menus. I try to always keep those items on hand. When I find one of our favorites in an unlikely place, I buy it and tuck it away. These items include peanuts, capers, olives, pimiento, chutney, pickle relish, raisins, wine vinegar, bottled lemon juice, Worcestershire sauce, Dijon mustard, olive oil, tarragon, basil, cumin, cornstarch, brown sugar, vanilla, oatmeal, popcorn, and honey.

Starbucks and its ilk have ruined Americans' ability to make a decent pot of coffee. I grew up in a household where we took drip coffee for granted. As a young homemaker, I learned to roast green coffee beans. It proved to be a wonderful accomplishment because green coffee beans last forever if they are kept dry.

One of the best shopping experiences we ever had was locating green coffee in Port Sudan where no one spoke English. We wandered into a small, dark store where we spied burlap bags of coffee. Stamped on the gunnysacks was the word "Kenya." Two old men sat in a corner watching us. When I spoke, they just shook their heads. When Jim asked, they looked less surly but still shook their heads. A little boy slid out of a corner and came to a battered desk. It had an old-fashioned pan balance on top. He took a weight, put it on the desk, and then put two ancient paper bills next to it. Brilliant! He was telling us that 1 kilo of beans cost 2 Sudanese pounds. When we purchased 20 kilos, he was all smiles, and so were the sour old guys in the corner.

I roast the beans in a heavy skillet on a flame tamer over a medium flame. Depending on how much I put in the skillet, it takes about 30 to 40 minutes. When the beans cool, they are ready to use. Green beans are easy to use, and we are the morning coffee stop for many cruisers.

Foreign Finds

Cruising in countries without freezers, microwaves, and prepackaged meals opens up new opportunities. The lack of what we call convenience foods is replaced by food products that are ideal for cruisers.

UHT milk is treated with heat so it can be kept without refrigeration for up to six months. It is common throughout the world, and it is available as whole, skim, and part-skim milk in liter boxes. I had more difficulty finding box milk in the United States than in any other country.

One spin-off product I found, and use a great deal, is cream in a box. I have used a 250-milliliter box of whipping cream to make ice cream.

Canned butter is occasionally found in the United States (and nearly everywhere else). Both Holland and New Zealand produce excellent canned butter. Other canned products I have found in the South Pacific, Australia, Asia, and Europe include cheese, bacon, ham, beef, hot dogs, and whole chickens. In the United States, our microwaves and freezers have made many canned goods hard to find.

I found dried vegetables in Australia. These were dehydrated, not freeze-dried. When reconstituted in cooking, they tasted like fresh vegetables. Varieties included peas, string beans, peas with carrots, and peas with corn. I stocked up on those vegetables before I left Australia, but I wasn't able to find them in Asia, Africa, Europe, or the Americas.

A popular item in Mexico is shredded, dried meat. It can be kept on the shelf, just like the dried vegetables. I use it for spaghetti sauce, chili, and stew.

Prepackaged mixes and convenience foods common in American supermarkets are becoming more available in other parts of the world.

There are biscuit mixes, pancake mixes, and cookie mixes similar to American products. The drawback for me is cost; items imported from the States, or made to appeal to a small portion of the population, are expensive. Consequently, I do without or make substitutes. With experimentation I have learned to make biscuit mix, instant hot chocolate mix, piecrust mix, peanut butter, and more.

The one item I have missed and found no real substitute for is American pickle relish. In Australia, I bought something that looked like the slime from a fish tank. It was tasteless. In some parts of Mexico, I found jars of pickle relish that looked as if they had been on the shelf since the time of Zapata. As a result, everyone who came to visit us brought pickle relish.

Bright Copper Kettles

My prize possession is a copper teakettle with a fast-heating coil in the bottom. I don't recommend copper for everyone, but I do recommend equipping your galley with certain pots that work in every galley—large or small.

The most frequently used item is the teakettle. Many cruisers prefer to boil water in a saucepan, but a teakettle is safer—if it spills or falls off the stove, the contents are less likely to scald bystanders. In addition, less heat and moisture escape into the atmosphere.

I find a pressure cooker the most valuable pot in the galley. Modern pressure cookers are quite safe, perform a variety of functions, and are ideal for cooking one-pot meals. Select a pressure cooker with at least a 4-quart capacity; unless you have a huge crew or plan to do canning, there is no need for a giant cooker. I prefer stainless steel—it is easy to maintain, particularly with saltwater washing. The rubber seals will deteriorate in the saltwater environment, so be sure to buy spares. Most pressure cookers come with instruction booklets and recipes. Practice with the unit before you leave home so you are comfortable with its basic functions. You can learn to cook nearly anything in a pressure cooker, including bread.

Another basic pot is a deep skillet (or *sauteuse*). In a kitchen you might use a skillet or crepe pan for doing a variety of chores, from frying eggs to sautéing fish. Those same chores can be done in a similar pan at sea, but the pan should have higher sides.

Stainless steel equipment is great, because it is easy to clean and does not corrode. If you have aluminum, there is no reason to throw it out until it is worn out. In a saltwater environment, it takes more effort to keep aluminum from corroding. Iron kettles and pots rust too quickly for my taste, so I don't keep them on board. Enameled iron is very nice, until the enamel chips.

I believe in having one good thermos bottle on board. I can heat water, coffee, soup, or a variety of liquids and keep them hot in a thermos bottle without using fuel to reheat liquids. Night watches and rough weather are more tolerable with a cup of something hot. Cold beverages can also be stored in a thermos bottle and kept cold in hot climates. It is important to buy a high-quality bottle to assure getting the best insulation.

I also have a griddle in my galley. This may seem redundant with a deep skillet on board, but a griddle can be used for French toast, pancakes, or grilled cheese sandwiches, and its primary value is its efficiency. My griddle covers two burners and can accommodate ten slices of French toast or six chops. When you have a hungry crowd aboard, a griddle is a lifesaver.

Space is always a consideration, so I try to have pots and pans that nest inside each other. The same rule applies to oven pans, if you have an oven.

Be careful when choosing oven pans. Sailboat stoves have small ovens, and oven size will restrict your choices when you buy pans. Measure your oven interior carefully before buying equipment. I make lots of pizza on board. I was often tempted to buy a pizza pan, but the diameter of a standard pizza pan was an inch too big for my oven on the sailboat, so I made rectangular pizzas instead. The oven on the trawler is larger, but we're used to rectangular pizzas now!

I store sharp knives in a knife block screwed down to the counter; the knives can be kept in place in bad weather by using shock cord across the handles. Never leave knives on a counter, because they will fly off with the least provocation. I store all other utensils in a drawer near the stove.

The utensils in the galley are the same ones you use in your kitchen, except they should be made of stainless steel: spatulas, can openers, tongs, graters, measuring spoons, cups, etc. Plastic and wooden utensils are great, although less sturdy. My measuring utensils are both English and metric, to match my varied cookbooks.

The standard home appliances I use as a liveaboard—blender, mixer, coffeemaker, toaster, microwave—may not be practical on some boats. If you can generate the electricity to operate these appliances and keep them from rusting, that's fine. But if you are like many cruisers, you need to find reasonable substitutes.

On the sailboat, I whipped egg whites or cream with a wire whisk. I made toast in the oven or on the griddle. My stainless steel drip coffeepot worked fine on the stove. I used a plastic jar with a snug-fitting lid and lots of arm motion to approximate a blender. The trawler allows us to have more kitchen luxuries, such as a blender that operates on 110 volts, a wok and wok burner, and a toaster.

My two concessions on the sailboat were a coffee grinder and a food processor, which I still use. As mentioned above, I roast and grind my own coffee beans. I enjoy real coffee at breakfast, and this is my way of having it every day. My backup is a hand grinder, in case the batteries are down. My food processor gets lots of use if I'm in a marina. Underway, I use it to make bread. It takes 3 minutes to make and knead dough. The dough rises in a zip-top bag and goes directly to the bread pans for final rise and bake. This system permits me to make fresh bread, even in the roughest conditions, without a big mess.

If you take electric appliances to use when you are plugged into shore power, remember that most of the world operates on 220 volts, 50 cycles. Once you leave the Western Hemisphere you will need a converter.

Tableware

For years, I used Corelle plates and cups. For variety, I began adding dinner plates of local handcrafted pottery. Stainless steel was our material of choice for soup bowls, wine glasses, and flatware.

I had stainless tumblers, but I replaced them with plastic; ice cubes melted rapidly in hot climates, and in cold climates the cups were uncomfortable to hold when filled with hot beverages. We have a pair of stainless thermal mugs that are all-purpose containers during watches. On the trawler, we use glass dishes and our stainless mugs.

Plastic dishes are practical on board, but they have two drawbacks: they cannot be preheated to a high temperature, and the surfaces show scratches after time. If you can find plastic that does not have these problems, let us know!

Our engraved, stainless flatware was easy to maintain. It was rugged and looked good. The only problem I had was the occasional loss of pieces when they disappeared overboard by accident, either with leftovers or in a bucket of saltwater dishwater. When we moved to the trawler, I retrieved our silver from our eldest child, and now we use it at every meal. An occasional bath in an aluminum foil pan filled with baking soda and boiling water keeps it tarnish free.

I use cloth napkins and placemats rather than disposable ones. Crew napkins, identified with different colored napkin rings, are used for several days before they are washed. (I tell everyone that I boil the napkins once a week to make soup.) I like cloth napkins because they are more attractive, require less stowage space than disposable goods, are cheaper to maintain, and do not create garbage.

Stowage

Perishables should be refrigerated. But the definition of a perishable depends on where you shop. If you purchase fresh produce and eggs, they stay fresh for a number of days without refrigeration. Those same items from a supermarket have been in cold storage and will not last unless maintained in the same conditions. Whenever you are concerned about the longevity of an item, purchase it from the source rather than from a store.

Eggs are a classic example. Fresh eggs straight from the chicken can be covered with a light coat of Vaseline and stored for a month;

you should turn them over every couple of days. This permits you to store eggs in a drawer, locker, or bilge rather than use precious space in the refrigerator. Don't wash the eggs until you are ready to use them, or you'll remove the coating that protects them from rotting and/or developing salmonella. (You should wash the eggs before using them because the shells can be dirty and have stray feathers on them.)

On the sailboat, until I reached tropical waters I used our bilges for storing perishables such as margarine and cheese. The water temperature against the hull made the bilges cool enough to keep these items. When the water temperature climbed above 65°F (18°C), I bought less, stored it in the refrigerator, and used it up in a short space of time. On the trawler, we use the refrigerator pretty much as we would a house refrigerator.

Handle stowed items in a refrigerator the same way you would at home; the only difference is that a top-loading refrigerator will be colder on the bottom, and items that need the coldest temperature should be kept at the bottom. Remember, however, that each time you add items to the refrigerator, they will raise the temperature until the box cools down again. Frequent changes in temperature will ruin some items rapidly (for example, dairy products).

You can use a separate box, such as a picnic cooler, in hot climates for drinks and snacks. If you have frozen food, you can put it in the cooler to defrost.

Mixing unlike items together is a basic mistake in food stowage. The traditional fruit bowl—with bananas, grapes, oranges—looks terrific. But it is rot in the making. You can put lemons, oranges, and grapefruit together, but adding the bananas or apples can cost you the whole bunch. When you store items such as potatoes, onions, carrots, beets, and turnips, separate them to prevent contact. Avocados and bananas will ripen quickly if they share a basket or bowl with a lemon. If you buy a stem of bananas, take a few at a time and ripen them with a lemon so you don't need to eat 150 bananas in a day or two.

I have seen many cruising boats with net slings used for food stowage. This is a good method of storage, because air can circulate around the items. Some things, such as potatoes, should be kept in the dark to prevent premature sprouting. You can hang a sling in a lazarette.

It is easy to manage tomatoes. Wrap each one in newspaper or brown paper. They will ripen slowly. When you are ready to eat one or two, unwrap them and set them out for a day or two. They will be ready to eat without all ripening at once. Don't stow tomatoes in a refrigerator at any time, because the cold will change the chemical composition.

Plastic containers in your lockers for staples allow you to get rid of paper containers, which can carry roach eggs and get "mushy" in the saltwater environment. You may want to invest in Tupperware containers. I use various plastic containers that I acquire as I travel. Many items are packaged in plastic jars, and they work just fine to keep out moisture and prevent bug infestation.

Bugs are a problem. Try keeping bugs off the boat. Because cockroaches live in paper boxes and bags, I unload everything in the dinghy and do not bring the sacks or boxes aboard. If I suspect that staples have weevils, I use bay leaves to keep the inhabitants from moving into other inventory. Bombing the boat with an insecticide may be one solution. One woman suggested I winter in an arctic climate to get rid of bugs, but that approach was too extreme for us. Several women recommended Roach Hotels, and others use boric acid.

The biggest stowage problem is garbage. There are international rules regarding the disposal of garbage, and it is necessary to abide by them. Even so, a long passage can present real problems. If you have the space and power, consider installing a garbage compactor.

The best way to avoid the disposal problem is to not have trash. If you can avoid the "overpackaging" that is part of the modern world, then you will not have to be concerned about plastic, foam, and all the rest of the garbage that pollutes the world. Putting the items into other containers and disposing of the wrappers before you leave the dock is the best solution. You may not be able to get rid of all of the packaging, but you can reduce it substantially.

Meat, fruit, and other supermarket staples come in foam trays with plastic covering, and I transfer those items to resealable plastic bags. I use the bags over and over again. If I cannot get rid of the foam trays, I use them for other purposes, such as snack servers. I rinse them in salt water and hang them with clothespins to a lifeline so they can be reused and disposed of at the next port.

You can dispose of biodegradable garbage overboard. Specific rules under the MARPOL treaty state what can and cannot be discarded at set distances from land. The placard specifying those limits should be prominently displayed on your boat. There is no place where it is acceptable to dispose of plastic-based materials except on land.

I flatten and break down nonbiodegradable garbage and stow it in plastic bags that are tied shut. When sailing between uninhabited places, I burn this type of trash on shore below the high tide line and then bury it. Be sure to remain upwind of fires with plastic and foams in them.

In many countries, shoreside garbage containers are ultimately dumped into the water, which is a very frustrating experience. If you can avoid acquiring trash-making materials, your life will be much easier.

The Voyage
Continues

When cruisers return from voyages, they may be at a point where they want to try a different boat, have more creature comforts, or move ashore. Deep down, though, most of them share an addiction to living an unfettered and simple life. Their voyage may be at an end, but many can hardly wait to get underway again.

I have found that some cruisers have difficulty returning after being away for more than a year. They no longer fit into the community they once called home.

If I am gone for a short period of time, I stay in touch with friends, neighbors, business connections, and social contacts. Few things change in my absence. And a cruise of a few weeks or months is less likely to take me to isolated and unfamiliar places that challenge my value system.

Some women are able to circumnavigate while still returning at regular intervals so they don't lose touch with their communities.

Patricia Miller Rains and Irene Hampshire, both professionals in yacht services, make trips of several months' duration and return to a home base to care for family (Patricia cared for her ailing mother), continue jobs, and raise children (Irene sometimes stayed at home with her sons rather than take them on less desirable jobs).

"If you go for a year, you can come home again," says Lin Pardey. "More than two years, you can't come home again. You will have changed and your community will have changed."

After a lengthy absence of two or more years, returning is indeed hard. Going back to the same place, the same house, the same friends, and the same job after a sustained absence is a tough adjustment. For some of us, it is impossible.

Even if a cruise is interrupted for a necessary trip home—because you are over budget, have a family emergency, or develop health problems—friends and family can seem oddly aloof. Time and distance have made them strangers.

Several solutions to this problem have been suggested. Lin recommends, "Come back someplace else. You can rent in a new location or buy a place in a new town. . . . Come back and start over."

When we tried returning to our home port after seven years, it had changed. We were greeted with the question, "When are you moving ashore?" Our joint response was, "We aren't."

Like many other cruisers, the first long voyage had simply whetted our appetite for another one. But our friends at home had assumed that we had seen everything, done everything, and been everywhere we wanted to go. To them, our trip was a mountain to be climbed. Once we scaled to the summit, we would return to normalcy.

Friends saw our life on the boat as hard, fearful, exciting, and inspiring. Still, they expected us to rejoin them in their world. We couldn't fit. We had changed. We no longer had the common ground to keep those friendships going.

Our friends became all the people out on boats around the world. Our mailbox was a stamp collector's dream, filled with letters from everywhere telling us what we were missing. Our boat became a floating boardinghouse for earthbound cruisers passing through. We worked hard for three years so we could finally set out again.

We finally realized in 2003 that we would have to change our lifestyle a little bit. We loved our beautiful *Nalu IV*, but we were getting too old to manage her. Several friends suggested that we modify her with roller furling, lazyjacks, and electric winches. Others thought we should have a bigger engine and larger fuel capacity. Our sailboat was and is perfect. We loved cruising, racing, and living aboard. Modification was not something we were willing to do. We sold her, and her new owner sent us an e-mail after sailing her to her new home in Long Beach: "I have just had the most awesome ride, aboard the most awesome boat. Thank you."

The trawler came into our lives suddenly. She was for sale in Chesapeake Bay. Years of neglect and unskilled repairs had taken a serious toll. We took her down the Intracoastal Waterway, put her on a dry-dock ship (where boats are floated aboard rather than lifted) to Ensenada, Mexico, and brought her up the coast on her own bottom to San Francisco. She is now structurally sound but needs some cosmetic work to return her to original condition.

Our new boat, the *MV Nalu*, is a 1974 Grand Banks Alaskan 53, built with mahogany hull and teak decks and pilothouse. Twin John Deere engines have replaced sails, and Naiad stabilizers steady her motion at sea.

We don't have a home base. Everything we own is now on our trawler because our boat is home—our real home. It's comfortable, and it suits us. We talk about what we will do when we get old, but we haven't made a firm plan. There is still too much for us to see and do.

I believe each of us chooses what we want to do with our lives. Even going along without making a conscious choice is a way of choosing.

Women who choose to cruise make a commitment to do something they believe will be more fulfilling, more satisfying, more fun, and more rewarding than anything else they can do with their lives. Best of all, cruising doesn't preclude other wonderful events and choices. You can still be a parent, an artist, a mechanic, a chef, a musician, or a minister—or you can be all those things at once! Cruising changes your world and challenges you. Those are the reasons why cruising is the choice I made, and why I encourage you to make the same choice.

APPENDIX

RESOURCES FOR CRUISING INFORMATION AND SERVICES

Associations/Cruising

Boat Owners Association of the United States (BoatU.S.)
800 South Pickett Street
Alexandria, VA 22304
703-823-9550
Fax: 703-461-2847
www.boatus.com

National Women's Sailing Association (NWSA)
70A Pleasant Street
Marblehead, MA 01945
866-631-NWSA (866-631-6972)
Fax: 781-631-2889
www.womensailing.org

U.S. Coast Guard Auxiliary
877-875-6296
www.cgaux.org

U.S. Power Squadrons
888-FOR-USPS (888-367-8777)
www.usps.org

US Sailing
P.O. Box 1260
15 Maritime Drive
Portsmouth, RI 02871-0907
800-USSAIL1 (800-877-2451)
Fax: 401-683-0840
www.ussailing.org

Women Aboard
816 Executive Drive
Oviedo, FL 32765
877-WMN-ABRD (877-966-2273); 407-328-1744
Fax: 407-323-8051
www.waboard.com

Ham Radio Contacts

American Radio Relay League (ARRL)
225 Main Street
Newington, CT 06111-1494
860-594-0200
Fax: 865-594-0259
www.arrl.org

Federal Communications Commission (FCC)
445 12th St., SW
Washington, DC 20554
888-225-5322
Fax: 866-418-0232
www.fcc.gov

Health Insurance/Health Agencies

Centers for Disease Control (CDC)
1600 Clifton Road, NE
Atlanta, GA 30333
800-311-3435; 404-639-3311 (general)
877-FYI-TRIP (877-394-8747) (Travelers' Health Automated
    Information Line)
www.cdc.gov

Global Insurance Net.com
7700 North Kendall Drive, Suite 505
Miami, FL 33156
800-975-7363; 305-274-0284
Fax: 305-675-6134
www.globalinsurancenet.com

International Association of Medical Assistance to
    Travellers (IAMAT)
U.S. office:
1623 Military Road, #279
Niagara Falls, NY 14304-1745
716-754-4883
www.iamat.org

International Health Insurance danmark a/s
8 Palaegade
1261 Copenhagen K
Denmark
(45) 33 15 30 99
Fax: (45) 33 32 25 60
www.ihi.com

MedAire
80 East Rio Salado Parkway, Suite 610
Tempe, AZ 85281

480-333-3700
Fax: 480-333-3592
www.medaire.com

Medex
8501 La Salle Road, Suite 200
Baltimore, MD 21286
800-732-5309; 410-453-6300
Fax: 410-453-6301
www.medexassist.com

Travel Assistance International
P.O. Box 668
Millersville, MD 21108
800-821-2828
www.travelassistance.com

Wallach & Co.
107 West Federal Street
P.O. Box 480
Middleburg, VA 20118-0480
800-237-6615; 540-687-3166
Fax: 540-687-3172
www.wallach.com

Home-Study Courses

American School
2200 East 170th Street
Lansing, IL 60438
800-531-9268; 708-418-2800
www.americanschoolofcorr.com

Brigham Young University
Department of Independent Study
206 Harman Continuing Education Building
Provo, UT 84602
800-914-8931; 801-422-2868
Fax: 801-422-0102
http://ce.byu.edu/is

Calvert Education Services
10713 Gilroy Road, Suite B
Hunt Valley, MD 21031
888-487-4652; 410-785-3400
www.calvertschool.org

Keystone National High School
420 West 5th Street
Bloomsburg, PA 17815-1564
800-255-4937; 570-784-5220
Fax: 570-784-2129
www.keystonehighschool.com

Marine Surveyor Information

National Association of Marine Surveyors (NAMS)
P.O. Box 9306
Chesapeake VA 23321-9306
800-822-6267; 757-638-9638
Fax: 757-638-9639
www.nams-cms.org

Society of Accredited Marine Surveyors (SAMS)
4605 Cardinal Boulevard
Jacksonville, FL 32210
800-344-9077; 904-384-1494
Fax: 904-388-3958
www.marinesurvey.org

Sailing and/or Powerboating Schools/Instruction

Offshore Sailing School
16731 McGregor Boulevard
Fort Myers, FL 33908
800-221-4326
Fax: 239-454-1191
www.offshore-sailing.com

Sea Sense
P.O. Box 1961
St. Petersburg, FL 33731
800-332-1404; 727-865-1404
www.seasenseboating.com
Offers sailing and powerboating.

Sistership Sailing School
PMB 3508
P.O. Box 8309
Cruz Bay, USVI 00831
Phone/fax: 284-495-1002
www.sailsistership.com

Womanship
137 Conduit Street
Annapolis, MD 21401
800-342-9295; 410-267-6661
Fax: 410-263-2036
www.womanship.com

BIBLIOGRAPHY

RECOMMENDED READING FOR CONFIDENCE AND PREPARATION

Please note: Some of these books may be hard to find or may no longer be in print. You can check your public library; you may get lucky. But the Internet has made locating such books a lot easier. Try a general website, such as Amazon (www.amazon.com) or AbeBooks (www.abebooks.com), or a specialty marine bookseller, such as Armchair Sailor (www.bluewaterweb.com).

Armstrong, Bob. *Getting Started in Powerboating.* 3rd ed. Camden, Maine: International Marine, 2005.

Calder, Nigel. *Marine Diesel Engines.* 3rd ed. Camden, Maine: International Marine, 2007.

Eastman, Peter F. Edited by John M. Levinson. *Advanced First Aid Afloat.* 5th ed. Centreville, Maryland: Cornell Maritime Press, 2000.

Farrington, Tony. *Rescue in the Pacific: A True Story of Disaster and Survival in a Force 12 Storm.* Camden, Maine: International Marine, 1996.

Giesemann, Suzanne. *It's Your Boat Too: A Woman's Guide to Greater Enjoyment on the Water.* Arcata, California: Paradise Cay, 2006.

Hamilton, Gene, and Katie Hamilton. *Coastal Cruising Under Power: How to Choose, Equip, Operate, and Maintain Your Boat.* Camden, Maine: International Marine, 2006.

Jeffers, Susan. *Feel the Fear . . . and Do It Anyway.* 20th anniv. ed. New York: Ballantine, 2007.

Jessie, Diana, et al. *Bareboat Cruising: The National Standard for Quality Sailing Instruction.* 2nd ed. Portsmouth, Rhode Island: United States Sailing Association, 2002.

————. *Basic Cruising: The National Standard for Quality Sailing Instruction.* 2nd ed. Portsmouth, Rhode Island: United States Sailing Association, 2002.

————. *Cruising with Your Four-Footed Friends: The Basics of Boat Travel with Your Cat or Dog.* Port Washington, Wisconsin: Seaworthy Publications, 2003.

Leonard, Beth A. *Blue Horizons: Dispatches from Distant Seas.* Camden, Maine: International Marine, 2007.

Loomis, Janette, and James H. Bryan. *The Healthy Cruiser's Handbook: Prevention and Treatment Medical Resource.* Trout Lake, Washington: Meridian Passage Consulting, 2002.

Marrett, Barbara, and John Neal. *Mahina Tiare: Pacific Passages.* Friday Harbor, Washington: Pacific International, 1993.

Marshall, Roger. *Rough Weather Seamanship for Sail and Power: Design, Gear, and Tactics for Coastal and Offshore Waters.* Camden, Maine: International Marine, 2006.

McEwen, Thomas. *Boater's Pocket Reference: Your Comprehensive Resource for Both Boats and Boating.* Littleton, Colorado: Anchor Cove, 2006.

Meisel, Tony. *On-Board Emergency Handbook: Your Indispensable Guide for Handling Any Challenge at Sea.* Camden, Maine: International Marine, 2006.

Morgan, Lael. *The Woman's Guide to Boating and Cooking.* Rev. ed. New York: Doubleday, 1974.

Pardey, Lin, with Larry Pardey. *The Care and Feeding of Sailing Crew.* 3rd ed, Arcata, California: Paradise Cay, 2006.

————. *Storm Tactics Handbook: Modern Methods of Heaving-To for Survival in Extreme Conditions.* Arcata, California: Paradise Cay Publications, 1995.

Parsons, Karen. *French for Cruisers: The Boater's Complete Language Guide for French Waters.* Hallettsville, Texas: Aventuras, 2004.

————. *Spanish for Cruisers: Boat Repairs and Maintenance Phrase Book.* Hallettsville, Texas: Aventuras, 2000.

Riley, Dawn, with Cynthia Flanagan. *Taking the Helm.* Boston: Little, Brown, 1995.

Roth, Hal. *How to Sail Around the World: Advice and Ideas for Voyaging Under Sail.* Camden, Maine: International Marine, 2004.

Rousmaniere, John. *The Annapolis Book of Seamanship.* 3rd rev. ed. New York: Simon and Schuster, 1999.

————. *Fastnet, Force 10.* New York: Norton, 2000.

Smeeton, Miles. *Once Is Enough.* Camden, Maine: International Marine, 2001, 2004. Originally published London: Hart-Davis, 1959.

United Kingdom Hydrographic Office. *Ocean Passages for the World.* 5th ed. Taunton, Somerset, England: UK Hydrographic Office, 2004.

United States Sailing Association. *Start Powerboating Right! The National Standard for Quality On-the-Water Instruction.* Portsmouth, Rhode Island: United States Sailing Association, 2003.

University Continuing Education Association. *Independent Study Catalog.* 7th ed. Princeton, New Jersey: Peterson's Guides, 1998.

Weiss, Eric, and Michael Jacobs. *A Comprehensive Guide to Marine Medicine.* Oakland, California: Adventure Medical Kits, 2005.

Werner, David, with Carol Thuman and Jane Maxwell. *Where There Is No Doctor: A Village Health Care Handbook.* New rev. ed. Palo Alto, California: Hesperian Foundation, 2006.

I've included the following two books because they demonstrate two very different cruising relationships. Both couples sailed Cape Horn, a challenging part of the world. But they brought with them very different skills, attitudes, and partnerships. For books about cruising, these titles are just the tip of the iceberg.

Hemingway-Douglass, Réanne. *Cape Horn: One Man's Dream, One Woman's Nightmare.* 2nd ed. Anacortes, Washington: Fine Edge, 2003.

Roth, Hal. *Two Against Cape Horn.* New York: W.W. Norton, 1978. This is now a part of *The Hal Roth Seafaring Trilogy: Three True Stories of Adventure Under Sail.* Camden, Maine: International Marine, 2006.

INDEX

Numbers in **bold** refer to pages with illustrations